AF486799

The Cosmic Kama Sutra

The Cosmic Kama Sutra

Matthew Petchinsky

The Cosmic Kama Sutra: An Astrological Guide to Sexual Positions
By: Matthew Petchinsky

Part 1: Foundations of Sexual Astrology

Introduction to Sexual Astrology: Understanding the Basics and the Connection to Sexual Energy

Astrology, an ancient practice rooted in the observation of celestial bodies, offers profound insights into human nature, behavior, and relationships. While many are familiar with astrology's influence on personality traits, career paths, and general life events, fewer may realize its deep connection to sexual energy and expression. Sexual astrology delves into this intimate aspect of our lives, revealing how the stars and planets can shape our desires, attractions, and the way we connect with others on a sensual level.

The Foundations of Astrology: A Brief Overview

To fully grasp sexual astrology, it is essential to first understand the basics of astrology itself. Astrology is based on the premise that the positions and movements of celestial bodies—such as the Sun, Moon, planets, and stars—at the time of our birth influence our personality, behaviors, and life experiences. The natal chart, also known as a birth chart, is a snapshot of the sky at the exact moment and location of your birth. This chart is divided into twelve houses, each representing different areas of life, and is populated by the zodiac signs and planets.

The zodiac is composed of twelve signs, each with unique characteristics and elemental associations (fire, earth, air, and water). The planets, in their respective positions, interact with these signs and houses, influencing various aspects of our being, including our approach to relationships and sexuality.

The Connection Between Astrology and Sexual Energy

Sexual energy is one of the most powerful forces in human nature. It is not merely about physical attraction or sexual activity; it encompasses our creative drive, passion, and the way we express intimacy and desire. In astrology, this energy is primarily governed by several key elements: the sign and placement of Venus (the planet of love and beauty), Mars (the planet of passion and aggression), and the Moon (which governs emotions and instincts). Together, these planets, along with the influence of the Sun and other celestial bodies, shape our sexual identity and behavior.

- **Venus** represents how we love, what we find beautiful and attractive, and our capacity for pleasure. In sexual astrology, Venus' position in the natal chart reveals our romantic preferences, the type of partner we are drawn to, and the ways we express affection.
- **Mars** governs our primal desires, sexual energy, and how we assert ourselves in pursuit of what we want. It reflects our sexual drive, the intensity of our passions, and the way we handle conflict and competition in relationships.
- **The Moon** symbolizes our emotional needs, instincts, and how we nurture ourselves and others. In the context of sexual astrology, the Moon's placement can indicate what we need to feel safe and fulfilled in intimate relationships.

The Role of the Zodiac Signs in Sexual Astrology

Each zodiac sign brings its unique qualities to our sexual expression. Understanding the characteristics of your Sun sign, as well as the signs where Venus, Mars, and the Moon reside in your natal chart, can provide valuable insights into your sexual nature.

For example:

- **Aries** (a fire sign ruled by Mars) is typically bold, passionate, and assertive in its approach to sex. Those with strong Aries influence may crave excitement, spontaneity, and a partner who can match their energy and intensity.
- **Taurus** (an earth sign ruled by Venus) values sensuality, comfort, and a slow, steady approach to intimacy. Stability, touch, and physical pleasure are often paramount for Taureans in their sexual relationships.
- **Gemini** (an air sign ruled by Mercury) brings a playful, communicative, and curious nature to sex. Intellectual stimulation and variety are key for Geminis, who may thrive on verbal foreplay and new experiences.
- **Cancer** (a water sign ruled by the Moon) is deeply emotional, nurturing, and protective in sexual relationships. Cancers often seek a strong emotional bond and security with their partners, and their sexuality is closely tied to their feelings of love and attachment.

These are just a few examples, but every sign has its distinct way of expressing and experiencing sexual energy. Understanding your sign's influence can help you navigate your sexual relationships with greater awareness and confidence.

Aspects, Houses, and Their Influence on Sexuality

In addition to the signs, the aspects (the angles formed between planets) and the houses in the natal chart play significant roles in shaping sexual astrology.

- **Aspects** can amplify or diminish the sexual energy associated with certain planets. For instance, a harmonious aspect (like a trine or sextile) between Venus and Mars may indicate a balanced and fulfilling sex life, while a challenging aspect (like a square or opposition) might suggest struggles with expressing desire or reconciling romantic and sexual needs.
- **The Eighth House** is particularly significant in sexual astrology, as it is associated with transformation, intimacy, and shared resources. Often referred to as the house of sex, death, and rebirth, the Eighth House reveals deep psychological patterns related to sexual experiences, including issues of power, control, and the merging of energies with another person.
- **The Fifth House** governs creativity, pleasure, and romantic relationships, offering insights into more casual, playful aspects of sexual expression. It highlights how we approach love affairs, flirtation, and the joys of physical connection.

The Interplay of Sexuality, Astrology, and Personal Growth

Sexual astrology is not just about understanding your sexual preferences; it is also a tool for personal growth and self-discovery. By exploring how the planets and signs influence your sexual energy, you can gain a deeper understanding of yourself and your relationships. This awareness can help you address any challenges or blockages in your sexual expression, leading to healthier, more fulfilling connections with others.

Moreover, sexual astrology encourages us to embrace our authentic selves, celebrating the diversity of sexual expression across the zodiac. Whether you are passionate and adventurous like an Aries, or nurturing and deeply connected like a Cancer, sexual astrology affirms that there is no "right" way to experience and express your sexuality—only the way that is true to you.

Conclusion

As you embark on your journey into sexual astrology, remember that it is a deeply personal and nuanced exploration. The insights gained from your natal chart can serve as a guide to understanding your desires, overcoming challenges, and cultivating a richer, more satisfying sexual life. By aligning with the cosmic forces that influence your sexual energy, you can enhance your connection to yourself and others, creating a more harmonious and passionate existence.

Chapter 1: The Role of Planets in Sexuality

Astrology offers a rich framework for understanding the complexities of human sexuality. By examining the influence of each planet in the natal chart, we can gain profound insights into how we express sexual desires, approach intimacy, and find compatibility with others. Each planet governs specific aspects of our sexual nature, shaping our desires, techniques, and the way we connect with others on a sensual level. This chapter provides an in-depth exploration of how the planets influence sexuality, offering a comprehensive guide to understanding your sexual self and how you relate to others.

The Sun: The Core of Sexual Identity and Expression

The Sun represents the essence of who we are—the core of our identity, vitality, and life force. In sexual astrology, the Sun's placement in the natal chart highlights how our sexual identity is intertwined with our overall sense of self. It influences how we project our sexual energy, the confidence we bring to our sexual encounters, and the way we express our desires as part of our fundamental nature.

- **Sun in Aries**: Those with the Sun in Aries approach sexuality with enthusiasm and a desire to take the lead. Aries is a sign known for its boldness, passion, and directness, often driving individuals to seek excitement and novelty in their sexual experiences. They thrive in relationships where spontaneity and intensity are key.
- **Sun in Taurus**: Individuals with the Sun in Taurus are drawn to the sensual pleasures of life. They value stability, comfort, and physical touch, often favoring a slow, steady approach to intimacy. Taurus is ruled by Venus, the planet of love and beauty, which enhances their appreciation for the aesthetic and sensual aspects of sexuality.

The Sun's influence on sexuality is integral to understanding how we express our sexual desires as part of our core identity. It reveals the level of confidence we bring to our sexual relationships and how we integrate our sexual nature into our overall persona.

The Moon: Emotional Needs and Sexual Fulfillment

The Moon governs our emotions, instincts, and subconscious mind. In sexual astrology, the Moon's placement reveals our emotional approach to sex, what we need to feel secure and nurtured in intimate relationships, and how our past experiences influence our sexual behavior. The Moon's influence is deeply tied to our need for emotional connection and intimacy in sexual relationships.

- **Moon in Cancer**: Those with the Moon in Cancer are deeply emotional and seek security and comfort in their sexual relationships. Cancer is ruled by the Moon, making individuals with this placement particularly sensitive and nurturing. They are likely to prioritize emotional intimacy and may require a strong emotional bond with their partner to feel sexually fulfilled.
- **Moon in Scorpio**: Individuals with the Moon in Scorpio experience their emotions with great intensity. They approach sexuality with depth and passion, often seeking profound, transformative experiences. Scorpio's influence can make them drawn to the mysteries of sex and intimacy, sometimes exploring the darker, more complex aspects of their desires.

The Moon's role in sexuality is crucial for understanding the emotional foundation of our sexual behavior. It highlights the importance of emotional security, past experiences, and subconscious needs in shaping our sexual desires and fulfillment.

Mercury: Communication and Intellectual Connection in Sexuality

Mercury, the planet of communication and intellect, plays a significant role in how we express and understand sexual desires. Mercury's placement in the natal chart influences how we communicate our needs, our approach to sexual discussions, and the importance of mental stimulation in our sexual relationships.

- **Mercury in Gemini**: With Mercury in Gemini, individuals are likely to approach sexuality with curiosity and a need for intellectual engagement. They may enjoy playful banter, verbal foreplay, and the exploration of new ideas with their partners. Mental stimulation is often as important as physical attraction for those with this placement.
- **Mercury in Virgo**: Those with Mercury in Virgo are analytical and detail-oriented in their approach to sexuality. They may prefer clear communication about desires and expectations, often focusing on perfecting techniques and ensuring that their partner's needs are met. Virgo's influence can lead to a practical and methodical approach to sex.

Mercury's influence on sexuality highlights the importance of communication and intellectual connection in sexual relationships. It reveals how we articulate our desires and the role of mental stimulation in our sexual expression.

Venus: Love, Attraction, and Sensuality

Venus is the planet of love, beauty, and pleasure, making it one of the most important influences in sexual astrology. Venus governs what we find attractive, how we express love and affection, and our approach to physical pleasure and sensuality. The placement of Venus in the natal chart reveals our romantic preferences, the qualities we seek in a partner, and how we experience and express sexual desire.

- **Venus in Libra**: Individuals with Venus in Libra are romantics who value harmony, balance, and beauty in their sexual relationships. They are drawn to partners who are charming, refined, and aesthetically pleasing. Venus in Libra often seeks a partnership that is both emotionally and physically satisfying, with a focus on creating a harmonious connection.
- **Venus in Scorpio**: Those with Venus in Scorpio approach love and sexuality with intensity and passion. Scorpio's influence makes them drawn to deep, transformative experiences in their relationships. They seek a partner who can match their emotional depth and are often attracted to the mysterious and powerful aspects of sexuality.

Venus' role in sexuality is central to understanding how we experience love, attraction, and sensual pleasure. It guides our desires for connection and intimacy, influencing how we attract and relate to others on a sexual level.

Mars: Passion, Drive, and Sexual Energy

Mars is the planet of action, aggression, and desire, governing our sexual drive and the way we pursue what we want in our sexual relationships. Mars' placement in the natal chart reveals how we express our sexual passions, the intensity of our desires, and our approach to asserting ourselves in sexual encounters.

- **Mars in Aries**: Those with Mars in Aries are driven by a strong sexual appetite and a desire to take the lead. Aries is ruled by Mars, making individuals with this placement particularly assertive and eager to pursue their desires with vigor. They are often attracted to partners who can match their energy and enthusiasm.
- **Mars in Capricorn**: Individuals with Mars in Capricorn approach sexuality with discipline and control. They may be slow to initiate but are determined and focused once engaged. Capricorn's influence can make them seek stability and commitment in their sexual relationships, often aiming for long-term satisfaction.

Mars' influence on sexuality is vital for understanding our sexual energy, drive, and how we take action in our sexual lives. It shapes our approach to pursuing desires and the intensity of our passions.

Jupiter: Expansion, Exploration, and Sexual Adventure

Jupiter, the planet of expansion, growth, and abundance, influences how we approach sexual exploration and the pursuit of pleasure. Jupiter's placement in the natal chart reveals our openness to new experiences, our desire for sexual adventure, and the ways in which we seek to grow and expand our sexual horizons.

- **Jupiter in Sagittarius**: Individuals with Jupiter in Sagittarius are adventurous and freedom-loving, often eager to explore new sexual experiences. They are drawn to partners who share their love of adventure and are open to experimenting with different forms of sexual expression. Sagittarius' influence encourages a broad-minded approach to sexuality.
- **Jupiter in Pisces**: Those with Jupiter in Pisces approach sexuality with a sense of spirituality and emotional depth. They may be drawn to partners who share their desire for a transcendental connection, often seeking experiences that go beyond the physical to touch the soul.

Jupiter's role in sexuality encourages us to seek growth, exploration, and expansion in our sexual lives. It guides us to embrace the abundance of pleasure and the possibilities that life has to offer.

Saturn: Structure, Discipline, and Boundaries in Sexuality

Saturn, the planet of structure, discipline, and boundaries, plays a significant role in shaping our approach to sexuality, particularly in terms of responsibility, commitment, and control. Saturn's placement in the natal chart reveals where we may face challenges or limitations in our sexual expression, as well as how we can develop sexual discipline and maturity.

- **Saturn in Capricorn**: Responsible and disciplined, those with Saturn in Capricorn approach sexuality with a sense of duty and control. They may focus on achieving mastery in their sexual relationships and are often drawn to partners who value stability and commitment. Capricorn's influence can lead to a practical and determined approach to sex.
- **Saturn in Aquarius**: Individuals with Saturn in Aquarius may approach sexuality with a focus on innovation and breaking away from traditional norms. They may face challenges related to balancing freedom and responsibility in their sexual relationships, often seeking partners who share their desire for individuality and independence.

Saturn's influence on sexuality encourages us to establish boundaries, take responsibility for our actions, and develop a mature and disciplined approach to our sexual lives.

Uranus: Innovation, Freedom, and Sexual Experimentation

Uranus, the planet of innovation, rebellion, and sudden change, influences how we approach sexual experimentation and the pursuit of freedom in our sexual relationships. Uranus' placement in the natal chart reveals our desire for unconventional experiences, our need for sexual freedom, and our willingness to break away from traditional norms.

- **Uranus in Aries**: Bold and pioneering, those with Uranus in Aries are often eager to explore new and unconventional forms of sexual expression. They are drawn to partners who share their adventurous spirit and are open to experimenting with new ideas and techniques.
- **Uranus in Libra**: Those with Uranus in Libra may approach sexuality with a focus on breaking away from traditional relationship structures and exploring new ways of connecting with others. They may be drawn to partners who share their desire for freedom and equality in sexual relationships.

Uranus' role in sexuality is to encourage us to embrace change, explore new possibilities, and seek freedom in our sexual lives, guiding us to break away from traditional norms and embrace our unique sexual expression.

Neptune: Fantasy, Illusion, and Spiritual Sexuality

Neptune, the planet of dreams, illusions, and spirituality, influences how we approach sexual fantasy and the pursuit of transcendental sexual experiences. Neptune's placement in the natal chart reveals our desire for spiritual connection, our tendency to idealize or escape through sexuality, and our attraction to the mystical and the unseen.

- **Neptune in Pisces**: Deeply empathetic, intuitive, and spiritual, those with Neptune in Pisces may approach sexuality with a focus on transcendental experiences and emotional depth. They are often drawn to partners who share their desire for spiritual connection and are open to exploring the mystical aspects of sexuality.
- **Neptune in Scorpio**: Intense, passionate, and magnetic, individuals with Neptune in Scorpio may approach sexuality with a focus on exploring the darker, more mysterious aspects of their desires. Scorpio's influence can lead to a fascination with the transformative power of sex.

Neptune's influence on sexuality is profound, guiding us to explore the spiritual, fantastical, and illusory aspects of our sexual experiences. It encourages us to connect with our partners on a soul level and to seek deeper meaning in our sexual relationships.

Pluto: Transformation, Power, and Sexual Intensity

Pluto, the planet of transformation, power, and regeneration, plays a significant role in shaping our approach to sexuality, particularly in terms of intensity, control, and the potential for deep, transformative experiences. Pluto's placement in the natal chart reveals where we seek to transform ourselves through sexuality and how we navigate issues of power and control in our sexual relationships.

- **Pluto in Scorpio**: Those with Pluto in Scorpio experience sexuality with unparalleled intensity and passion. Scorpio is the natural ruler of Pluto, making individuals with this placement drawn to deep, transformative sexual experiences. They may seek to explore the darker, more powerful aspects of their desires and are often attracted to partners who can match their intensity.
- **Pluto in Capricorn**: Individuals with Pluto in Capricorn approach sexuality with a focus on control and mastery. They may be driven by a desire to achieve power in their sexual relationships, often seeking partners who respect their need for structure and discipline. Capricorn's influence can lead to a calculated and determined approach to sex.

Pluto's influence on sexuality is transformative, guiding us to explore the depths of our desires and to seek power and control in our sexual experiences. It encourages us to embrace the potential for transformation and regeneration in our sexual lives.

Conclusion

The planets in our natal chart play a crucial role in shaping our sexual desires, techniques, and compatibility with others. By understanding the influence of each planet, we can gain valuable insights into our sexual nature and how we relate to others on a sensual level. Whether it's the confidence of the Sun, the emotional needs of the Moon, or the transformative power of Pluto, each planet offers a unique perspective on our sexuality, guiding us to embrace our true sexual selves and to navigate our intimate relationships with greater awareness and understanding.

Chapter 2: The Influence of Zodiac Signs

Astrology provides a fascinating framework for understanding sexual expression, and each zodiac sign brings its own unique approach to sex. The signs of the zodiac are associated with specific qualities, preferences, and inclinations that shape how individuals experience and express their sexuality. In this chapter, we will delve into the sexual characteristics of each zodiac sign, exploring their preferences, turn-ons, turn-offs, and the overall approach they take to intimacy.

Aries: The Passionate Pioneer

Element: Fire

Ruling Planet: Mars

Keywords: Bold, Assertive, Energetic

Aries, the first sign of the zodiac, is ruled by Mars, the planet of passion and desire. Those born under Aries approach sex with enthusiasm and a pioneering spirit. They are known for their boldness, assertiveness, and a strong desire to take the lead in sexual encounters.

- **Preferences:** Aries individuals crave excitement and spontaneity in their sexual experiences. They are drawn to partners who can match their energy and who are open to trying new things. Aries loves the thrill of the chase and often enjoys being the initiator in a relationship.
- **Turn-Ons:** A confident partner who isn't afraid to take risks and explore new sexual territories is a major turn-on for Aries. They are also attracted to physical displays of affection, such as passionate kissing and playful teasing.
- **Turn-Offs:** Routine and predictability can quickly dampen Aries' sexual enthusiasm. They are easily bored by partners who are too passive or hesitant to try new things. Aries also dislikes any form of emotional manipulation or games.

Taurus: The Sensual Lover

Element: Earth

Ruling Planet: Venus

Keywords: Sensual, Patient, Reliable

Taurus, ruled by Venus, the planet of love and beauty, is all about sensuality and physical pleasure. Taureans approach sex with patience and a deep appreciation for the sensory experiences it offers. They are known for their reliability and their preference for creating a comfortable, luxurious environment for intimacy.

- **Preferences:** Taurus individuals are drawn to slow, sensual sexual experiences that engage all the senses. They enjoy physical touch, soft textures, and a warm, inviting atmosphere. Stability and trust are key for Taurus, who prefers long-term, committed relationships.
- **Turn-Ons:** A partner who takes the time to create a romantic and comfortable setting is a major turn-on for Taurus. They are also aroused by tactile sensations, such as gentle massages, soft fabrics, and warm, lingering touches.
- **Turn-Offs:** Taurus is turned off by rushed or overly aggressive sexual encounters. They dislike anything that disrupts their sense of comfort and security, such as sudden changes or unpredictability. Being too forceful or pushy is a major no-no with Taurus.

Gemini: The Playful Communicator
Element: Air
Ruling Planet: Mercury
Keywords: Curious, Playful, Versatile

Gemini, ruled by Mercury, the planet of communication, is known for its playful and curious approach to sex. Geminis are highly versatile and enjoy experimenting with different aspects of sexuality. They are intellectually driven and often seek a mental connection as much as a physical one.

- **Preferences:** Gemini individuals thrive on variety and mental stimulation in their sexual experiences. They enjoy partners who can engage them in witty conversation and who are open to trying new things. For Gemini, sex is as much about the mind as it is about the body.
- **Turn-Ons:** Verbal communication, including dirty talk and playful banter, is a major turn-on for Gemini. They also enjoy role-playing, exploring fantasies, and being in situations that challenge their intellect.
- **Turn-Offs:** Gemini is turned off by predictability and routine. They dislike partners who are too serious or who fail to engage them mentally. Boredom is the biggest enemy of Gemini, and they need constant stimulation to stay interested.

Cancer: The Emotional Intimate
Element: Water
Ruling Planet: Moon
Keywords: Nurturing, Emotional, Protective

Cancer, ruled by the Moon, is deeply emotional and nurturing. Those born under Cancer seek emotional intimacy and security in their sexual relationships. They are known for their caring and protective nature, often seeking to create a deep emotional bond with their partners before engaging in physical intimacy.

- **Preferences:** Cancer individuals are drawn to partners who can provide emotional security and who are willing to form a deep, meaningful connection. They prefer sex that is tender and emotionally fulfilling, often prioritizing the emotional bond over the physical act.
- **Turn-Ons:** A partner who is attentive, nurturing, and emotionally available is a major turn-on for Cancer. They also appreciate acts of affection, such as cuddling, gentle touches, and expressions of love and care.
- **Turn-Offs:** Cancer is turned off by partners who are emotionally distant or dismissive of their feelings. They dislike anything that feels cold or impersonal, and they are particularly sensitive to rejection or criticism. Cancer also avoids superficial encounters that lack emotional depth.

Leo: The Confident Performer

Element: Fire

Ruling Planet: Sun

Keywords: Confident, Charismatic, Passionate

Leo, ruled by the Sun, is known for its confidence and charisma. Leos approach sex with a sense of passion and creativity, often enjoying the spotlight and seeking to impress their partners. They are generous lovers who take pride in their ability to please.

- **Preferences:** Leo individuals are drawn to partners who admire and appreciate them. They enjoy sexual experiences that are passionate, creative, and full of drama. Leos love to be adored and often enjoy being the center of attention in the bedroom.
- **Turn-Ons:** Flattery, admiration, and affectionate attention are major turn-ons for Leo. They also enjoy playful competition and sexual encounters that allow them to showcase their talents and creativity.
- **Turn-Offs:** Leo is turned off by partners who fail to appreciate or acknowledge their efforts. They dislike being ignored or taken for granted and are particularly sensitive to criticism. Routine and lack of excitement can also dampen Leo's sexual enthusiasm.

Virgo: The Meticulous Lover
Element: Earth
Ruling Planet: Mercury
Keywords: Analytical, Perfectionist, Attentive

Virgo, ruled by Mercury, is known for its analytical and perfectionist nature. In sexual relationships, Virgos are attentive and detail-oriented, often seeking to perfect their techniques and ensure their partner's satisfaction. They approach sex with a sense of responsibility and a desire to serve.

- **Preferences:** Virgo individuals are drawn to partners who are clean, well-groomed, and respectful. They appreciate sexual experiences that are well-planned and executed with precision. Virgos often enjoy sex that is focused on mutual satisfaction and improvement.
- **Turn-Ons:** A partner who is attentive to detail and willing to communicate openly about desires and preferences is a major turn-on for Virgo. They also appreciate acts of service, such as a partner who takes care of their needs or helps them relax.
- **Turn-Offs:** Virgo is turned off by disorder, messiness, and lack of hygiene. They dislike anything that feels rushed or chaotic, and they are particularly sensitive to criticism or judgment. Virgo also avoids partners who are overly aggressive or insensitive to their needs.

Libra: The Harmonious Lover
Element: Air
Ruling Planet: Venus
Keywords: Diplomatic, Romantic, Balanced

Libra, ruled by Venus, is all about harmony, balance, and romance. Those born under Libra seek to create a balanced and aesthetically pleasing sexual experience. They are known for their diplomatic nature and their ability to create a peaceful and loving environment in their relationships.

- **Preferences:** Libra individuals are drawn to partners who are charming, refined, and fair-minded. They enjoy sexual experiences that are romantic and balanced, often prioritizing the needs and desires of both partners. Libras value equality and mutual respect in their relationships.
- **Turn-Ons:** A partner who is attentive to their needs and who values harmony and balance is a major turn-on for Libra. They also appreciate beauty, whether it's in their partner's appearance or in the environment where the sexual experience takes place.
- **Turn-Offs:** Libra is turned off by conflict, aggression, and anything that disrupts their sense of balance. They dislike partners who are overly demanding or who fail to consider their feelings. Libra also avoids chaotic or unappealing environments that lack aesthetic appeal.

Scorpio: The Intense Lover
Element: Water
Ruling Planet: Pluto
Keywords: Intense, Passionate, Mysterious

Scorpio, ruled by Pluto, is known for its intensity and passion. Those born under Scorpio approach sex with a deep, transformative energy, often seeking to explore the depths of their desires and connect with their partner on a profound level. Scorpios are mysterious and magnetic, often drawing others in with their allure.

- **Preferences:** Scorpio individuals are drawn to partners who are willing to explore the deeper, more intense aspects of sexuality. They appreciate sexual experiences that are passionate, transformative, and emotionally charged. Scorpios often seek to dominate or be dominated in the bedroom, exploring power dynamics.
- **Turn-Ons:** A partner who is intense, passionate, and willing to explore the darker sides of sexuality is a major turn-on for Scorpio. They are also attracted to mystery, secrets, and anything that challenges their sense of control.
- **Turn-Offs:** Scorpio is turned off by superficiality and lack of depth. They dislike partners who are emotionally distant or who fail to engage them on a deep level. Scorpio also avoids anything that feels fake or inauthentic.

Sagittarius: The Adventurous Explorer
Element: Fire
Ruling Planet: Jupiter
Keywords: Adventurous, Optimistic, Free-Spirited

Sagittarius, ruled by Jupiter, is known for its adventurous and optimistic **nature.** Those born under Sagittarius approach sex with a sense of freedom and exploration. They are enthusiastic, open-minded, and always ready to try something new. Sagittarians seek variety and excitement in their sexual experiences, often valuing the journey as much as the destination.

- **Preferences:** Sagittarius individuals are drawn to partners who share their love of adventure and are open to exploring new horizons in and out of the bedroom. They enjoy spontaneous and unplanned sexual encounters, often seeking experiences that are fun, light-hearted, and full of energy.
- **Turn-Ons:** A partner who is adventurous, optimistic, and open to new experiences is a major turn-on for Sagittarius. They are also aroused by the idea of travel, exotic locations, and the thrill of the unknown. Intellectual stimulation and philosophical discussions can also be very appealing to them.
- **Turn-Offs:** Sagittarius is turned off by possessiveness, jealousy, and anything that feels restrictive or confining. They dislike routine and predictability, preferring partners who can keep up with their need for variety and excitement. Clinginess and overly emotional displays can also be a turn-off for Sagittarius.

Capricorn: The Disciplined Lover
Element: Earth
Ruling Planet: Saturn
Keywords: Responsible, Ambitious, Controlled

Capricorn, ruled by Saturn, is known for its disciplined and responsible approach to life, and this extends to their sexual relationships. Capricorns often approach sex with a sense of purpose and determination, seeking to master the art of intimacy. They are ambitious and goal-oriented, often viewing sex as another area where they can achieve excellence.

- **Preferences:** Capricorn individuals are drawn to partners who are reliable, mature, and serious about commitment. They appreciate sexual experiences that are well-planned and executed with precision. Capricorns often prefer long-term relationships where they can build a deep, enduring connection with their partner.
- **Turn-Ons:** A partner who is disciplined, ambitious, and shares their goals and values is a major turn-on for Capricorn. They also appreciate a strong work ethic and a sense of responsibility, both in and out of the bedroom. Subtle power dynamics and a controlled, measured approach to sex can be particularly appealing.
- **Turn-Offs:** Capricorn is turned off by irresponsibility, laziness, and anything that disrupts their sense of order and control. They dislike partners who are overly emotional or who fail to take their relationship seriously. Capricorn also avoids chaotic or unpredictable situations that make them feel insecure.

Aquarius: The Unconventional Lover
Element: Air
Ruling Planet: Uranus
Keywords: Innovative, Independent, Humanitarian

Aquarius, ruled by Uranus, is known for its innovative and unconventional approach to life. Those born under Aquarius often bring a unique, forward-thinking perspective to their sexual relationships. They are independent, open-minded, and often seek to explore new and unconventional aspects of sexuality.

- **Preferences:** Aquarius individuals are drawn to partners who are intellectually stimulating, open to experimentation, and willing to break away from traditional norms. They enjoy sexual experiences that are innovative and unconventional, often seeking to push boundaries and explore new ideas.
- **Turn-Ons:** A partner who is independent, creative, and willing to explore unconventional sexual experiences is a major turn-on for Aquarius. They are also attracted to intellectual discussions, humanitarian ideals, and the idea of making a positive impact on the world, even in their intimate relationships.
- **Turn-Offs:** Aquarius is turned off by conformity, narrow-mindedness, and anything that feels overly traditional or restrictive. They dislike partners who are overly emotional or who try to impose conventional expectations on them. Aquarius also avoids possessiveness and jealousy, as they highly value their independence.

Pisces: The Dreamy Romantic
Element: Water
Ruling Planet: Neptune
Keywords: Empathetic, Intuitive, Compassionate

Pisces, ruled by Neptune, is known for its dreamy, romantic, and empathetic nature. Those born under Pisces approach sex with a sense of spirituality and emotional depth. They are intuitive lovers who often seek to merge emotionally and spiritually with their partner, creating a profound and transcendent experience.

- **Preferences:** Pisces individuals are drawn to partners who are gentle, compassionate, and capable of deep emotional connection. They appreciate sexual experiences that are romantic, imaginative, and spiritually fulfilling. Pisces often seeks to create a fantasy world where they can escape with their partner, finding solace in the depth of their connection.
- **Turn-Ons:** A partner who is emotionally available, empathetic, and shares their desire for spiritual connection is a major turn-on for Pisces. They are also attracted to artistic expression, music, and the idea of escaping reality together. Acts of kindness and selflessness in the bedroom can be particularly appealing to them.
- **Turn-Offs:** Pisces is turned off by harshness, insensitivity, and anything that disrupts their sense of emotional harmony. They dislike partners who are overly critical or dismissive of their feelings. Pisces also avoids overly aggressive or domineering behavior, preferring a gentle, compassionate approach to intimacy.

Conclusion

Each zodiac sign brings its own unique qualities, preferences, and tendencies to sexual relationships. Understanding the influence of your sign—and the signs of your partners—can provide valuable insights into your approach to sex, including what turns you on, what turns you off, and how you can create more fulfilling and harmonious intimate experiences. By exploring the sexual characteristics of each sign, you can deepen your understanding of yourself and your partners, leading to more satisfying and meaningful connections.

Chapter 3: Celestial Bodies and Their Energies

In addition to the planets and zodiac signs, astrology considers a wide array of celestial bodies that influence human behavior and sexuality. Stars, asteroids, and other cosmic entities contribute to the intricate tapestry of astrological influences that shape our sexual experiences, desires, and compatibility. This chapter delves into the roles these celestial bodies play in sexual astrology, providing insights into how their energies manifest in our intimate lives.

The Role of Fixed Stars in Sexual Astrology

Fixed stars, ancient and powerful celestial bodies, have been studied for millennia in astrology. Unlike the wandering planets, fixed stars hold specific positions in the sky and exert a more subtle but profound influence on our natal charts. Many fixed stars are associated with mythological figures and carry specific energies that can enhance or challenge our sexual expression.

- **Antares (15° Sagittarius):** Known as the "Heart of the Scorpion," Antares is a star of intensity, passion, and desire. When this star is prominent in a natal chart, it can amplify sexual magnetism and drive, often leading to a life marked by intense and transformative sexual experiences. Those with strong Antares influences may find themselves drawn to deep, passionate relationships that push the boundaries of their desires.
- **Algol (26° Taurus):** Algol, often associated with the myth of Medusa, is a star that embodies themes of power, seduction, and danger. In sexual astrology, Algol's influence can manifest as a powerful, almost hypnotic allure, but it can also bring challenges related to jealousy, obsession, and sexual power dynamics. Individuals with Algol prominent in their charts may need to navigate intense sexual energies carefully, ensuring they use their power wisely.
- **Spica (23° Libra):** Spica is a star of grace, beauty, and harmony. In the context of sexuality, Spica's influence brings a refined, elegant approach to love and intimacy. Those with strong Spica placements are often drawn to relationships that emphasize balance, mutual respect, and aesthetic pleasure. Spica can enhance a person's ability to attract and maintain harmonious sexual relationships.

Fixed stars add another layer of complexity to sexual astrology, influencing how we express our sexual nature and how we interact with others in intimate relationships. By understanding the specific energies of these stars, we can gain deeper insights into the nuances of our sexual lives.

The Influence of Asteroids in Sexual Astrology

Asteroids, smaller celestial bodies primarily located between Mars and Jupiter in the asteroid belt, play a significant role in modern astrology. In sexual astrology, certain asteroids are particularly relevant, offering insights into specific aspects of love, desire, and intimacy.

- **Eros (433 Eros):** Eros is the asteroid of erotic desire and passion. Named after the Greek god of love, Eros represents sexual attraction, infatuation, and the erotic thrill of new love. When Eros is strongly placed in a natal chart, it can indicate a person who experiences intense, often overwhelming sexual desires. Eros' influence is about the raw, primal force of attraction and the pursuit of pleasure.

- **Psyche (16 Psyche):** Psyche, representing the soul, explores the intersection of love and the psyche. In sexual astrology, Psyche's placement reveals how emotional and spiritual connections enhance sexual experiences. Psyche's influence is about deep, soulful love that transcends mere physical attraction, emphasizing the importance of emotional intimacy in sexual relationships.

- **Juno (3 Juno):** Juno is the asteroid associated with marriage, commitment, and partnership. In sexual astrology, Juno's placement in the natal chart can reveal our preferences for long-term sexual relationships, the qualities we seek in a committed partner, and how we approach fidelity and loyalty. Juno's influence helps us understand the role of commitment and stability in our sexual lives.

- **Lilith (1181 Lilith):** Lilith, often referred to as the "Dark Moon," represents the untamed, primal aspects of sexuality. In mythology, Lilith is a figure of rebellion and independence, and in astrology, her influence can signify sexual liberation, taboo desires, and the rejection of traditional sexual roles. Those with strong Lilith influences may find themselves drawn to exploring the darker, more unconventional aspects of sexuality.

Asteroids like Eros, Psyche, Juno, and Lilith offer specific insights into the different facets of our sexual expression, from raw desire to soulful connections, from commitment to sexual liberation. By examining the placement of these asteroids in the natal chart, we can gain a more nuanced understanding of our sexual nature.

The Nodes of the Moon: Karmic Sexual Lessons

The North and South Nodes of the Moon, also known as the "Nodes of Destiny," represent our karmic path and the lessons we are meant to learn in this lifetime. In sexual astrology, the Nodes provide insights into our sexual past (South Node) and the growth we are meant to achieve in our sexual relationships (North Node).

- **South Node:** The South Node represents our past lives, habits, and tendencies that we may fall back on out of comfort. In sexual astrology, the South Node can reveal patterns of sexual behavior that we are familiar with, but which may no longer serve our growth. Understanding the South Node's influence can help us identify and overcome negative sexual patterns or unhealthy relationship dynamics.
- **North Node:** The North Node represents the qualities and experiences we are meant to develop in this lifetime. In sexual astrology, the North Node indicates the sexual experiences and relationships that will lead to our growth and fulfillment. It encourages us to step out of our comfort zone and embrace new ways of relating to others on a sexual level.

The Nodes of the Moon provide a karmic perspective on sexuality, helping us understand the deeper lessons we are meant to learn through our sexual experiences. By aligning with the energies of the North Node, we can move towards more fulfilling and evolved sexual relationships.

Chiron: The Wounded Healer in Sexuality

Chiron, often referred to as the "Wounded Healer," is a celestial body that represents our deepest wounds and the potential for healing. In sexual astrology, Chiron's placement in the natal chart can reveal areas of vulnerability, pain, and healing related to our sexual experiences.

- **Chiron in Aries:** Chiron in Aries may indicate wounds related to sexual assertiveness and confidence. Individuals with this placement might struggle with expressing their desires or asserting themselves in sexual relationships. Healing comes through developing self-confidence and embracing one's sexual identity.

- **Chiron in Scorpio:** Chiron in Scorpio can signify deep wounds related to power, control, and intimacy. Those with this placement may have experienced trauma or betrayal in their sexual relationships, leading to issues of trust and vulnerability. Healing involves reclaiming personal power and learning to trust in intimate connections.

Chiron's influence in sexual astrology is about recognizing and healing our deepest wounds, allowing us to move towards healthier and more fulfilling sexual relationships. By working with Chiron's energy, we can transform our sexual experiences into opportunities for profound healing and growth.

Black Moon Lilith: The Dark Feminine and Sexual Power

Black Moon Lilith, different from the asteroid Lilith, represents the wild, untamed aspects of the feminine and the hidden power of sexuality. In sexual astrology, Black Moon Lilith's placement in the natal chart reveals where we may experience themes of sexual power, taboo, and the rejection of societal norms.

- **Black Moon Lilith in Leo:** Black Moon Lilith in Leo may manifest as a strong desire for recognition and power in sexual relationships. Individuals with this placement may seek to express their sexuality in bold, dramatic ways, challenging traditional norms and embracing their sexual sovereignty.
- **Black Moon Lilith in Pisces:** Black Moon Lilith in Pisces can indicate a deep connection to the mystical and spiritual aspects of sexuality. Those with this placement may be drawn to explore the boundaries between the physical and spiritual realms, seeking transcendental sexual experiences that defy conventional understanding.

Black Moon Lilith's influence in sexual astrology encourages us to embrace the darker, more mysterious aspects of our sexuality. It challenges us to confront societal taboos and reclaim our sexual power in ways that are authentic and liberating.

The Part of Fortune: Sexual Fulfillment and Joy

The Part of Fortune, an Arabic Part in astrology, represents areas of life where we are likely to find happiness, success, and fulfillment. In sexual astrology, the Part of Fortune's placement in the natal chart can reveal where we are most likely to find joy and satisfaction in our sexual relationships.

- **Part of Fortune in Taurus:** With the Part of Fortune in Taurus, sexual fulfillment is likely to be found through sensual experiences and a deep connection to the physical body. Individuals with this placement may find joy in creating a comfortable, luxurious environment for intimacy and indulging in the pleasures of the senses.
- **Part of Fortune in Sagittarius:** The Part of Fortune in Sagittarius suggests that sexual fulfillment comes through exploration, adventure, and a sense of freedom. Those with this placement may find joy in expanding their sexual horizons, trying new things, and embracing the excitement of the unknown.

The Part of Fortune's influence in sexual astrology highlights where we can find the most joy and fulfillment in our sexual lives. By aligning with this energy, we can enhance our sexual experiences and create more meaningful, pleasurable connections.

Conclusion

The vast array of celestial bodies beyond the traditional planets offers a rich tapestry of influences that shape our sexual experiences. From the passionate intensity of fixed stars like Antares to the healing potential of Chiron, these celestial entities add depth and complexity to our understanding of sexual astrology. By exploring the roles of stars, asteroids, and other celestial bodies, we can gain a more comprehensive understanding of our sexual nature and how to navigate the intimate relationships in our lives. Whether through the raw desire of Eros, the karmic lessons of the Moon's Nodes, or the powerful allure of Black Moon Lilith, these cosmic influences guide us towards a deeper, more fulfilling exploration of our sexual selves. Understanding the energies of these celestial bodies allows us to integrate their influences into our lives, helping us to navigate the complexities of sexuality with greater awareness and intention.

As we delve deeper into sexual astrology, it's important to recognize that these celestial bodies offer both challenges and opportunities. They reveal where we might experience difficulties or wounds in our sexual expression, as well as where we can find healing, empowerment, and joy. By acknowledging and working with these energies, we can transform our sexual experiences into profound journeys of self-discovery and growth.

Each of these celestial bodies—whether they are fixed stars, asteroids, or points like the Part of Fortune—carries its own unique energy and symbolism. These energies interact with the more commonly known planets and zodiac signs to create a complex, multi-dimensional picture of our sexual nature. For example, while the Sun and Mars might tell us about our core sexual identity and drive, the placement of Eros or Psyche can reveal how we experience erotic desire or deep emotional connections.

Incorporating the influences of these celestial bodies into your understanding of sexual astrology can enrich your self-awareness and enhance your relationships. It encourages you to look beyond the surface, to explore the deeper layers of your desires, and to understand the forces that drive your sexual behavior. Whether you're seeking to heal past wounds, break free from restrictive patterns, or simply enjoy a more fulfilling sexual relationship, the energies of these celestial bodies provide valuable guidance and insight.

As you continue to explore sexual astrology, consider how these celestial influences manifest in your own life and relationships. Reflect on the lessons they offer, the challenges they present, and the opportunities they create for growth and fulfillment. By embracing the full spectrum of astrological influences, you can develop a more holistic understanding of your sexual self and create more harmonious and satisfying intimate connections.

In the chapters that follow, we will build upon this foundation, exploring how these celestial bodies interact with the planets, zodiac signs, and houses in the natal chart to shape your overall sexual profile. We will also look at how these influences play out in synastry—the comparison of two charts to understand relationship dynamics—and in transits, which reveal how current celestial movements impact your sexual life. By the end of this journey, you will have a comprehensive understanding of how the cosmos influences every aspect of your sexuality, empowering you to embrace your desires, navigate challenges, and create the fulfilling sexual experiences you seek.

Chapter 4: Moon Phases and Sexual Energy

The Moon, a powerful celestial body, governs our emotions, instincts, and inner world. Its influence on Earth is undeniable, from the ebb and flow of the tides to the cycles of human behavior. In astrology, the Moon is closely associated with our emotional life, our subconscious, and our deepest desires. It is no surprise, then, that the Moon's phases—waxing, waning, full, and new—have a profound impact on our sexual energy, libido, and intimate connections. This chapter explores how each phase of the Moon affects our sexual experiences and how we can align our intimate lives with the natural rhythms of the lunar cycle.

The New Moon: Beginnings and Introspection

The New Moon marks the beginning of the lunar cycle. During this phase, the Moon is not visible from Earth, as it is positioned between the Earth and the Sun. The energy of the New Moon is one of new beginnings, introspection, and planting seeds for the future. This phase is a time for setting intentions and exploring what we truly desire.

- **Sexual Energy:** The New Moon is a time of lower energy levels and introspection, which can translate into a more subdued approach to sexuality. Libido may be lower during this phase, as the focus shifts inward. However, this can also be a powerful time for exploring deeper emotional connections and setting new intentions for your sexual life. The New Moon is ideal for intimate, quiet moments with a partner where you can discuss your desires, fantasies, and what you want to manifest in your sexual relationship.

- **Intimacy:** This phase encourages emotional intimacy and the strengthening of bonds. It's a good time to engage in activities that promote trust and connection, such as deep conversations, shared goals, and mutual understanding. Sexual experiences during the New Moon may be more about emotional connection than physical passion, focusing on the quality of the bond rather than the intensity of the act.

- **Rituals and Practices:** Consider using the energy of the New Moon to set intentions for your sexual life. You might write down your desires, goals, or areas of your sexual relationship that you wish to explore or improve. Meditation, journaling, and quiet reflection can be powerful tools during this time to align your inner desires with your sexual energy.

The Waxing Moon: Growth and Desire

As the Moon begins to grow from a sliver of light to a fuller crescent, it enters the waxing phase. This period is associated with growth, momentum, and increasing energy. The waxing Moon is a time of action, building upon the intentions set during the New Moon and moving toward manifestation.

- **Sexual Energy:** The waxing Moon is a time of increasing sexual energy and desire. As the Moon grows, so too does our libido and our appetite for connection. This phase is characterized by a rising sense of excitement and anticipation, making it an ideal time for exploring new aspects of your sexual relationship, trying new things, and taking more initiative in intimacy.
- **Intimacy:** The energy during the waxing Moon is dynamic and forward-moving, encouraging you to take steps toward achieving your sexual and intimate goals. Whether it's deepening your connection with a partner or exploring new fantasies, this phase supports growth and exploration. It's a time to be proactive in your sexual relationship, nurturing the seeds planted during the New Moon.
- **Rituals and Practices:** During the waxing Moon, focus on actions that support your sexual growth. This might include trying new techniques, experimenting with different forms of intimacy, or even taking steps to improve your physical health and well-being, which can enhance your sexual vitality. Affirmations, goal-setting, and positive visualization can help you harness the growing energy of this phase.

The Full Moon: Peak Energy and Passion

The Full Moon is the climax of the lunar cycle, when the Moon is fully illuminated by the Sun and visible in its entirety. This phase is associated with peak energy, heightened emotions, and a sense of completion. The Full Moon is often linked to increased activity, both physically and emotionally, and is a time of celebration and fulfillment.

- **Sexual Energy:** The Full Moon is a period of heightened sexual energy and passion. Libido is at its peak, and there is often a strong desire for connection, intimacy, and physical expression.

This phase can bring out intense emotions and a deep need to merge with a partner, making it a powerful time for sexual encounters that are both passionate and transformative.

- **Intimacy:** The energy of the Full Moon is all about fullness, abundance, and expression. This is a time when emotions run high, and intimate connections can reach their peak. The Full Moon encourages openness, honesty, and a willingness to fully engage with your partner. It's a time for celebrating your sexual relationship, exploring your desires fully, and embracing the intensity of your connection.
- **Rituals and Practices:** The Full Moon is an ideal time for rituals that involve release, celebration, and full expression. You might engage in practices that allow you to fully express your desires, such as dance, movement, or creative activities. This is also a time to celebrate your sexual self and the connection you share with your partner, perhaps through a romantic evening or a ritual that honors your bond.

The Waning Moon: Reflection and Letting Go

After the Full Moon, the lunar cycle enters the waning phase, as the Moon gradually diminishes in light and energy. The waning Moon is a time of reflection, introspection, and releasing what no longer serves you. This phase is about winding down, letting go, and preparing for the next cycle.

- **Sexual Energy:** The waning Moon brings a decrease in sexual energy and a shift towards a more reflective, introspective approach to intimacy. Libido may decrease as the focus turns inward, and there may be a desire for rest and recuperation. This phase is a time to assess what is working in your sexual relationship and what needs to be released or transformed.
- **Intimacy:** The waning Moon encourages reflection and the letting go of old patterns or behaviors that no longer serve your relationship. It's a time for healing and closure, whether that involves resolving conflicts, forgiving past hurts, or simply taking a step back to recharge. Intimacy during this phase may be more about emotional support and nurturing than physical connection.
- **Rituals and Practices:** Use the waning Moon to engage in rituals that promote healing and release. This might include letting go of past grievances, clearing out emotional or physical clutter, or engaging in practices that restore balance and harmony. Meditation, forgiveness rit-

uals, and activities that promote relaxation and inner peace can be particularly beneficial during this phase.

The Lunar Eclipse: Intensified Energy and Transformation

Lunar eclipses, which occur during the Full Moon when the Earth comes between the Sun and the Moon, blocking the Moon's light, are significant astrological events that amplify the effects of the Full Moon. Eclipses are associated with sudden changes, revelations, and powerful transformations.

- **Sexual Energy:** During a lunar eclipse, sexual energy can be incredibly intense, often bringing hidden desires and emotions to the surface. This phase can catalyze major shifts in your sexual relationship, sometimes revealing truths that have been suppressed or ignored. Eclipses can be both disruptive and transformative, pushing you to confront deep-seated issues in your intimate life.
- **Intimacy:** The energy of a lunar eclipse can bring about profound changes in how you relate to your partner. This is a time for confronting and releasing old patterns that no longer serve you, making way for new growth. Eclipses often bring about endings or beginnings, so it's a time to be open to whatever changes may come in your sexual relationship.
- **Rituals and Practices:** Eclipses are powerful times for transformation and release. Consider engaging in rituals that help you let go of the past and embrace new beginnings. This might include shadow work, journaling about your deepest desires and fears, or engaging in symbolic acts of release and renewal.

The Void of Course Moon: A Pause in Sexual Energy

The Void of Course Moon is a period when the Moon has completed its last major aspect before changing signs and is no longer making significant contacts with other planets. This phase is often seen as a time of stillness, when activities may not proceed as planned, and energy can feel stagnant or directionless.

- **Sexual Energy:** During the Void of Course Moon, sexual energy may feel unfocused or lacking in direction. This is not typically a time for initiating new sexual experiences or making significant changes in your relationship. Instead, it's a time to pause, reflect, and allow things to unfold naturally.
- **Intimacy:** The Void of Course Moon is a good time for rest and relaxation rather than intense intimacy. It's a phase for being present with your partner without the need for action or decision-making. Embrace the stillness and use this time to recharge and rejuvenate.
- **Rituals and Practices:** During the Void of Course Moon, engage in gentle, calming activities that allow you to rest and reflect. Meditation, quiet time with your partner, or solo self-care rituals can be particularly beneficial. Avoid making significant decisions or taking bold actions during this time, as the energy is not conducive to forward movement.

Conclusion

The Moon's phases offer a powerful framework for understanding how our sexual energy ebbs and flows throughout the lunar cycle. By aligning your intimate life with the natural rhythms of the Moon, you can enhance your sexual experiences, deepen your connections, and gain greater insight into your desires and needs. Each phase of the Moon—whether it's the introspective New Moon, the passionate Full Moon, or the reflective waning Moon—offers unique opportunities for growth, healing, and fulfillment in your sexual relationships. Embrace the wisdom of the lunar cycle, and let it guide you toward a more harmonious and satisfying sexual life.

Chapter 5: Celestial Events and Their Impact

Astrology not only considers the influence of planets, zodiac signs, and lunar phases but also the significant impact of various celestial events. These events—eclipses, solar flares, and meteor showers—create shifts in cosmic energy that can profoundly affect our emotions, behavior, and sexual energy. This chapter explores how these celestial phenomena influence our intimate lives and how we can harness or navigate their energies to enhance our sexual experiences.

Eclipses: Catalysts for Transformation

Eclipses are powerful astrological events that occur when the Sun, Moon, and Earth align in such a way that one celestial body temporarily obscures another. Solar eclipses happen during a New Moon when the Moon passes between the Earth and the Sun, while lunar eclipses occur during a Full Moon when the Earth is between the Sun and the Moon. Eclipses are often seen as times of heightened energy, dramatic change, and revelation.

- **Sexual Energy:** Eclipses are known for their ability to bring hidden emotions and desires to the surface. During an eclipse, you might experience a surge in sexual energy that feels intense, unpredictable, or even overwhelming. This heightened energy can lead to a greater need for intimacy and connection, but it can also bring unresolved issues in your sexual relationship to light.

- **Transformation and Revelation:** Eclipses often act as catalysts for change, pushing you to confront aspects of your sexual life that need transformation. This might involve facing unresolved conflicts with a partner, exploring new desires that have been suppressed, or making significant decisions about your relationship. The energy of an eclipse can be both disruptive and liberating, offering an opportunity for profound growth and renewal.

- **Rituals and Practices:** To harness the transformative energy of an eclipse, consider engaging in rituals that focus on release and renewal. For a solar eclipse, which marks new beginnings, you might set intentions for your sexual life, focusing on what you wish to manifest or change. For a lunar eclipse, which is more about endings and culmination, consider rituals that involve letting go of old patterns or emotional baggage that no longer serves you.

Solar Flares: Surges of Cosmic Energy

Solar flares are bursts of intense radiation from the Sun that can impact the Earth's electromagnetic field. While they are primarily known for their effects on technology, solar flares also have a significant impact on human energy levels, emotions, and behavior. In astrology, solar flares are associated with sudden surges of energy that can heighten emotions, increase tension, and amplify sexual desires.

- **Sexual Energy:** During periods of solar flare activity, you might experience heightened sexual energy and a strong desire for physical connection. The intense energy of a solar flare can amplify libido, making you more eager for sexual encounters. However, this energy can also lead to restlessness or irritability if not properly channeled.
- **Intensified Emotions:** Solar flares can magnify emotions, leading to passionate, intense interactions in your sexual relationship. This energy can be thrilling and invigorating, but it can also lead to conflicts or power struggles if emotions are not managed effectively. It's important to be mindful of how you and your partner are feeling during these periods and to communicate openly about any heightened emotions or desires.
- **Rituals and Practices:** To make the most of the energetic boost from a solar flare, consider engaging in activities that allow you to channel this energy constructively. Physical exercise, creative expression, or passionate sexual encounters can help you release any pent-up energy. Meditation and grounding exercises can also be beneficial in maintaining balance and preventing emotional overwhelm.

Meteor Showers: Celestial Magic and Inspiration

Meteor showers occur when the Earth passes through the trail of debris left by a comet, creating a spectacular display of shooting stars. While meteor showers are not traditionally a focus in astrology, their occurrence is often seen as a time of heightened inspiration, magic, and the potential for wishes to be fulfilled. In the context of sexual energy, meteor showers can bring a sense of wonder, creativity, and new possibilities.

- **Sexual Energy:** The energy of a meteor shower is more subtle and mystical than that of an eclipse or solar flare. It can inspire a sense of romanticism and creativity in your sexual relationship, encouraging you to explore new fantasies, deepen your emotional connection, or try something new and exciting with your partner. The magic of a meteor shower can infuse your intimate life with a sense of wonder and possibility.

- **Creative Exploration:** Meteor showers are an excellent time for exploring the more imaginative and playful aspects of your sexuality. This might involve trying out new fantasies, engaging in role play, or simply spending time with your partner under the stars, allowing the celestial display to inspire your connection. The energy of a meteor shower supports creativity and experimentation, making it a great time to try something out of the ordinary.

- **Rituals and Practices:** To harness the magical energy of a meteor shower, consider planning a romantic evening under the stars. This could involve setting up a cozy outdoor space where you can watch the meteor shower with your partner, perhaps incorporating elements like candlelight, soft music, or shared storytelling. You might also use this time to make wishes or set intentions for your sexual relationship, using the energy of the shooting stars to manifest your desires.

Cosmic Alignments: The Synergy of Multiple Events

Sometimes, multiple celestial events coincide, creating a powerful synergy of energies that can have a profound impact on our sexual lives. For example, a solar eclipse might occur during a period of heightened solar flare activity, or a meteor shower might align with a Full Moon. These cosmic alignments can intensify the effects of individual events, leading to significant shifts in energy and behavior.

- **Amplified Sexual Energy:** When multiple celestial events align, the impact on sexual energy can be dramatic. You might experience a surge in libido, a deeper emotional connection with your partner, or a heightened sense of urgency to address unresolved issues in your relationship. These periods can be both exhilarating and challenging, as the combined energies push you toward transformation and growth.

- **Navigating Complexity:** The combined influence of multiple celestial events can create a complex emotional landscape. It's important to stay attuned to your own feelings and those of your partner, recognizing that these energies can bring both opportunities and challenges. Open communication, mindfulness, and a willingness to embrace change are key to navigating these intense periods.
- **Rituals and Practices:** During cosmic alignments, consider engaging in rituals that honor the unique combination of energies at play. This might involve combining elements from different rituals, such as setting intentions, releasing old patterns, and celebrating your sexual connection. Embrace the complexity of these moments, allowing the synergy of celestial events to guide you toward deeper understanding and connection.

Conclusion

Celestial events like eclipses, solar flares, and meteor showers offer unique opportunities to explore and enhance your sexual energy and intimate relationships. Each event brings its own distinct energy, whether it's the transformative power of an eclipse, the intense surge of a solar flare, or the magical inspiration of a meteor shower. By understanding how these cosmic phenomena affect your sexual energy, you can align with their rhythms and harness their power to create more fulfilling and meaningful sexual experiences. Embrace the influence of these celestial events as part of your astrological journey, and let them guide you toward greater connection, passion, and intimacy in your relationships.

Part 2: Planetary Influence on Sexual Positions

Chapter 6: Sun: Vitality and Ego in Sex

Positions that boost confidence and showcase individuality.

The Sun, the center of our solar system, represents the core of our being, radiating vitality, ego, and self-expression. In astrology, the Sun governs our identity, how we shine in the world, and how we express our individuality. When it comes to sexuality, the Sun's influence is all about confidence, passion, and the celebration of self. Understanding the role of the Sun in sexual dynamics can help individuals and couples harness their inner power, boost their confidence, and showcase their unique identities in the bedroom.

This chapter explores the connection between the Sun's energy and sexual expression, offering a variety of positions that enhance self-assurance, allow for self-expression, and create a powerful connection between partners. These positions are designed to help you tap into your solar energy, embrace your individuality, and shine brightly in your intimate encounters.

The Sun's Influence on Sexuality

In astrology, the Sun represents our ego, identity, and the way we express our true selves. It governs our vitality, drive, and the desire to be seen and recognized. When the Sun's energy is positively channeled in sexual relationships, it can lead to a vibrant, confident, and fulfilling experience. The Sun encourages us to take pride in our sexual identity, to be confident in our desires, and to express ourselves fully with our partners.

- Vitality: The Sun's influence brings energy, enthusiasm, and a zest for life into sexual experiences. It fuels our desire for connection and pleasure, making us feel alive and invigorated.
- Ego and Self-Expression: The Sun governs our sense of self-worth and how we present ourselves to others. In sexual relationships, this translates to a strong sense of confidence and the ability to express one's desires, preferences, and individuality without hesitation.

• Showcasing Individuality: The Sun's energy encourages us to embrace our unique qualities and to celebrate what makes us special. In the context of sex, this means exploring positions and practices that allow for personal expression, creativity, and the celebration of our distinct sexual identities.

Positions that Boost Confidence and Showcase Individuality

The following positions are designed to enhance confidence, allow for self-expression, and make you feel like the star of your own sexual experience. These positions are ideal for those looking to tap into their solar energy, whether they're seeking to boost their self-esteem, express their desires, or simply enjoy a passionate, ego-boosting encounter.

1. The Sun Worshipper
   ◦ Description: This position involves one partner lying back with their chest lifted, while the other partner kneels or stands over them, taking a dominant yet adoring stance. The partner on top radiates confidence and power, while the partner lying back is celebrated and admired.
   ◦ Benefits: The Sun Worshipper position is perfect for boosting confidence and allowing both partners to feel valued and appreciated. The partner on top takes on a role of dominance, showcasing their strength and vitality, while the partner below basks in the attention and adoration.
   ◦ How to Perform: The receiving partner lies on their back, propped up on their elbows or a cushion to lift their chest. The other partner kneels or stands above them, maintaining eye contact and using their hands to caress and explore the receiving partner's body. This position is all about mutual admiration and celebrating each other's bodies.
2. The Star Performer
   ◦ Description: In this position, one partner stands with their back against a wall, while the other partner supports them from below. The standing partner is free to move their hips, control the rhythm, and showcase their sexual prowess, while the supporting partner provides stability and encouragement.

- Benefits: The Star Performer position is ideal for those who want to take control and express their sexual confidence. It allows the standing partner to take the lead, moving in a way that feels empowering and expressive.
- How to Perform: The standing partner leans against a wall for support, while the other partner kneels or sits beneath them, holding their hips or thighs for stability. The standing partner controls the pace and movement, using their body to express their desires and showcase their sexual energy.

3. The Radiant Embrace
- Description: This position involves both partners sitting facing each other, with their legs wrapped around one another. They maintain eye contact and synchronize their movements, creating a powerful connection that allows each partner to express their individuality while staying in tune with their partner.
- Benefits: The Radiant Embrace is perfect for those who want to celebrate their connection while also expressing their unique sexual energy. The position allows for deep intimacy, mutual support, and the opportunity to explore different rhythms and movements together.
- How to Perform: Both partners sit facing each other, legs wrapped around each other's waists. They hold each other's hands or shoulders for support, maintaining eye contact as they move together. This position encourages both partners to express themselves freely while remaining connected.

4. The Solar Flare
- Description: The Solar Flare is a dynamic position where one partner lies on their back with their legs raised, while the other partner kneels between their legs, leaning forward to create a powerful, intimate connection. This position allows the kneeling partner to take control, showcasing their strength and confidence.
- Benefits: The Solar Flare position is ideal for those who want to feel powerful and in control while also maintaining a deep connection with their partner. It allows for assertive movements and self-expression, making it perfect for boosting confidence and showcasing individuality.

- How to Perform: The receiving partner lies on their back with their legs raised, either resting on the kneeling partner's shoulders or held in the air. The kneeling partner leans forward, using their body weight to control the pace and depth of penetration. This position emphasizes strength, control, and a powerful connection.

5. The Sun Chariot
   - Description: Inspired by the mythological chariots of the Sun gods, this position involves one partner sitting on top of the other, straddling them like a charioteer. The top partner controls the movement, while the bottom partner provides support and stability, creating a dynamic and empowering experience.
   - Benefits: The Sun Chariot is perfect for those who want to feel in control and showcase their sexual confidence. It allows the top partner to take charge, exploring different rhythms and angles, while the bottom partner supports and enjoys the ride.
   - How to Perform: The bottom partner lies on their back or sits up slightly, providing a stable base. The top partner straddles them, sitting upright and holding onto their partner's shoulders or chest for support. The top partner controls the movement, using their hips to set the pace and intensity.

Embracing Your Solar Energy in Sexual Relationships

The Sun's influence in sexual relationships is all about embracing your individuality, radiating confidence, and celebrating your unique identity. Whether you're looking to boost your self-esteem, express your desires, or simply enjoy a passionate encounter, these positions can help you tap into your solar energy and shine brightly in your sexual experiences.

- Self-Expression: Don't be afraid to express your desires, preferences, and boundaries in the bedroom. The Sun encourages you to be bold and unapologetic in your sexual identity, allowing you to explore what makes you feel confident and fulfilled.
- Confidence Building: Use these positions to build your confidence and self-esteem. By taking on roles that allow you to feel powerful and in control, you can enhance your sense of self-worth and enjoy a more satisfying sexual relationship.

- Celebrating Individuality: Celebrate what makes you unique in your sexual relationships. Whether it's your physical appearance, your sexual preferences, or your personality, the Sun encourages you to embrace and showcase your individuality in the most intimate of settings.

Conclusion

The Sun's energy in astrology is a powerful force that drives our vitality, ego, and self-expression. By incorporating positions that boost confidence and showcase individuality, you can tap into this solar energy, creating a sexual relationship that is both empowering and deeply satisfying. Embrace your inner Sun, and let it shine brightly in all aspects of your intimate life.

Chapter 7: Moon: Emotional Intimacy and Sensuality

The Moon is a celestial body that has long been associated with emotions, instincts, and the subconscious. In astrology, the Moon governs our emotional needs, nurturing tendencies, and the ways we seek comfort and security. When it comes to sexuality, the Moon plays a crucial role in shaping our desires for emotional intimacy and sensual connection. This chapter explores the Moon's influence on our sexual relationships, focusing on nurturing and intimate positions that deepen emotional bonds and create a sense of security and closeness with a partner.

The Moon's Influence on Emotional Intimacy

The Moon's energy is deeply tied to our emotional well-being and how we connect with others on a deeply personal level. In sexual relationships, the Moon represents the need for emotional closeness, security, and a sense of being cared for. Understanding the Moon's influence on your sexual life can help you create more fulfilling and emotionally resonant experiences with your partner.

- **Emotional Security:** The Moon governs our need for emotional security in relationships. This security is often built through trust, vulnerability, and a willingness to share one's innermost thoughts and feelings. In the context of sexuality, the Moon's influence encourages partners to create a safe and supportive environment where both can express their desires without fear of judgment.
- **Nurturing and Care:** The Moon's energy is also associated with nurturing and care. In a sexual relationship, this can manifest as a desire to take care of your partner, to ensure they feel loved and valued. This nurturing aspect of the Moon can deepen the emotional connection between partners, making sex not just a physical act but a profound expression of love and care.
- **Emotional Connection:** For those with a strong Moon influence in their natal chart, emotional connection is often a prerequisite for satisfying sexual experiences. They may find that their sexual desires are closely linked to their emotional state and that true satisfaction comes from connecting with their partner on a deeper, more intimate level.

Sensuality and the Moon: The Role of Touch and Comfort

Sensuality, governed by the Moon, is about engaging the senses to create a deeply satisfying and emotionally fulfilling experience. The Moon encourages us to slow down, to savor the moment, and to prioritize comfort and emotional connection over mere physical gratification.

- **The Importance of Touch:** The Moon's influence heightens the importance of touch in sexual relationships. Gentle, nurturing touch can create a sense of security and connection, helping partners feel more emotionally aligned. Whether it's through soft caresses, holding hands, or simply lying close to one another, touch is a powerful way to deepen emotional intimacy.
- **Creating a Comforting Environment:** The Moon's energy thrives in environments that feel safe, warm, and comforting. In the context of sexuality, this might involve creating a cozy, inviting space where both partners feel relaxed and secure. Soft lighting, warm blankets, and soothing music can all contribute to an atmosphere that nurtures emotional connection.
- **Savoring the Moment:** Sensuality under the Moon's influence is about slowing down and savoring each moment of intimacy. Instead of rushing through the experience, partners are encouraged to take their time, to explore each other's bodies with care and attention, and to focus on the emotional connection that arises from shared sensual pleasure.

Nurturing and Intimate Positions for Emotional Connection

Certain sexual positions naturally lend themselves to deeper emotional connections, allowing partners to nurture each other and build a strong emotional bond. The following positions are particularly suited to enhancing the Moon's influence in a sexual relationship, fostering emotional intimacy, and creating a sense of security and care.

- **Spooning:**
    - **Description:** Spooning is a position where one partner lies behind the other, their bodies closely aligned. This position is inherently nurturing, as it allows for full-body contact and creates a sense of closeness and protection.
    - **Emotional Benefits:** Spooning fosters a deep sense of security and emotional connection. The partner in front may feel safe and cared for, while the partner behind can ex-

press their love and support through gentle, nurturing touch. This position is ideal for couples who want to feel close and emotionally connected during sex.

- **Face-to-Face Missionary:**
    - ◦ **Description:** In this variation of the traditional missionary position, both partners maintain eye contact, with their bodies aligned and close together. The position allows for deep emotional connection through visual and physical intimacy.
    - ◦ **Emotional Benefits:** Face-to-face missionary enhances emotional intimacy by allowing partners to look into each other's eyes, creating a powerful sense of connection. This position also allows for close physical contact, making it easier to share gentle touches and whispered words of affection.
- **Lotus Position:**
    - ◦ **Description:** In the Lotus position, one partner sits cross-legged while the other straddles them, wrapping their legs around their partner's waist. This position is highly intimate, with both partners facing each other and their bodies fully intertwined.
    - ◦ **Emotional Benefits:** The Lotus position is excellent for fostering deep emotional intimacy. The close physical contact and face-to-face orientation allow partners to feel fully connected, both emotionally and physically. This position is ideal for slow, sensual lovemaking where the focus is on nurturing the emotional bond.
- **Cradling Position:**
    - ◦ **Description:** In the Cradling position, one partner lies on their back while the other lies on top, resting their head on their partner's chest. This position allows for gentle rocking movements and close physical contact.
    - ◦ **Emotional Benefits:** The Cradling position is highly nurturing, as it mimics the comforting experience of being held and cradled. This position is ideal for moments when one partner needs reassurance, care, and emotional support. It fosters a deep sense of security and love, making it perfect for emotionally intimate encounters.
- **Yab-Yum:**
    - ◦ **Description:** Similar to the Lotus position, Yab-Yum involves one partner sitting cross-legged while the other sits on their lap, facing them. In this position, the partners' hearts are aligned, and they can maintain close eye contact.

- **Emotional Benefits:** Yab-Yum is a deeply spiritual and emotionally connected position. It aligns the partners' energies, allowing for a profound sense of unity and oneness. This position is often used in Tantric practices to deepen emotional and spiritual connection through sexual intimacy.

Enhancing Emotional Intimacy Through Rituals and Practices

The Moon's influence on emotional intimacy can be further enhanced through rituals and practices that align with its nurturing energy. These activities can help you and your partner deepen your emotional connection, making your sexual relationship more fulfilling and harmonious.

- **Moonlit Rituals:** Consider engaging in rituals that involve the Moon's energy, such as spending time together under the light of the Full Moon or New Moon. You might set intentions for your relationship, meditate together, or simply enjoy each other's company in the peaceful glow of the Moon.
- **Sensual Massage:** Incorporate sensual massage into your intimate routine. Using oils and gentle touch, take turns giving each other massages that focus on relaxation and emotional connection. This practice can help you both feel more connected and cared for, enhancing the Moon's nurturing influence.
- **Shared Baths:** A warm, shared bath can be a deeply nurturing and intimate experience. Light candles, add soothing essential oils, and take the time to relax together in the warm water. This shared experience can help you both feel more emotionally connected and cared for.
- **Gratitude Practices:** Expressing gratitude for each other can enhance emotional intimacy. Take a moment each day to share something you appreciate about your partner, whether it's a kind gesture, a loving touch, or simply their presence in your life. This practice aligns with the Moon's energy by fostering emotional closeness and connection.

Conclusion

The Moon's influence on emotional intimacy and sensuality is profound, guiding us to seek deeper connections with our partners that go beyond physical attraction. By understanding and honoring the Moon's energy in your sexual relationship, you can create a more nurturing, emotionally fulfilling bond with your partner. The positions and practices outlined in this chapter are designed to enhance the Moon's influence, helping you and your partner connect on a deeper, more intimate level. Embrace the nurturing power of the Moon, and let it guide you toward a more harmonious and emotionally satisfying sexual relationship.

Chapter 8: Mercury: Communication and Playfulness

Mercury, the planet of communication, intellect, and curiosity, plays a vital role in our sexual relationships by influencing how we express our desires, engage in verbal exchange, and infuse playfulness into our intimate interactions. In astrology, Mercury governs the way we think, speak, and connect with others on a mental level. When it comes to sexuality, Mercury's influence encourages open communication, intellectual stimulation, and playful exploration. This chapter delves into how Mercury shapes our sexual experiences and introduces positions that foster verbal exchange and playful interaction, enhancing both mental and physical intimacy.

The Role of Mercury in Sexual Relationships

Mercury's energy is dynamic, curious, and intellectually driven. It encourages us to communicate our thoughts and desires clearly and to engage in playful, stimulating interactions with our partners. In sexual relationships, Mercury's influence can enhance the connection between partners by facilitating better understanding, fostering curiosity, and bringing an element of fun and spontaneity to intimate moments.

- **Communication:** Mercury emphasizes the importance of clear and open communication in sexual relationships. This includes discussing desires, boundaries, and fantasies, as well as providing feedback during intimate moments. When partners are able to communicate effectively, they can create a more satisfying and harmonious sexual relationship.

- **Intellectual Stimulation:** For those with a strong Mercury influence in their natal chart, intellectual connection can be just as important as physical attraction. Engaging in mentally stimulating conversations, sharing ideas, and exploring fantasies together can enhance the overall sexual experience, making it more fulfilling and enjoyable.

- **Playfulness:** Mercury's energy is light-hearted and playful, encouraging partners to have fun and explore their sexuality with a sense of curiosity and adventure. Incorporating playfulness into your sexual relationship can help reduce tension, build rapport, and create a more relaxed and enjoyable atmosphere.

Positions That Encourage Verbal Exchange

Certain sexual positions naturally lend themselves to verbal exchange, allowing partners to communicate openly and share their thoughts, desires, and feelings during intimacy. These positions can help deepen the mental and emotional connection between partners, making the sexual experience more engaging and interactive.

- **Face-to-Face Sitting:**
    - **Description:** In this position, both partners sit facing each other, with one partner straddling the other's lap. This close, face-to-face orientation allows for easy verbal communication and eye contact.
    - **Verbal Interaction:** The face-to-face sitting position is ideal for intimate conversations and whispered exchanges during sex. Partners can share their thoughts, express their desires, and offer feedback in real-time, enhancing the emotional and mental connection.
    - **Playfulness:** This position also allows for playful interaction, such as teasing, kissing, and exploring each other's reactions to different touches and movements.
- **Reverse Cowgirl:**
    - **Description:** In the reverse cowgirl position, one partner lies on their back while the other straddles them, facing away. This position provides a unique angle and allows the partner on top to control the pace and depth of penetration.
    - **Verbal Interaction:** The reverse cowgirl position encourages verbal communication as the partner on top can easily guide the experience by expressing their preferences and desires. The partner on the bottom can also offer feedback and encouragement, creating a dynamic exchange of verbal cues.
    - **Playfulness:** The position's playful nature allows for a sense of fun and experimentation, as partners can explore different rhythms and techniques while maintaining an open line of communication.
- **Doggy Style with Mirror:**
    - **Description:** In this variation of the doggy style position, one partner is on all fours while the other penetrates from behind. The addition of a mirror in front of the re-

ceiving partner allows both partners to maintain eye contact and observe each other's reactions.

- **Verbal Interaction:** The presence of the mirror facilitates verbal exchange, as partners can communicate what they see and feel, enhancing the overall experience. This position allows for playful comments, dirty talk, and expressions of pleasure, making it a highly interactive experience.
- **Playfulness:** The visual element adds a layer of excitement and playfulness, as partners can watch each other and engage in fun, teasing banter during the act.

- **Side-by-Side Spooning:**
  - **Description:** In the side-by-side spooning position, both partners lie on their sides, facing each other or in a spooning arrangement. This close, intimate position allows for gentle movements and easy verbal communication.
  - **Verbal Interaction:** The side-by-side position is perfect for soft, intimate conversations. Partners can whisper sweet nothings, share their feelings, and express their desires in a relaxed, comforting environment. This position is particularly suited for moments of deep emotional connection.
  - **Playfulness:** The spooning position also allows for playful interactions, such as light tickling, gentle caresses, and experimenting with different rhythms, all while maintaining a close, intimate connection.

Playful Positions That Enhance the Mercury Influence

Mercury's playful energy encourages exploration, fun, and spontaneity in sexual relationships. The following positions are designed to bring out the light-hearted, adventurous side of intimacy, making sex an enjoyable and dynamic experience for both partners.

- **Standing Up:**
  - **Description:** In this position, both partners stand facing each other, with one partner lifting the other's leg or holding them up for deeper penetration. This position is dynamic and requires balance and coordination.

- ◦ **Playfulness:** The standing position is playful and spontaneous, often requiring partners to communicate and adjust to maintain balance. This can lead to laughter, teasing, and a sense of adventure as partners explore different angles and movements.
- **The Wheelbarrow:**
  - ◦ **Description:** In the wheelbarrow position, one partner stands or kneels while holding the other partner's legs, who supports themselves with their hands on the floor. This position is challenging and requires strength and coordination.
  - ◦ **Playfulness:** The wheelbarrow is a playful position that encourages partners to work together, communicate, and have fun experimenting with different dynamics. The unconventional nature of this position often leads to laughter and a sense of shared adventure.
- **Chair Straddle:**
  - ◦ **Description:** In the chair straddle position, one partner sits on a chair while the other straddles them, facing away or towards them. This position allows for a range of movements and angles.
  - ◦ **Playfulness:** The chair straddle is a versatile and playful position, allowing for different levels of control and exploration. Partners can switch between playful and intimate interactions, making it a dynamic and enjoyable experience.
- **The Frog:**
  - ◦ **Description:** In the frog position, the receiving partner lies on their back with their legs bent and spread wide, while the other partner kneels between their legs for penetration. This position is open and allows for a playful approach to intimacy.
  - ◦ **Playfulness:** The frog position is playful and allows for experimentation with depth, speed, and rhythm. Partners can easily communicate their preferences, making this a fun and interactive position.

Enhancing Communication and Playfulness Through Rituals and Practices

In addition to incorporating Mercury-inspired positions into your sexual relationship, there are rituals and practices that can further enhance communication and playfulness. These activities encourage partners to explore their sexuality with curiosity and openness, fostering a deeper connection.

- **Verbal Games:** Engage in verbal games that encourage communication and playfulness. This could include truth-or-dare, asking each other intimate questions, or playing a game of "Would You Rather?" tailored to your sexual preferences. These games can help partners explore their desires and boundaries in a fun, light-hearted way.
- **Role Play:** Role-playing is a powerful way to bring Mercury's playful energy into your sexual relationship. Choose characters or scenarios that excite both partners and engage in a playful exploration of different roles. This can help you step outside of your usual dynamics and explore new aspects of your sexuality.
- **Dirty Talk Practice:** Practice dirty talk with your partner to enhance verbal communication during sex. Start with simple phrases and gradually explore more explicit language that excites both partners. Dirty talk can add an element of excitement and playfulness, making your sexual experiences more dynamic and engaging.
- **Intellectual Foreplay:** Engage in intellectual foreplay by discussing fantasies, sharing erotic stories, or debating topics that interest both partners before transitioning into physical intimacy. This mental stimulation can heighten arousal and create a deeper connection between partners, aligning with Mercury's influence.

Conclusion

Mercury's influence on communication and playfulness in sexual relationships is profound, encouraging partners to engage in open dialogue, intellectual exploration, and light-hearted interaction. By incorporating positions that foster verbal exchange and playful dynamics, you can enhance both the mental and physical aspects of your sexual connection. Whether through face-to-face conversations, playful banter, or intellectual foreplay, Mercury's energy can help you create a more satisfying and interactive sexual relationship. Embrace the power of communication and playfulness, and let Mercury guide you toward deeper connection, greater intimacy, and more joyful sexual experiences.

Chapter 9: Venus: Love and Sensual Pleasure

Venus, the planet of love, beauty, and pleasure, plays a central role in shaping our romantic and sexual experiences. In astrology, Venus governs our desires for love, intimacy, and sensual enjoyment, guiding how we express affection and experience pleasure in our relationships. This chapter explores Venus's influence on our sexual lives, focusing on romantic and pleasure-centric positions that emphasize love, beauty, and deep connection. By aligning with Venus's energy, you can create a more fulfilling and harmonious sexual relationship that celebrates both emotional intimacy and physical pleasure.

The Role of Venus in Romantic and Sexual Relationships

Venus is often associated with the archetype of the lover, representing our capacity for love, attraction, and the appreciation of beauty. In sexual relationships, Venus's energy encourages us to seek out experiences that are not only physically satisfying but also emotionally enriching and aesthetically pleasing.

- **Love and Affection:** Venus governs how we express love and affection in our relationships. This includes the ways we show appreciation for our partners, how we cultivate romance, and the importance we place on emotional connection. Venus's influence encourages a loving, nurturing approach to sexuality, where both partners feel valued and cherished.
- **Sensual Pleasure:** Venus is also the planet of sensual pleasure, emphasizing the importance of physical touch, beauty, and the enjoyment of the senses. In sexual relationships, Venus encourages us to slow down and savor the experience, focusing on the pleasure that comes from connecting with our partners in a loving, intimate way.
- **Aesthetic Appreciation:** Venus is closely linked to the appreciation of beauty, both in our surroundings and in our partners. Creating a beautiful, romantic environment can enhance the sexual experience, making it more pleasurable and emotionally fulfilling. Venus's influence reminds us to pay attention to the details that make an intimate encounter special, such as soft lighting, gentle music, and tactile sensations.

Romantic and Pleasure-Centric Positions

Certain sexual positions are particularly well-suited to enhancing Venus's energy in a relationship, focusing on romantic connection, sensual pleasure, and the beauty of the shared experience. These positions are designed to emphasize love, intimacy, and the enjoyment of physical touch, creating a deeply satisfying and harmonious sexual connection.

- **The Lovers' Embrace:**
  - **Description:** In the Lovers' Embrace, both partners lie facing each other, with their legs intertwined and bodies pressed close together. This position allows for deep eye contact, gentle caresses, and a slow, rhythmic movement that emphasizes connection and intimacy.
  - **Romantic Benefits:** The Lovers' Embrace is ideal for fostering emotional closeness and expressing love through physical touch. The close contact allows partners to feel each other's heartbeat, breathe together, and maintain a deep, loving connection throughout the encounter.
  - **Sensual Pleasure:** This position encourages slow, deliberate movements that allow both partners to savor the sensations and fully enjoy the pleasure of the experience. The emphasis is on tenderness and the shared enjoyment of the moment.
- **The Butterfly:**
  - **Description:** In the Butterfly position, one partner lies on their back with their legs raised and spread, while the other partner kneels between their legs, holding their ankles or thighs for support. This position allows for deep penetration and a close, intimate connection.
  - **Romantic Benefits:** The Butterfly position allows for close eye contact and the opportunity to share loving words and gentle kisses. The open, vulnerable posture of the receiving partner encourages trust and emotional intimacy, making it a deeply romantic experience.
  - **Sensual Pleasure:** The angle of penetration in the Butterfly position allows for enhanced pleasure, particularly for the receiving partner. The slow, controlled movements

that this position encourages can lead to a deeply satisfying and pleasurable experience for both partners.

- **The Rocking Horse:**
  - **Description:** In the Rocking Horse position, one partner sits on a sturdy surface, such as the edge of a bed or a chair, while the other partner straddles them, facing forward. This position allows for a gentle rocking motion that can be both soothing and stimulating.
  - **Romantic Benefits:** The Rocking Horse position is perfect for a romantic, intimate encounter. The face-to-face orientation allows for deep eye contact, shared smiles, and the exchange of loving words. The slow, rocking motion can create a sense of harmony and connection between partners.
  - **Sensual Pleasure:** The Rocking Horse position allows both partners to control the rhythm and depth of penetration, making it easy to find a pace that is mutually satisfying. The gentle, rhythmic movement is ideal for prolonged, sensual lovemaking that emphasizes the enjoyment of the experience.
- **The Venus Shell:**
  - **Description:** Inspired by the famous painting "The Birth of Venus," the Venus Shell position involves one partner lying on their side with their legs slightly bent, while the other partner spoons them from behind. This position allows for close physical contact and a sense of protection and care.
  - **Romantic Benefits:** The Venus Shell position is deeply romantic and nurturing, with the spooning partner providing a sense of security and warmth. This position allows for whispered words of affection, gentle kisses on the neck and shoulders, and a deep emotional connection.
  - **Sensual Pleasure:** The Venus Shell position is perfect for slow, sensual lovemaking that emphasizes tenderness and care. The close physical contact allows both partners to enjoy the warmth and softness of each other's bodies, creating a deeply pleasurable and intimate experience.

- **The Heart-to-Heart:**
  - **Description:** In the Heart-to-Heart position, one partner lies on their back while the other partner lies on top, aligning their chests and hearts. This position allows for full-body contact and the opportunity to synchronize breathing and movements.
  - **Romantic Benefits:** The Heart-to-Heart position is ideal for creating a deep emotional bond between partners. The close physical contact and the alignment of the hearts and chests symbolize a union of both body and soul. This position is perfect for expressing love and devotion.
  - **Sensual Pleasure:** The Heart-to-Heart position encourages slow, rhythmic movements that allow both partners to fully enjoy the physical and emotional connection. The full-body contact enhances the sensual pleasure, making it a deeply satisfying and intimate experience.

Enhancing Venusian Energy Through Rituals and Practices

In addition to incorporating Venus-inspired positions into your sexual relationship, there are rituals and practices that can further enhance the energy of love, beauty, and sensual pleasure. These activities encourage partners to connect on a deeper level, fostering a romantic and harmonious atmosphere that aligns with Venus's influence.

- **Romantic Rituals:** Engage in rituals that celebrate love and romance, such as lighting candles, playing soft music, or creating a beautiful, inviting environment for your intimate encounters. These rituals can help set the mood and enhance the overall experience, making it more pleasurable and emotionally fulfilling.
- **Shared Baths:** Taking a bath together can be a deeply romantic and sensual experience. Add rose petals, essential oils, or bath salts to the water, and take the time to relax and enjoy each other's company. The soothing warmth of the water and the close physical contact can help deepen your emotional connection and enhance the sensual pleasure of the experience.
- **Gifting:** Venus loves beauty and luxury, so consider surprising your partner with a small, thoughtful gift that reflects your appreciation for them. This could be something as simple

as a flower, a piece of jewelry, or a handwritten love note. The act of giving and receiving can strengthen your emotional bond and add a touch of romance to your relationship.

- **Massage and Touch:** Incorporate massage and gentle touch into your intimate routine. Use scented oils and take turns giving each other massages that focus on relaxation and sensual pleasure. This practice can help you both feel more connected and cherished, enhancing the Venusian energy in your relationship.

Conclusion

Venus's influence on love and sensual pleasure is central to creating a deeply satisfying and harmonious sexual relationship. By embracing the romantic and pleasure-centric positions outlined in this chapter, you can enhance the emotional and physical connection with your partner, making your intimate encounters more meaningful and fulfilling. Whether through the tender embrace of the Lovers' Embrace, the rhythmic motion of the Rocking Horse, or the nurturing warmth of the Venus Shell, Venus's energy encourages you to celebrate love, beauty, and the joy of sensual pleasure. Let Venus guide you toward a more loving, romantic, and pleasurable sexual relationship, where both partners feel cherished, valued, and deeply connected.

Chapter 10: Mars: Passion and Aggression

Mars, the planet of action, desire, and aggression, is the driving force behind our sexual energy and passion. In astrology, Mars represents our primal instincts, our capacity for assertiveness, and our pursuit of what we desire. When it comes to sexuality, Mars fuels our drive for physical connection, excitement, and intensity. This chapter explores Mars's influence on our sexual experiences, focusing on high-energy positions that unleash raw passion and assertiveness. By aligning with Mars's dynamic energy, you can bring a powerful, fiery intensity to your sexual relationship, creating thrilling and unforgettable experiences.

The Role of Mars in Sexual Relationships

Mars is often associated with the warrior archetype, symbolizing strength, courage, and the will to pursue what one wants. In sexual relationships, Mars's influence encourages us to embrace our desires boldly, to be assertive in expressing our needs, and to channel our physical energy into passionate encounters. Mars is the planet that pushes us to take action, to explore new territories, and to engage in sexual experiences that are exhilarating and full of intensity.

- **Passion and Desire:** Mars governs our sexual drive and the intensity of our desires. When Mars is strong in a natal chart, individuals are often driven by a powerful need for physical connection and sexual satisfaction. Mars's energy brings heat, excitement, and urgency to sexual relationships, making encounters more dynamic and thrilling.

- **Aggression and Assertiveness:** Mars also represents the assertive, sometimes aggressive side of our sexuality. This isn't about harmful aggression, but rather about the confidence and willingness to take the lead, to initiate, and to express one's desires without hesitation. In a healthy sexual relationship, Mars's energy encourages both partners to be bold and direct in their pursuit of pleasure.

- **Physical Energy:** Mars is the source of our physical vitality and stamina, which are crucial for high-energy sexual experiences. Mars-driven sexuality is often characterized by a need for action, movement, and the physical expression of desire. This energy can lead to vigorous, adventurous sexual encounters that are both satisfying and empowering.

High-Energy Positions That Unleash Raw Passion

Certain sexual positions are particularly well-suited to channeling Mars's intense, fiery energy. These high-energy positions emphasize physical exertion, deep connection, and the expression of raw passion and assertiveness. They are designed to ignite the flames of desire, creating powerful and exhilarating sexual experiences.

- **Standing Dog:**
    - **Description:** In the Standing Dog position, one partner bends forward, supporting themselves with their hands on a sturdy surface, while the other partner stands behind and penetrates from a standing position. This position allows for deep penetration and a strong, rhythmic thrusting motion.
    - **Passion and Assertiveness:** The Standing Dog position is ideal for unleashing raw passion and assertiveness. The standing partner can take full control of the pace and intensity, allowing for a powerful, driving rhythm that channels Mars's energy. This position also encourages the use of hands for added stimulation or to assert dominance.
    - **Physical Energy:** This position requires strength and stamina, making it perfect for those moments when you want to fully engage in a high-energy, physically demanding encounter.
- **The Press:**
    - **Description:** In the Press position, one partner lies on their back with their legs raised and pressed against their partner's chest, while the other partner kneels or stands and penetrates. This position allows for deep, forceful penetration and close physical contact.
    - **Passion and Assertiveness:** The Press position allows the penetrating partner to take control and drive the intensity of the encounter. The close physical contact heightens the sense of connection and allows for deep, powerful thrusts that emphasize raw passion.

- **Physical Energy:** The Press position requires physical strength and control, particularly for the penetrating partner, who must maintain balance and rhythm while delivering deep, assertive movements.

- **The Piledriver:**
  - **Description:** In the Piledriver position, one partner lies on their back with their hips lifted and legs bent back over their head, while the other partner kneels and penetrates from above. This position allows for deep penetration and intense physical exertion.
  - **Passion and Assertiveness:** The Piledriver is a highly assertive position that allows for maximum control and intensity. The penetrating partner can deliver powerful, deep thrusts, fully channeling Mars's aggressive energy. The receiving partner is in a vulnerable, yet highly stimulated position, which can heighten the overall intensity of the experience.
  - **Physical Energy:** This position is physically demanding for both partners, requiring flexibility, strength, and stamina. It's perfect for those moments when you want to fully embrace the raw, physical side of your sexuality.

- **The Cowgirl's Revenge:**
  - **Description:** In this variation of the classic cowgirl position, the receiving partner straddles the penetrating partner while facing away, taking control of the movement and intensity. This position allows the receiving partner to set the pace and fully engage in the rhythm.
  - **Passion and Assertiveness:** The Cowgirl's Revenge position empowers the receiving partner to take charge, fully expressing their desires and asserting control over the encounter. The penetrating partner can also engage in assertive movements by gripping the hips or guiding the rhythm, creating a dynamic exchange of power and passion.
  - **Physical Energy:** This position is ideal for those who enjoy an active, high-energy experience. It requires strength and coordination from both partners, making it a physically engaging and passionate encounter.

- **The Thrusting Bridge:**
  - **Description:** In the Thrusting Bridge position, one partner lies on their back with their hips lifted in a bridge pose, supported by their feet and shoulders. The other partner kneels between their legs and penetrates while maintaining a deep, rhythmic thrust.
  - **Passion and Assertiveness:** The Thrusting Bridge allows the penetrating partner to take control of the intensity and rhythm, delivering deep, powerful thrusts that channel Mars's fiery energy. The lifted position of the receiving partner enhances the depth and impact of each movement, intensifying the overall experience.
  - **Physical Energy:** This position requires strength and stamina from both partners. The receiving partner must maintain the bridge pose while the penetrating partner delivers strong, assertive movements. It's a position that fully engages the body, making it perfect for high-energy, passionate encounters.

Enhancing Mars's Energy Through Rituals and Practices

To fully harness Mars's energy in your sexual relationship, consider incorporating rituals and practices that emphasize physical exertion, assertiveness, and passion. These activities can help you tap into Mars's dynamic energy, enhancing the intensity and excitement of your sexual experiences.

- **Physical Fitness:** Maintaining physical fitness is key to harnessing Mars's energy. Regular exercise, strength training, and activities that build stamina can enhance your ability to engage in high-energy sexual encounters. Physical fitness not only improves your endurance but also boosts your confidence and assertiveness, aligning you with Mars's influence.
- **Role Play and Power Dynamics:** Engage in role play or explore power dynamics in your sexual relationship to channel Mars's assertive energy. Whether you take on the role of the dominant partner or the one who actively pursues their desires, role-playing can help you express Mars's energy in a playful, exciting way.
- **Breathwork and Visualization:** Practice breathwork and visualization techniques that focus on building and directing your sexual energy. Visualize the fiery, assertive energy of Mars filling your body, fueling your desires, and empowering you to take bold, confident actions during your sexual encounters.

- **Adventurous Encounters:** Mars thrives on excitement and new challenges, so consider adding an element of adventure to your sexual relationship. This might include trying new locations, experimenting with different positions, or introducing toys and props that enhance the physical and sensory experience. The goal is to keep the energy dynamic and thrilling, fully embracing Mars's influence.

Conclusion

Mars's influence on passion and aggression is a powerful force in sexual relationships, driving us to pursue our desires with intensity, confidence, and assertiveness. By incorporating the high-energy positions outlined in this chapter, you can unleash the raw, fiery energy of Mars, creating sexual experiences that are both exhilarating and deeply satisfying. Whether through the intense thrusts of the Piledriver, the assertive control of the Cowgirl's Revenge, or the powerful connection of the Thrusting Bridge, Mars's energy encourages you to embrace your primal instincts and fully engage in the physical expression of your desires. Let Mars guide you toward more passionate, dynamic, and empowering sexual encounters that celebrate the strength, courage, and intensity of your love and connection.

Chapter 11: Jupiter: Exploration and Expansion

Jupiter, the planet of expansion, exploration, and growth, brings a sense of adventure and curiosity to every aspect of life, including sexuality. In astrology, Jupiter represents the desire to explore new horizons, to learn and grow through experience, and to embrace opportunities for expansion. When it comes to sexual relationships, Jupiter's influence encourages partners to step out of their comfort zones, try new things, and cultivate a sense of adventure and discovery. This chapter explores Jupiter's role in sexuality, focusing on adventurous positions that promote exploration, growth, and the joy of shared experiences.

The Role of Jupiter in Sexual Relationships

Jupiter is often associated with the archetype of the explorer, representing the quest for knowledge, wisdom, and new experiences. In sexual relationships, Jupiter's energy encourages us to approach intimacy with a sense of curiosity and openness, to seek out new adventures with our partners, and to grow through the shared exploration of our desires.

- **Exploration and Adventure:** Jupiter governs the desire for exploration and adventure in all aspects of life, including sexuality. This energy drives us to try new positions, experiment with different dynamics, and explore uncharted territories in our sexual relationships. Under Jupiter's influence, partners are more likely to embrace novelty and take risks, leading to exciting and fulfilling experiences.

- **Growth and Expansion:** Jupiter's expansive energy encourages growth, both individually and as a couple. In the context of sexuality, this means pushing boundaries, learning from each experience, and continuously seeking ways to deepen the connection with your partner. Jupiter's influence fosters an open-minded approach to sex, where growth and learning are central to the experience.

- **Joy and Optimism:** Jupiter is also associated with joy, optimism, and a positive outlook on life. This energy infuses sexual relationships with a sense of fun, playfulness, and enthusiasm.

Under Jupiter's influence, sex becomes an adventure filled with possibilities, where the focus is on enjoying the journey as much as the destination.

Adventurous Positions That Promote Exploration and Growth

Certain sexual positions are particularly well-suited to channeling Jupiter's adventurous, expansive energy. These positions encourage partners to explore new dynamics, try different angles, and embrace the thrill of discovery. They are designed to promote growth, both physically and emotionally, making each encounter a learning experience that deepens the connection between partners.

- **The Standing Wheelbarrow:**
  - **Description:** In the Standing Wheelbarrow position, one partner stands while the other supports themselves with their hands on the floor, their legs held by the standing partner. This position allows for deep penetration and a unique angle, requiring strength and coordination from both partners.
  - **Exploration and Growth:** The Standing Wheelbarrow is an adventurous position that requires balance, trust, and teamwork. It encourages partners to explore new physical dynamics and push their limits, fostering a sense of shared accomplishment and growth.
  - **Joy and Optimism:** The novelty and challenge of this position make it a fun and exciting experience, filled with the optimism and enthusiasm that Jupiter inspires. The shared effort to maintain balance and rhythm adds an element of playfulness to the encounter.
- **The Lotus Lift:**
  - **Description:** In the Lotus Lift position, one partner sits in the traditional Lotus position with their legs crossed, while the other partner straddles them, lifting slightly off the ground using their arms for support. This position allows for close physical contact and a deep, rhythmic movement.
  - **Exploration and Growth:** The Lotus Lift combines intimacy with physical challenge, encouraging partners to explore different levels of control and intensity. The position

promotes growth by requiring both strength and flexibility, allowing partners to discover new ways to connect and enjoy each other.

- ◦ **Joy and Optimism:** The close contact and mutual support in this position create a sense of unity and shared joy, reflecting Jupiter's expansive, optimistic energy. The rhythmic movement can be both soothing and exhilarating, making the experience deeply satisfying.

- **The Crossroads:**
  - ◦ **Description:** In the Crossroads position, one partner lies on their back with their legs spread wide, while the other partner kneels between their legs, positioning their body perpendicular to their partner's. This position allows for a wide range of motion and angles, making it highly versatile.
  - ◦ **Exploration and Growth:** The Crossroads position encourages exploration by allowing partners to experiment with different angles and depths of penetration. The versatility of this position promotes growth as partners learn to communicate their preferences and adapt to each other's needs.
  - ◦ **Joy and Optimism:** The playful nature of the Crossroads position makes it a joyful experience, filled with opportunities for laughter and shared discovery. The flexibility and variety it offers align with Jupiter's energy, making each encounter an adventure.

- **The Reverse Scoop:**
  - ◦ **Description:** In the Reverse Scoop position, one partner lies on their side with their back to their partner, while the other partner spoons them from behind, with both partners' legs scissored in opposite directions. This position allows for deep penetration and close physical contact.
  - ◦ **Exploration and Growth:** The Reverse Scoop is an exploratory position that encourages partners to try different movements and angles, promoting a sense of discovery and growth. The close contact and unique positioning foster a deeper connection and a sense of shared exploration.
  - ◦ **Joy and Optimism:** The intimate and slightly unconventional nature of the Reverse Scoop adds a playful element to the encounter, making it a joyful and optimistic experience that reflects Jupiter's expansive energy.

- **The Chair Lift:**
  - **Description:** In the Chair Lift position, one partner sits on the edge of a chair, while the other partner stands in front, lifting their legs to straddle the seated partner. This position allows for deep penetration and requires strength and coordination from both partners.
  - **Exploration and Growth:** The Chair Lift is a physically demanding position that encourages partners to push their limits and explore new physical dynamics. It promotes growth by requiring both partners to work together and adapt to the demands of the position.
  - **Joy and Optimism:** The challenge and novelty of the Chair Lift position make it an exciting and adventurous experience, filled with the optimism and enthusiasm that Jupiter inspires. The shared effort and accomplishment add to the joy of the encounter.

Enhancing Jupiter's Energy Through Rituals and Practices

In addition to incorporating Jupiter-inspired positions into your sexual relationship, there are rituals and practices that can further enhance the energy of exploration, growth, and joy. These activities encourage partners to embrace new experiences, cultivate a sense of adventure, and continuously seek ways to expand their connection.

- **Travel-Inspired Encounters:** Embrace Jupiter's love of travel and exploration by incorporating elements from different cultures or locations into your sexual relationship. This could involve trying out new positions inspired by different parts of the world, exploring fantasies that involve travel or adventure, or even planning a romantic getaway to a new destination where you can explore your sexuality in a fresh, exciting environment.
- **Sexual Journaling:** Keep a journal of your sexual experiences and the new things you try with your partner. Reflect on what you enjoyed, what you learned, and how each experience contributed to your growth as a couple. This practice aligns with Jupiter's energy by encouraging continuous learning and self-improvement in your sexual relationship.
- **Learning Together:** Engage in activities that allow you and your partner to learn and grow together, such as taking a Tantra workshop, reading books on sexual exploration, or watching

educational videos on new techniques. The goal is to continuously expand your knowledge and skills, fostering a deeper connection and a more fulfilling sexual relationship.

- **Setting Sexual Goals:** Just as Jupiter is associated with expansion and growth, consider setting sexual goals that you and your partner can work toward together. These goals might include trying a certain number of new positions, exploring a specific fantasy, or deepening your emotional connection through shared experiences. Setting goals and working toward them together can enhance your sense of adventure and accomplishment.

Conclusion

Jupiter's influence on exploration and expansion encourages us to approach our sexual relationships with a sense of curiosity, openness, and a desire for growth. By incorporating the adventurous positions outlined in this chapter, you can harness Jupiter's dynamic energy to create sexual experiences that are both thrilling and deeply satisfying. Whether through the challenge of the Standing Wheelbarrow, the intimacy of the Lotus Lift, or the versatility of the Crossroads, Jupiter's energy encourages you to embrace new experiences, push boundaries, and continuously seek ways to expand your connection with your partner. Let Jupiter guide you toward a more adventurous, growth-oriented, and joyful sexual relationship, where each encounter is an opportunity for exploration and discovery.

Chapter 12: Saturn: Discipline and Structure

Saturn, the planet of discipline, structure, and responsibility, represents the aspects of life that require control, endurance, and a methodical approach. In astrology, Saturn is often associated with boundaries, limitations, and the lessons that come from persistence and hard work. When applied to sexuality, Saturn's influence encourages a disciplined, structured approach that emphasizes control, endurance, and the cultivation of deep, lasting connections. This chapter explores Saturn's role in sexual relationships, focusing on structured positions that enhance control and endurance, making the sexual experience more meaningful and profound.

The Role of Saturn in Sexual Relationships

Saturn's energy is often perceived as challenging, but it brings a necessary sense of discipline and structure to various aspects of life, including sexuality. Saturn's influence in sexual relationships is not about restriction but about creating a strong foundation through control, endurance, and a methodical approach to pleasure.

- **Discipline and Control:** Saturn emphasizes the importance of discipline and control in sexual relationships. This includes the ability to regulate one's desires, to maintain focus, and to exercise restraint when necessary. Saturn's energy encourages partners to approach sex with intentionality, ensuring that each encounter is meaningful and purposeful.
- **Endurance and Patience:** Saturn is associated with time, endurance, and the ability to persevere. In the context of sexuality, this translates to the capacity for prolonged, sustained pleasure, where the focus is on endurance and the slow, deliberate buildup of intensity. Saturn teaches that true satisfaction often comes from patience and the ability to maintain control over extended periods.
- **Structure and Boundaries:** Saturn also represents the importance of structure and boundaries in sexual relationships. This might involve setting clear expectations, understanding each other's limits, and creating a safe, secure environment where both partners feel respected and valued. Saturn's influence ensures that the relationship is built on a solid foundation, with

both partners understanding and honoring the boundaries that support mutual trust and respect.

Structured Positions That Emphasize Control and Endurance

Certain sexual positions are particularly well-suited to channeling Saturn's disciplined, structured energy. These positions focus on control, endurance, and the methodical buildup of pleasure, creating a sexual experience that is both deeply satisfying and aligned with Saturn's teachings.

- **The Slow Grind:**
  - **Description:** In the Slow Grind position, one partner lies on their back while the other straddles them, slowly grinding their hips in a controlled, rhythmic motion. The focus is on maintaining a steady pace and deep connection, rather than rapid movement.
  - **Discipline and Control:** The Slow Grind requires both partners to exercise control over their movements, maintaining a deliberate, unhurried rhythm. This position emphasizes the importance of discipline in sustaining pleasure over time, allowing both partners to fully experience each sensation.
  - **Endurance:** The Slow Grind is ideal for prolonged, enduring encounters. The slow pace allows for a gradual buildup of intensity, making it a perfect position for exploring the depths of pleasure and connection.
- **The Bridge:**
  - **Description:** In the Bridge position, one partner lies on their back with their hips lifted into a bridge pose, supported by their feet and shoulders. The other partner kneels or stands between their legs, maintaining a deep, controlled thrusting motion.
  - **Discipline and Control:** The Bridge position requires significant control and strength, particularly from the partner holding the bridge pose. The penetrating partner must also exercise discipline to maintain a steady, powerful rhythm, aligning with Saturn's emphasis on structure and endurance.
  - **Endurance:** The Bridge is a physically demanding position that challenges both partners to sustain their energy and focus over an extended period. It's ideal for those who

want to explore the boundaries of their physical endurance and experience the rewards of sustained effort.

- **The Plank:**
  - **Description:** In the Plank position, one partner supports themselves in a plank pose, holding their body straight and parallel to the ground, while the other partner kneels behind and penetrates. This position requires significant strength and control from both partners.
  - **Discipline and Control:** The Plank is a highly disciplined position that demands focus and control from both partners. The partner in the plank pose must maintain their form, while the penetrating partner must control the depth and rhythm of their movements. This position embodies Saturn's emphasis on structure and discipline.
  - **Endurance:** The Plank position is an endurance challenge, requiring both partners to sustain their efforts over time. It's perfect for those who want to test their limits and experience the satisfaction that comes from pushing through physical challenges together.
- **The Reverse Missionary:**
  - **Description:** In the Reverse Missionary position, one partner lies on their back with their legs raised and bent at the knees, while the other partner lies on top, facing their partner's feet. This position allows for deep penetration and a slow, controlled thrusting motion.
  - **Discipline and Control:** The Reverse Missionary position emphasizes control and precision. The penetrating partner must carefully manage the depth and pace of their movements, ensuring that each thrust is deliberate and well-executed. This aligns with Saturn's teachings on discipline and structure.
  - **Endurance:** The Reverse Missionary is ideal for prolonged encounters where endurance and sustained effort are key. The position encourages a slow buildup of intensity, making it a deeply satisfying and rewarding experience for both partners.

- **The Tortoise:**
  - **Description:** In the Tortoise position, one partner lies flat on their stomach with their legs slightly apart, while the other partner lies on top, penetrating from behind. This position allows for deep, controlled penetration and close physical contact.
  - **Discipline and Control:** The Tortoise position requires both partners to exercise control over their movements, maintaining a slow, steady rhythm that emphasizes connection and endurance. The focus is on the methodical buildup of pleasure, rather than quick, rapid movements.
  - **Endurance:** The Tortoise is a position that rewards patience and endurance, allowing both partners to fully immerse themselves in the experience. It's perfect for those who appreciate the slow, deliberate buildup of intensity that Saturn encourages.

Enhancing Saturn's Energy Through Rituals and Practices

To fully harness Saturn's energy in your sexual relationship, consider incorporating rituals and practices that emphasize discipline, structure, and endurance. These activities can help you align with Saturn's teachings, making your sexual experiences more intentional, meaningful, and deeply satisfying.

- **Mindful Breathing:** Practice mindful breathing techniques during sex to maintain focus and control over your energy and movements. This aligns with Saturn's emphasis on discipline and helps you sustain your efforts over time. Deep, controlled breathing can also enhance your endurance, making it easier to maintain a steady rhythm and pace.
- **Meditative Touch:** Incorporate meditative touch into your intimate routine. This involves slowing down and focusing on the sensations of touch, exploring your partner's body with deliberate, intentional movements. Meditative touch aligns with Saturn's teachings by emphasizing control, focus, and the methodical buildup of pleasure.
- **Setting Boundaries:** Saturn's energy is closely tied to the concept of boundaries. Take the time to discuss and establish clear boundaries in your sexual relationship, ensuring that both partners feel safe, respected, and valued. Setting and honoring boundaries creates a strong foundation for trust and mutual respect, aligning with Saturn's influence.

- **Strength and Endurance Training:** Incorporate physical training into your routine to build strength and endurance, which are key to embracing Saturn's energy. This might involve weightlifting, yoga, or other forms of exercise that enhance your physical capabilities. Building strength and endurance will help you fully engage in the structured positions that emphasize control and sustained effort.

Conclusion

Saturn's influence on discipline and structure brings a sense of control, endurance, and intentionality to sexual relationships. By incorporating the structured positions outlined in this chapter, you can harness Saturn's energy to create sexual experiences that are deeply satisfying, meaningful, and aligned with your values. Whether through the controlled movements of the Slow Grind, the physical challenge of the Plank, or the deliberate rhythm of the Tortoise, Saturn's energy encourages you to embrace discipline, structure, and endurance in your sexual encounters. Let Saturn guide you toward a more intentional, structured, and rewarding sexual relationship, where every encounter is an opportunity to build a strong, lasting connection with your partner.

Chapter 13: Uranus: Innovation and Experimentation

Uranus, the planet of innovation, rebellion, and sudden change, brings a dynamic and unconventional energy to every aspect of life, including sexuality. In astrology, Uranus represents the desire for freedom, individuality, and the breaking of traditional boundaries. When applied to sexual relationships, Uranus's influence encourages partners to experiment, embrace spontaneity, and explore new and unconventional ways of connecting. This chapter delves into Uranus's role in sexuality, focusing on positions that foster innovation, creativity, and the thrill of the unexpected.

The Role of Uranus in Sexual Relationships

Uranus is often associated with the archetype of the revolutionary, representing the impulse to innovate, disrupt the status quo, and embrace change. In sexual relationships, Uranus's energy encourages us to step outside of our comfort zones, to challenge traditional norms, and to explore new dimensions of intimacy and pleasure.

- **Innovation and Creativity:** Uranus governs innovation and creativity, driving us to seek out new experiences and experiment with different forms of sexual expression. This energy inspires partners to try unconventional positions, explore new fantasies, and infuse their sexual relationship with a sense of creativity and originality.

- **Spontaneity and Excitement:** Uranus is also associated with spontaneity and the thrill of the unexpected. In the context of sexuality, this means being open to sudden impulses, trying new things on the spur of the moment, and embracing the excitement that comes from stepping into the unknown.

- **Breaking Boundaries:** Uranus's influence encourages the breaking of boundaries and the rejection of traditional constraints. This might involve exploring non-traditional dynamics, experimenting with role reversal, or trying out positions that challenge conventional ideas about sex. Uranus invites partners to redefine their sexual relationship in ways that reflect their unique desires and individuality.

Unconventional Positions That Embrace Spontaneity and Creativity

Certain sexual positions are particularly well-suited to channeling Uranus's innovative, rebellious energy. These positions emphasize creativity, spontaneity, and the exploration of new dynamics, making each encounter an exciting and unpredictable adventure.

- **The Side Saddle:**
  - **Description:** In the Side Saddle position, one partner lies on their back while the other partner straddles them sideways, positioning themselves perpendicular to their partner's body. This position allows for a unique angle of penetration and encourages creative movement.
  - **Innovation and Creativity:** The Side Saddle is an unconventional position that encourages partners to explore different angles and movements, fostering a sense of creativity and experimentation. The unique orientation allows for a fresh perspective on the sexual experience.
  - **Spontaneity and Excitement:** The novelty of the Side Saddle position adds an element of excitement and unpredictability to the encounter, aligning with Uranus's energy. The position's versatility makes it easy to switch between different movements and rhythms, keeping the experience dynamic and engaging.
- **The Standing Split:**
  - **Description:** In the Standing Split position, one partner stands while the other partner lifts one leg, holding it against their partner's body for support. The standing partner penetrates while maintaining balance and control.
  - **Innovation and Creativity:** The Standing Split is a physically demanding position that encourages partners to experiment with balance, flexibility, and strength. The position's unconventional nature fosters creativity and the exploration of new dynamics.
  - **Spontaneity and Excitement:** The Standing Split's challenging nature adds a sense of adventure and excitement to the encounter. The position's spontaneous energy aligns with Uranus's influence, making it perfect for those who enjoy pushing their limits and trying new things.

- **The Scissors:**
  - **Description:** In the Scissors position, both partners lie on their sides, with their legs interlocked in a scissor-like fashion. This position allows for close physical contact and a range of movement options.
  - **Innovation and Creativity:** The Scissors position is highly versatile, allowing partners to experiment with different angles, depths, and movements. The interlocking of legs creates a unique dynamic that encourages creativity and the exploration of new sensations.
  - **Spontaneity and Excitement:** The Scissors position's adaptability makes it ideal for spontaneous encounters. Partners can easily shift between different movements and positions, keeping the experience fresh and exciting. The position's unconventional nature reflects Uranus's energy, making it a playful and adventurous choice.
- **The Reverse Chair:**
  - **Description:** In the Reverse Chair position, one partner sits on a chair facing backward, while the other partner straddles them from behind, facing away. This position allows for deep penetration and a unique angle of contact.
  - **Innovation and Creativity:** The Reverse Chair is an innovative position that encourages partners to explore new dynamics and angles. The use of a chair adds an element of novelty and creativity, allowing for a fresh perspective on the sexual experience.
  - **Spontaneity and Excitement:** The Reverse Chair's unconventional nature adds an element of surprise and excitement to the encounter. The position's adaptability makes it easy to switch between different movements and rhythms, aligning with Uranus's energy of spontaneity and experimentation.
- **The Wheel of Fortune:**
  - **Description:** In the Wheel of Fortune position, one partner lies on their back with their legs lifted and bent at the knees, while the other partner stands and holds their legs, rotating their partner's hips in a circular motion during penetration.

- ◦ **Innovation and Creativity:** The Wheel of Fortune is a playful and creative position that encourages partners to experiment with different movements and rhythms. The rotating motion adds a unique dynamic to the encounter, fostering a sense of innovation and exploration.
- ◦ **Spontaneity and Excitement:** The Wheel of Fortune's dynamic nature adds a sense of adventure and unpredictability to the experience. The position's circular movement aligns with Uranus's energy, making it a fun and exciting choice for those who enjoy spontaneous, creative encounters.

Enhancing Uranus's Energy Through Rituals and Practices

To fully harness Uranus's energy in your sexual relationship, consider incorporating rituals and practices that emphasize innovation, spontaneity, and creativity. These activities can help you align with Uranus's dynamic energy, making your sexual experiences more exciting, unconventional, and deeply satisfying.

- **Creative Role Play:** Engage in role play that involves unconventional scenarios, characters, or dynamics. This practice aligns with Uranus's energy by encouraging partners to step outside of traditional roles and explore new aspects of their sexuality. The key is to be open to experimentation and to embrace the fun and spontaneity of the experience.
- **Spontaneous Encounters:** Embrace the thrill of the unexpected by planning spontaneous sexual encounters. This might involve surprising your partner with an unplanned rendezvous, trying out a new location, or experimenting with a new position on the spur of the moment. Spontaneity adds an element of excitement and unpredictability, aligning with Uranus's influence.
- **Incorporating Toys and Props:** Introduce toys, props, or other accessories into your sexual relationship to add a layer of innovation and creativity. Whether it's trying out a new toy, experimenting with different textures, or using furniture in unconventional ways, the goal is to keep the experience fresh, exciting, and aligned with Uranus's energy.
- **Fantasy Exploration:** Explore your fantasies together, particularly those that involve unconventional scenarios or dynamics. Sharing and acting out fantasies can help you connect with

Uranus's energy by encouraging openness, creativity, and the breaking of traditional boundaries. The key is to approach fantasy exploration with a sense of curiosity and a willingness to experiment.

Conclusion

Uranus's influence on innovation and experimentation brings a dynamic, unconventional energy to sexual relationships, encouraging partners to embrace spontaneity, creativity, and the thrill of the unexpected. By incorporating the innovative positions outlined in this chapter, you can harness Uranus's energy to create sexual experiences that are both exciting and deeply satisfying. Whether through the unique dynamics of the Side Saddle, the physical challenge of the Standing Split, or the playful rotation of the Wheel of Fortune, Uranus's energy invites you to break free from tradition and explore new dimensions of intimacy and pleasure. Let Uranus guide you toward a more innovative, spontaneous, and adventurous sexual relationship, where every encounter is an opportunity to experiment, discover, and grow together.

Chapter 14: Neptune: Fantasy and Mysticism

Neptune, the planet of dreams, illusions, and mysticism, is the gateway to the ethereal and the mysterious. In astrology, Neptune represents the realm of fantasy, spirituality, and the subconscious mind, where reality blurs with the imagination. When applied to sexual relationships, Neptune's influence encourages lovers to transcend the physical plane and explore the mystical, spiritual, and fantasy-driven aspects of intimacy. This chapter delves into Neptune's role in sexuality, focusing on positions that are dreamy, mystical, and capable of transporting lovers to another realm, where the boundaries between body, mind, and spirit dissolve.

The Role of Neptune in Sexual Relationships

Neptune's energy is deeply connected to the spiritual, the imaginative, and the transcendent. It invites us to explore the depths of our subconscious desires, to indulge in fantasies, and to connect with our partners on a spiritual and emotional level that goes beyond the physical.

- **Fantasy and Imagination:** Neptune governs the realm of fantasy and imagination, encouraging us to explore our deepest desires and to engage in sexual experiences that are infused with elements of the mystical and the surreal. Under Neptune's influence, sex becomes a dreamlike experience, where the imagination plays a central role in creating an atmosphere of enchantment and wonder.

- **Mysticism and Spirituality:** Neptune is also associated with spirituality and the search for higher meaning. In sexual relationships, this energy encourages partners to explore the spiritual dimensions of intimacy, to connect on a soul level, and to experience sex as a sacred, transcendent act. Neptune invites lovers to see their connection as part of a greater cosmic dance, where physical pleasure is intertwined with spiritual fulfillment.

- **Illusion and Dissolution:** Neptune's energy is elusive and fluid, dissolving the boundaries between self and other, between the physical and the spiritual. In the context of sexuality, this can lead to experiences where the lovers feel as though they are merging into one, losing themselves in the moment, and becoming part of something greater than themselves. Neptune invites us to surrender to the flow, to let go of control, and to embrace the beauty of the unknown.

Dreamy and Mystical Positions That Transport Lovers to Another Realm

Certain sexual positions are particularly well-suited to channeling Neptune's dreamy, mystical energy. These positions emphasize the blending of physical pleasure with spiritual connection, creating an experience that feels otherworldly, transcendent, and deeply fulfilling. They are designed to transport lovers to a place where time slows down, and the boundaries between body, mind, and spirit blur.

- **The Mermaid's Embrace:**
    - **Description:** In the Mermaid's Embrace position, both partners lie on their sides, facing each other, with their legs intertwined like the tail of a mermaid. This position allows for gentle, rhythmic movements and deep, soulful eye contact.
    - **Fantasy and Imagination:** The Mermaid's Embrace is a position that evokes the imagery of mythical creatures and underwater realms, where lovers are free to explore their fantasies in a fluid, dreamlike environment. The intertwined legs symbolize the merging of souls, creating a mystical connection that transcends the physical.
    - **Mysticism and Spirituality:** The close, face-to-face orientation of this position allows partners to connect on a deep emotional and spiritual level. The gentle movements and the slow, rhythmic pace encourage a meditative state, where both partners can lose themselves in the moment and experience a sense of unity and oneness.
- **The Lotus Blossom:**
    - **Description:** In the Lotus Blossom position, one partner sits cross-legged on the bed, while the other partner sits on their lap, wrapping their legs around their partner's waist. This position allows for close physical contact and a slow, circular rocking motion.
    - **Fantasy and Imagination:** The Lotus Blossom position is inspired by the symbolism of the lotus flower, which represents purity, enlightenment, and spiritual awakening. The circular rocking motion mirrors the cycles of the cosmos, creating a sense of har-

mony and balance. This position invites lovers to enter a state of deep relaxation and contemplation, where they can explore their fantasies and connect with the divine.

- **Mysticism and Spirituality:** The Lotus Blossom position is ideal for exploring the spiritual dimensions of sex. The close physical contact allows for the exchange of energy between partners, creating a sense of deep connection and spiritual intimacy. The position's meditative nature encourages both partners to focus on their breathing and to synchronize their movements, enhancing the sense of unity and oneness.

- **The Starry Night:**
  - **Description:** In the Starry Night position, one partner lies on their back, while the other partner lies on top, aligning their bodies so that they form a star shape. This position allows for slow, gentle movements and deep emotional connection.
  - **Fantasy and Imagination:** The Starry Night position is reminiscent of lying under the stars, where the vastness of the universe becomes a backdrop for the lovers' connection. The star shape symbolizes the expansive nature of the cosmos, inviting lovers to explore the infinite possibilities of their connection and to lose themselves in the beauty of the moment.
  - **Mysticism and Spirituality:** The Starry Night position encourages a sense of awe and wonder, as partners gaze into each other's eyes and feel the energy of the universe flowing through them. The slow, gentle movements allow both partners to enter a state of deep relaxation, where they can connect on a spiritual level and experience the profound beauty of their union.

- **The Dream Weaver:**
  - **Description:** In the Dream Weaver position, both partners lie on their sides, facing each other, with their arms wrapped around each other's bodies. This position allows for close physical contact and gentle, rhythmic movements.
  - **Fantasy and Imagination:** The Dream Weaver position is inspired by the idea of weaving dreams together, where lovers create a shared fantasy world that they can explore together. The close physical contact and the gentle movements create a sense of intimacy and connection, where the boundaries between reality and fantasy blur.

- **Mysticism and Spirituality:** The Dream Weaver position is perfect for exploring the spiritual dimensions of intimacy. The close, face-to-face orientation allows partners to connect on a deep emotional level, while the gentle movements encourage a state of relaxation and meditation. This position invites lovers to enter a dreamlike state, where they can explore their deepest desires and connect with the divine.

- **The Cosmic Spiral:**
  - **Description:** In the Cosmic Spiral position, one partner sits on the bed with their legs extended, while the other partner straddles them, wrapping their legs around their partner's waist. The partners then lean back, creating a spiral shape with their bodies. This position allows for deep penetration and a slow, circular rocking motion.
  - **Fantasy and Imagination:** The Cosmic Spiral position is inspired by the spiral patterns found in nature, from galaxies to seashells. The spiral shape symbolizes the continuous flow of energy and the interconnectedness of all things. This position invites lovers to explore the mysteries of the universe and to lose themselves in the rhythm of the cosmos.
  - **Mysticism and Spirituality:** The Cosmic Spiral position encourages a deep connection between partners, both physically and spiritually. The slow, circular rocking motion mirrors the cycles of the universe, creating a sense of harmony and balance. This position invites lovers to connect with the divine and to experience the transcendent beauty of their union.

Enhancing Neptune's Energy Through Rituals and Practices

To fully harness Neptune's energy in your sexual relationship, consider incorporating rituals and practices that emphasize fantasy, mysticism, and spiritual connection. These activities can help you align with Neptune's ethereal energy, making your sexual experiences more dreamlike, mystical, and deeply fulfilling.

- **Fantasy Exploration:** Explore your fantasies together, particularly those that involve mystical or spiritual themes. Sharing and acting out fantasies can help you connect with Neptune's energy by encouraging creativity and imagination. The key is to approach fantasy exploration with an open mind and a willingness to embrace the unknown.

- **Meditative Sex:** Incorporate meditation into your sexual relationship by practicing mindful breathing, visualization, and deep relaxation during sex. Meditative sex aligns with Neptune's energy by encouraging both partners to enter a state of deep relaxation and to connect on a spiritual level. The goal is to create a sense of unity and oneness, where the boundaries between self and other dissolve.
- **Sacred Space Creation:** Create a sacred space for your sexual encounters by incorporating elements that enhance the mystical atmosphere. This might include soft lighting, candles, incense, and soothing music. The goal is to create an environment that feels safe, sacred, and conducive to exploring the spiritual dimensions of intimacy.
- **Ritual Baths:** Take a ritual bath together before engaging in sexual activity. Add elements such as rose petals, essential oils, and crystals to the water, and take the time to relax and connect with each other. The ritual bath aligns with Neptune's energy by creating a sense of purification and preparation, allowing both partners to enter the sexual experience with a clear mind and an open heart.

Conclusion

Neptune's influence on fantasy and mysticism invites lovers to explore the spiritual, imaginative, and transcendent aspects of sexuality. By incorporating the dreamy and mystical positions outlined in this chapter, you can harness Neptune's energy to create sexual experiences that are both ethereal and deeply fulfilling. Whether through the fluid movements of the Mermaid's Embrace, the meditative stillness of the Lotus Blossom, or the cosmic alignment of the Starry Night, Neptune's energy invites you to transcend the physical and connect with your partner on a spiritual level. Let Neptune guide you toward a more mystical, dreamlike, and spiritually enriching sexual relationship, where every encounter is an opportunity to explore the depths of your connection and to experience the divine beauty of your union.

Chapter 15: Pluto: Transformation and Power

Pluto, the planet of transformation, power, and regeneration, is the force behind the profound changes and deep connections that define our lives. In astrology, Pluto represents the hidden, often unconscious forces that drive us to explore the depths of our desires, confront our fears, and undergo significant transformations. When applied to sexuality, Pluto's influence brings an intense, almost primal energy that evokes deep transformation and powerful connections between lovers. This chapter explores Pluto's role in sexual relationships, focusing on positions that are intense, transformative, and capable of fostering powerful, life-altering connections.

The Role of Pluto in Sexual Relationships

Pluto's energy is associated with the themes of power, control, and transformation. It is the force that compels us to dig deep, to face the darker aspects of our psyche, and to emerge stronger and more empowered. In sexual relationships, Pluto's influence encourages partners to explore the depths of their desires, to confront their fears, and to experience intimacy on a profoundly transformative level.

- **Transformation and Renewal:** Pluto governs transformation and renewal, driving us to explore the deeper, often hidden aspects of our sexuality. This energy encourages partners to confront and release old patterns, fears, and inhibitions, allowing for a rebirth of their sexual relationship. Pluto's influence brings a sense of catharsis, where sexual experiences become opportunities for profound personal and relational growth.
- **Power and Control:** Pluto is also associated with power and control, both in terms of self-mastery and the dynamics between partners. In sexual relationships, this energy manifests as a desire to explore power dynamics, to experience the intensity of surrender and dominance, and to find strength in vulnerability. Pluto encourages partners to embrace their power, to assert their desires, and to engage in a dance of control and surrender that deepens their connection.
- **Intensity and Passion:** Pluto's energy is intense, passionate, and often overwhelming. In the context of sexuality, this intensity can lead to experiences that are deeply satisfying, emotionally charged, and transformative. Pluto invites lovers to embrace the full spectrum of their de-

sires, to explore the edges of their comfort zones, and to experience the raw, unfiltered power of their connection.

Intense Positions That Evoke Deep Transformation and Powerful Connections

Certain sexual positions are particularly well-suited to channeling Pluto's intense, transformative energy. These positions emphasize deep physical and emotional connection, the exploration of power dynamics, and the potential for profound transformation through intimate encounters. They are designed to evoke powerful connections and to create experiences that leave a lasting impact on both partners.

- **The Dominant Embrace:**
  - **Description:** In the Dominant Embrace position, one partner stands or kneels with their partner sitting or lying in front of them, fully submitting to their control. The standing partner maintains physical control, guiding the pace and intensity of the encounter while maintaining eye contact.
  - **Transformation and Renewal:** The Dominant Embrace position is a powerful exploration of control and surrender, where both partners experience transformation through the exchange of power. The submissive partner may confront and release fears or inhibitions, while the dominant partner embraces their strength and assertiveness.
  - **Intensity and Passion:** This position is deeply intense, as it involves a high level of trust and vulnerability. The Dominant Embrace encourages a passionate connection that goes beyond the physical, tapping into the emotional and psychological depths of the relationship.
- **The Ravisher:**
  - **Description:** In the Ravisher position, one partner pins the other against a wall or flat surface, taking full control of the encounter. The penetrating partner asserts their dominance through deep, forceful thrusts, while the receiving partner surrenders to the intensity of the experience.
  - **Power and Control:** The Ravisher position is an exploration of power dynamics, where the dominant partner fully embraces their role, asserting control with confidence

and intensity. The receiving partner experiences the transformative power of surrender, trusting their partner to lead the encounter.

- ◦ **Transformation and Renewal:** The intense, almost primal nature of the Ravisher position can lead to a cathartic release of pent-up emotions, fears, and desires. This position encourages both partners to explore the darker, more intense aspects of their connection, leading to profound personal and relational growth.

- **The Binding Union:**
  - ◦ **Description:** In the Binding Union position, both partners are positioned in a way that restricts movement, either through the use of restraints or by intertwining their bodies tightly together. This position emphasizes stillness and deep connection, with minimal movement but maximum intensity.
  - ◦ **Intensity and Passion:** The Binding Union is a position that heightens intensity through restriction, forcing both partners to focus on the connection between them. The lack of movement amplifies the sensations, creating a powerful, almost meditative experience.
  - ◦ **Power and Control:** The Binding Union explores the dynamics of control and surrender in a unique way, where both partners are bound together, unable to escape the intensity of the moment. This position is an exploration of trust, power, and the willingness to be fully present with each other.

- **The Immersive Gaze:**
  - ◦ **Description:** In the Immersive Gaze position, one partner sits on top of the other, maintaining deep eye contact throughout the encounter. The focus is on the connection between their eyes, with movements that are slow, deliberate, and synchronized.
  - ◦ **Transformation and Renewal:** The Immersive Gaze position is an intense exploration of emotional and spiritual connection. The deep eye contact serves as a mirror, reflecting each partner's desires, fears, and vulnerabilities. This position encourages transformation through the act of truly seeing and being seen by one's partner.
  - ◦ **Intensity and Passion:** The Immersive Gaze is a position that heightens emotional intensity, as it requires both partners to maintain unwavering focus on each other. This

deepens the emotional connection, making the experience profoundly intimate and transformative.

- **The Phoenix Rising:**
  - **Description:** In the Phoenix Rising position, one partner supports the other as they rise from a kneeling or lying position, symbolizing the act of rebirth and renewal. This position can involve a slow, deliberate ascent, with the supporting partner providing both physical and emotional support.
  - **Transformation and Renewal:** The Phoenix Rising position is symbolic of Pluto's energy, representing the process of transformation and renewal. The act of rising together serves as a metaphor for overcoming challenges, releasing old patterns, and embracing a new chapter in the relationship.
  - **Intensity and Passion:** The Phoenix Rising position is both physically and emotionally intense, requiring strength, trust, and a willingness to embrace change. The slow, deliberate movements create a powerful sense of unity and connection, making the experience deeply transformative.

Enhancing Pluto's Energy Through Rituals and Practices

To fully harness Pluto's energy in your sexual relationship, consider incorporating rituals and practices that emphasize transformation, power, and deep connection. These activities can help you align with Pluto's intense energy, making your sexual experiences more profound, transformative, and deeply satisfying.

- **Shadow Work:** Engage in shadow work as a couple, exploring the darker aspects of your desires, fears, and emotions. Shadow work aligns with Pluto's energy by encouraging partners to confront and integrate the hidden parts of themselves, leading to profound personal and relational growth. This can involve journaling, therapy, or deep conversations about your deepest fears and desires.
- **Power Exchange Rituals:** Incorporate power exchange rituals into your sexual relationship, where one partner takes on a dominant role while the other surrenders. These rituals can include role play, bondage, or other forms of power exchange that emphasize control and

surrender. The key is to approach these rituals with mutual respect, trust, and clear communication.

- **Transformational Meditation:** Practice meditation focused on transformation and renewal before engaging in sexual activity. This can involve visualizing the release of old patterns, the shedding of emotional baggage, and the rebirth of your connection with your partner. Transformational meditation aligns with Pluto's energy by preparing both partners for a deeply transformative experience.
- **Sacred Space Creation:** Create a sacred space that reflects Pluto's energy, incorporating elements such as deep colors, candles, and symbols of transformation (e.g., phoenix, serpents, or symbols of death and rebirth). The goal is to create an environment that feels intense, powerful, and conducive to deep emotional and spiritual connection.

Conclusion

Pluto's influence on transformation and power brings an intense, primal energy to sexual relationships, encouraging partners to explore the depths of their desires and to experience intimacy on a profoundly transformative level. By incorporating the intense positions outlined in this chapter, you can harness Pluto's energy to create sexual experiences that are both powerful and deeply satisfying. Whether through the control and surrender of the Dominant Embrace, the cathartic intensity of the Ravisher, or the symbolic renewal of the Phoenix Rising, Pluto's energy invites you to embrace the full spectrum of your desires and to experience the profound transformation that comes from deep, meaningful connections. Let Pluto guide you toward a more intense, transformative, and empowered sexual relationship, where every encounter is an opportunity to explore the depths of your connection and to emerge stronger and more unified.

Part 3: Zodiac Signs and Sexual Techniques

Chapter 16: Aries: The Initiator

Aries, the first sign of the zodiac, is ruled by Mars, the planet of action, aggression, and desire. Known for its fiery energy and dynamic personality, Aries is the sign of the warrior, the leader, and the pioneer. In the realm of sexuality, Aries is the initiator—bold, passionate, and always ready to take the lead. This chapter explores Aries' approach to sex, focusing on bold and dynamic positions that channel Aries' fiery energy, allowing them to express their passion, assertiveness, and adventurous spirit.

The Aries Lover: Passionate, Bold, and Fearless

Aries is a sign driven by passion and a desire to conquer new territories, both in life and in love. As a fire sign, Aries is energetic, enthusiastic, and always eager to take the initiative. In sexual relationships, Aries brings this same boldness and dynamism, often taking the lead and driving the intensity of the encounter.

- **Passion and Desire:** Aries is ruled by Mars, the planet of desire and action, making them one of the most passionate signs of the zodiac. When Aries feels desire, they go after it with everything they have, unafraid to express their needs and take charge in the bedroom.
- **Boldness and Confidence:** Aries is known for their confidence and boldness, both in life and in love. They are not shy about taking risks, trying new things, or exploring new dynamics in their sexual relationships. For Aries, sex is an adventure—a chance to express their fiery energy and to connect with their partner in a powerful, dynamic way.
- **Initiation and Leadership:** As the first sign of the zodiac, Aries is the initiator—the one who takes the lead and sets things in motion. In sexual relationships, Aries often takes the initiative, whether it's making the first move, introducing a new idea, or setting the pace of the encounter. They thrive in positions that allow them to assert their dominance and take control of the experience.

Bold and Dynamic Positions for Aries' Fiery Energy

Certain sexual positions are particularly well-suited to channeling Aries' bold, dynamic energy. These positions emphasize movement, control, and intensity, allowing Aries to fully express their passion and assertiveness. They are designed to ignite the flames of desire and to create a sexual experience that is both thrilling and satisfying for both partners.

- **The Warrior's Stance:**
  - **Description:** In the Warrior's Stance position, one partner stands with their legs slightly apart, while the other partner straddles them, wrapping their legs around their waist. The standing partner supports their partner's weight while maintaining a strong, controlled stance.
  - **Passion and Boldness:** The Warrior's Stance is a bold, powerful position that allows Aries to take full control of the encounter. The standing partner's strong, assertive stance embodies the warrior spirit, while the close physical contact ignites passion and intensity.
  - **Initiation and Leadership:** This position is perfect for Aries' need to take the lead and assert their dominance. The standing partner sets the pace and rhythm, guiding the encounter with confidence and control. The Warrior's Stance is ideal for a passionate, high-energy encounter that leaves both partners feeling exhilarated.
- **The Charger:**
  - **Description:** In the Charger position, one partner lies on their back with their legs bent at the knees, while the other partner kneels between their legs, leaning forward with their arms braced against the bed. This position allows for deep penetration and a powerful, driving motion.
  - **Passion and Boldness:** The Charger is a dynamic, intense position that channels Aries' fiery energy into powerful, rhythmic movements. The kneeling partner's forward-leaning stance creates a sense of momentum and drive, embodying Aries' bold, unstoppable nature.

- **Initiation and Leadership:** The Charger position allows Aries to take control of the encounter, setting the pace and intensity of the experience. The kneeling partner's powerful movements create a thrilling, high-energy dynamic that is perfect for an Aries lover who thrives on passion and intensity.

- **The Spear:**
  - **Description:** In the Spear position, one partner stands at the edge of the bed, while the other partner lies on their back with their legs raised and resting on the standing partner's shoulders. This position allows for deep, controlled penetration and close physical contact.
  - **Passion and Boldness:** The Spear is a bold, assertive position that channels Aries' intense energy into deep, powerful movements. The standing partner's upright stance and the deep penetration create a sense of dominance and control, embodying Aries' fiery, passionate nature.
  - **Initiation and Leadership:** The Spear position allows Aries to take the lead, driving the intensity of the encounter with powerful, controlled movements. The standing partner sets the tone for the experience, using their strength and confidence to create a dynamic, satisfying connection.

- **The Ram's Charge:**
  - **Description:** In the Ram's Charge position, one partner stands behind the other, who is bent forward with their hands resting on the bed or a sturdy surface. This position allows for deep penetration and a strong, rhythmic thrusting motion.
  - **Passion and Boldness:** The Ram's Charge is an intense, high-energy position that channels Aries' fiery passion into powerful, driving movements. The standing partner's forceful thrusts embody Aries' bold, assertive nature, creating a dynamic, thrilling experience for both partners.
  - **Initiation and Leadership:** The Ram's Charge is perfect for an Aries lover who loves to take the lead and assert their dominance. The standing partner sets the pace and intensity of the encounter, using their strength and energy to drive the experience forward with confidence and power.

- **The Ascendant:**
  - **Description:** In the Ascendant position, one partner lies on their back with their legs bent and feet flat on the bed, while the other partner straddles them, facing away. This position allows for deep penetration and a strong, upward thrusting motion.
  - **Passion and Boldness:** The Ascendant is a powerful, dynamic position that channels Aries' bold energy into upward, forceful movements. The straddling partner's position allows them to take control of the depth and rhythm, embodying Aries' fiery, assertive nature.
  - **Initiation and Leadership:** The Ascendant position is ideal for an Aries lover who loves to take charge and lead the encounter. The straddling partner sets the pace and intensity, using their strength and energy to create a thrilling, high-energy experience.

Enhancing Aries' Energy Through Rituals and Practices

To fully harness Aries' fiery energy in your sexual relationship, consider incorporating rituals and practices that emphasize boldness, confidence, and dynamic movement. These activities can help you align with Aries' passionate energy, making your sexual experiences more thrilling, intense, and deeply satisfying.

- **Physical Fitness:** Aries is a sign associated with physical strength and energy, so maintaining physical fitness is key to fully embracing their dynamic nature. Regular exercise, strength training, and activities that build stamina can enhance your ability to engage in high-energy sexual encounters, aligning you with Aries' bold, assertive energy.
- **Spontaneous Encounters:** Embrace Aries' love of spontaneity by planning spontaneous sexual encounters. This might involve surprising your partner with an unplanned rendezvous, trying out a new location, or experimenting with a new position on the spur of the moment. Spontaneity adds an element of excitement and unpredictability, aligning with Aries' dynamic energy.

- **Role Play and Fantasy Exploration:** Engage in role play or explore fantasies that involve bold, assertive dynamics. Whether you take on the role of a warrior, a leader, or a conqueror, role-playing can help you express Aries' fiery energy in a playful, exciting way. The key is to be confident and bold in your approach, fully embracing the intensity of the experience.
- **Power Affirmations:** Incorporate power affirmations into your daily routine to boost your confidence and assertiveness. Affirmations such as "I am bold," "I am confident," and "I am a powerful leader" can help you tap into Aries' energy, enhancing your ability to take the lead and assert your desires in your sexual relationship.

Conclusion

Aries' influence on sexuality brings a bold, dynamic energy that drives passion, intensity, and the desire to take the lead. By incorporating the bold and dynamic positions outlined in this chapter, you can harness Aries' fiery energy to create sexual experiences that are both thrilling and deeply satisfying. Whether through the powerful movements of the Warrior's Stance, the driving intensity of the Charger, or the assertive control of the Ram's Charge, Aries' energy invites you to embrace your boldness, to take the lead, and to ignite the flames of passion in your sexual relationship. Let Aries guide you toward a more dynamic, adventurous, and empowered sexual relationship, where every encounter is an opportunity to express your passion, assert your desires, and experience the thrill of the moment.

Chapter 17: Taurus: The Sensualist

Taurus, the second sign of the zodiac, is ruled by Venus, the planet of love, beauty, and sensual pleasure. Known for its deep appreciation of luxury, comfort, and the finer things in life, Taurus is the ultimate sensualist. In the realm of sexuality, Taurus seeks experiences that are slow, indulgent, and deeply satisfying. This chapter explores Taurus' approach to sex, focusing on positions that emphasize sensuality, luxury, and the pleasure of taking one's time. These positions are designed to cater to Taurus' love of comfort and their desire for a rich, indulgent experience.

The Taurus Lover: Sensual, Patient, and Affectionate

Taurus is an earth sign, grounded in the physical world and deeply connected to the senses. As a lover, Taurus is patient, affectionate, and focused on creating a sexual experience that is as pleasurable as it is meaningful. Taurus values quality over quantity, preferring to indulge in long, luxurious encounters where every touch, taste, and sensation is savored.

- **Sensuality and Indulgence:** Taurus is ruled by Venus, making them naturally inclined toward sensual pleasure and indulgence. For Taurus, sex is not just about physical gratification; it's about creating an experience that engages all the senses. They appreciate soft fabrics, soothing aromas, and the warmth of a lover's touch, all of which contribute to a deeply satisfying encounter.

- **Patience and Persistence:** Taurus is known for their patience and persistence, qualities that they bring to their sexual relationships. They are not in a hurry to reach the climax; instead, they prefer to take their time, exploring every inch of their partner's body and building pleasure slowly and deliberately. This patient approach ensures that both partners fully enjoy the experience, making it deeply fulfilling.

- **Love of Comfort and Luxury:** Taurus is drawn to comfort and luxury, both in their everyday lives and in their sexual experiences. They prefer settings that are cozy, warm, and inviting, with plenty of soft pillows, warm blankets, and luxurious sheets. Taurus thrives in an environment where they can relax, unwind, and fully immerse themselves in the pleasures of the moment.

Slow and Indulgent Positions for Taurus' Love of Luxury

Certain sexual positions are particularly well-suited to channeling Taurus' sensual, indulgent energy. These positions emphasize slow movements, deep connection, and the enjoyment of physical pleasure in a luxurious, comfortable setting. They are designed to cater to Taurus' love of comfort and their desire to create a deeply satisfying, indulgent experience.

- **The Luxurious Linger:**
  - **Description:** In the Luxurious Linger position, both partners lie on their sides, facing each other, with their legs intertwined and bodies pressed close together. This position allows for gentle, rhythmic movements and deep eye contact, creating a slow, sensual connection.
  - **Sensuality and Indulgence:** The Luxurious Linger is a deeply sensual position that allows Taurus to fully indulge in the pleasure of close physical contact. The slow, deliberate movements encourage both partners to take their time, savoring each touch and caress. This position is perfect for creating a luxurious, intimate experience that engages all the senses.
  - **Love of Comfort:** The close, side-by-side orientation of this position is ideal for Taurus' love of comfort and coziness. Partners can wrap themselves in soft blankets, enjoy the warmth of each other's bodies, and fully relax into the experience.
- **The Velvet Embrace:**
  - **Description:** In the Velvet Embrace position, one partner sits with their back against a headboard or wall, while the other partner straddles them, facing forward. This position allows for slow, controlled movements and close physical contact, with both partners able to wrap their arms around each other.
  - **Sensuality and Indulgence:** The Velvet Embrace is a luxurious position that allows Taurus to fully immerse themselves in the pleasure of their partner's touch. The slow, rhythmic movements encourage both partners to take their time, building pleasure

gradually and savoring every sensation. This position is perfect for creating a deep, sensual connection.

- **Love of Comfort:** The seated orientation of this position is ideal for Taurus' love of comfort, as both partners can relax against soft pillows or cushions. The close physical contact and the ability to maintain eye contact create a warm, intimate atmosphere that Taurus thrives in.

- **The Sensual Spoon:**
  - **Description:** In the Sensual Spoon position, one partner lies on their side with their back pressed against their partner's chest, while the other partner lies behind them, spooning them closely. This position allows for gentle, rhythmic movements and close physical contact.
  - **Sensuality and Indulgence:** The Sensual Spoon is a deeply comforting and indulgent position that allows Taurus to fully relax and enjoy the warmth and closeness of their partner's body. The slow, rhythmic movements are perfect for building pleasure gradually, allowing both partners to savor each moment.
  - **Love of Comfort:** The spooning position is ideal for Taurus' love of comfort and security. Partners can wrap themselves in soft blankets, enjoy the warmth of each other's bodies, and fully relax into the experience. The Sensual Spoon is perfect for lazy mornings or quiet evenings, where the focus is on relaxation and connection.

- **The Reclining Lotus:**
  - **Description:** In the Reclining Lotus position, one partner lies on their back with their legs bent and feet flat on the bed, while the other partner straddles them, leaning back to rest on their partner's legs. This position allows for slow, gentle movements and close physical contact.
  - **Sensuality and Indulgence:** The Reclining Lotus is a luxurious position that allows Taurus to fully indulge in the pleasure of slow, controlled movements. The position encourages both partners to take their time, building pleasure gradually and savoring each sensation. This position is perfect for creating a deep, sensual connection.
  - **Love of Comfort:** The reclining orientation of this position is ideal for Taurus' love of comfort, as both partners can relax into the experience, supported by soft pillows

or cushions. The close physical contact and the ability to maintain eye contact create a warm, intimate atmosphere that Taurus thrives in.

- **The Lavish Lounge:**
  - **Description:** In the Lavish Lounge position, one partner reclines on a chaise lounge or sofa, while the other partner straddles them, facing forward. This position allows for slow, controlled movements and close physical contact, with both partners able to relax and enjoy the luxurious setting.
  - **Sensuality and Indulgence:** The Lavish Lounge is a luxurious position that allows Taurus to fully indulge in the pleasure of their partner's touch. The slow, rhythmic movements encourage both partners to take their time, building pleasure gradually and savoring each sensation. This position is perfect for creating a deep, sensual connection in a luxurious, comfortable setting.
  - **Love of Comfort:** The reclining orientation of this position is ideal for Taurus' love of comfort, as both partners can relax into the experience, supported by soft pillows or cushions. The close physical contact and the luxurious setting create a warm, intimate atmosphere that Taurus thrives in.

Enhancing Taurus' Energy Through Rituals and Practices

To fully harness Taurus' sensual energy in your sexual relationship, consider incorporating rituals and practices that emphasize indulgence, comfort, and the enjoyment of physical pleasure. These activities can help you align with Taurus' sensual energy, making your sexual experiences more luxurious, satisfying, and deeply fulfilling.

- **Sensory Rituals:** Engage in sensory rituals that enhance the pleasure of touch, taste, and smell. This might include using scented oils, soft fabrics, and delicious foods to create a luxurious, indulgent atmosphere. The goal is to engage all the senses, making the experience as pleasurable and satisfying as possible.
- **Bath Rituals:** Incorporate luxurious bath rituals into your sexual relationship, where both partners can relax and unwind in a warm, scented bath before engaging in intimacy. Add elements such as rose petals, essential oils, and candles to create a soothing, indulgent atmos-

phere. Bath rituals align with Taurus' love of luxury and comfort, helping both partners to relax and fully enjoy the experience.

- **Slow Touch Exploration:** Practice slow touch exploration, where both partners take turns exploring each other's bodies with slow, deliberate movements. This practice aligns with Taurus' love of indulgence and sensuality, allowing both partners to fully engage with the pleasure of touch and to build a deeper, more satisfying connection.
- **Creating a Luxurious Environment:** Create a luxurious, comfortable environment for your sexual encounters by incorporating soft fabrics, warm lighting, and soothing aromas. The goal is to create a space that feels cozy, inviting, and conducive to relaxation and indulgence, aligning with Taurus' love of comfort and luxury.

Conclusion

Taurus' influence on sexuality brings a sensual, indulgent energy that emphasizes comfort, luxury, and the slow, deliberate enjoyment of physical pleasure. By incorporating the slow and indulgent positions outlined in this chapter, you can harness Taurus' sensual energy to create sexual experiences that are deeply satisfying, luxurious, and fulfilling. Whether through the close contact of the Luxurious Linger, the comforting embrace of the Sensual Spoon, or the indulgent relaxation of the Lavish Lounge, Taurus' energy invites you to slow down, savor each moment, and fully immerse yourself in the pleasures of the senses. Let Taurus guide you toward a more sensual, indulgent, and luxurious sexual relationship, where every encounter is an opportunity to relax, unwind, and enjoy the beauty of the moment.

Chapter 18: Gemini: The Communicator

Gemini, the third sign of the zodiac, is ruled by Mercury, the planet of communication, intellect, and adaptability. Known for its dual nature, Gemini embodies the qualities of versatility, curiosity, and quick-wittedness. In the realm of sexuality, Gemini is the communicator—dynamic, playful, and always eager to explore new ideas and experiences. This chapter delves into Gemini's approach to sex, focusing on positions that emphasize communication, versatility, and the ability to adapt to the ever-changing flow of desire. These positions are designed to cater to Gemini's need for variety, intellectual stimulation, and connection through words and movement.

The Gemini Lover: Curious, Playful, and Expressive

Gemini is an air sign, which means they are naturally drawn to the realms of thought, communication, and ideas. As a lover, Gemini is curious, playful, and always eager to explore new possibilities. They thrive on intellectual stimulation and are often attracted to partners who can engage them in witty banter, deep conversations, and playful exchanges.

- **Curiosity and Exploration:** Gemini is ruled by Mercury, making them inherently curious and eager to explore new experiences. In sexual relationships, this translates to a desire for variety and experimentation. Gemini is not content with the same routine; they crave novelty and are always on the lookout for new positions, techniques, and dynamics to keep things exciting.

- **Communication and Connection:** Communication is central to Gemini's approach to sexuality. They are natural conversationalists and enjoy using words to express their desires, fantasies, and feelings. For Gemini, sex is as much about mental connection as it is about physical pleasure. They thrive in positions that allow for verbal exchange, eye contact, and playful interaction.

- **Versatility and Adaptability:** Gemini is known for their dual nature, which gives them the ability to adapt to different situations and moods. In the bedroom, this means they can easily switch between roles, positions, and dynamics, keeping the experience fresh and engaging.

Gemini enjoys positions that allow for quick transitions and adaptability, ensuring that both partners are always engaged and excited.

Versatile and Communicative Positions for Gemini's Dual Nature

Certain sexual positions are particularly well-suited to channeling Gemini's versatile, communicative energy. These positions emphasize flexibility, adaptability, and the opportunity for verbal exchange, allowing Gemini to fully express their dynamic nature. They are designed to keep the experience lively, engaging, and intellectually stimulating, catering to Gemini's need for variety and connection.

- **The Conversationalist:**
    - **Description:** In the Conversationalist position, both partners sit facing each other, with one partner straddling the other. This position allows for close physical contact, deep eye contact, and easy verbal communication.
    - **Communication and Connection:** The Conversationalist is ideal for Gemini's love of communication and connection. The face-to-face orientation allows for easy conversation, playful banter, and the exchange of fantasies or desires. This position is perfect for partners who enjoy talking during sex and want to maintain a strong intellectual and emotional connection.
    - **Versatility and Adaptability:** The Conversationalist position is highly versatile, allowing partners to switch between different rhythms and angles easily. Gemini will appreciate the ability to adapt the position to suit their changing moods and desires, keeping the experience fresh and exciting.
- **The Pivot:**
    - **Description:** In the Pivot position, one partner lies on their back with their legs bent at the knees, while the other partner straddles them, facing forward. This position allows for deep penetration and a wide range of movement options, with the straddling partner able to pivot from side to side.
    - **Versatility and Adaptability:** The Pivot position is perfect for Gemini's need for variety and adaptability. The straddling partner can easily switch between different angles

and movements, keeping the experience dynamic and engaging. The ability to pivot and change direction mirrors Gemini's dual nature, allowing them to explore different sensations and dynamics.

- ◦ **Communication and Connection:** The Pivot position also allows for verbal exchange and playful interaction, as the partners can maintain eye contact and engage in conversation. Gemini will appreciate the ability to communicate their desires and to adapt the position to suit their changing needs.

- **The Switch:**
  - ◦ **Description:** In the Switch position, both partners start in a standard missionary position, with the penetrating partner on top. At any point, the partners can switch roles, with the penetrating partner rolling onto their back and the receiving partner taking control on top. This position allows for seamless transitions and adaptability.
  - ◦ **Versatility and Adaptability:** The Switch is the ultimate position for Gemini's dual nature, allowing for quick and easy transitions between roles. Gemini will enjoy the opportunity to switch between being dominant and submissive, keeping the experience lively and engaging. The adaptability of this position ensures that both partners remain engaged and excited throughout.
  - ◦ **Communication and Connection:** The Switch position also encourages communication, as the partners must coordinate their movements and communicate their desires during the transition. This makes the experience more interactive and connected, catering to Gemini's love of verbal exchange and intellectual stimulation.

- **The Whisper:**
  - ◦ **Description:** In the Whisper position, one partner sits on a chair or the edge of the bed, while the other partner sits on their lap, facing away. This position allows for close physical contact, deep penetration, and easy access to whisper in each other's ears.
  - ◦ **Communication and Connection:** The Whisper is a highly communicative position that allows for intimate verbal exchange. The seated partner can whisper sweet nothings, fantasies, or playful remarks into their partner's ear, enhancing the sense of connection and intimacy. This position is perfect for Gemini's love of words and the power of verbal expression.

- **Versatility and Adaptability:** The Whisper position is also versatile, allowing the seated partner to control the depth and rhythm of the experience. Gemini will appreciate the ability to adapt the position to suit their changing desires, keeping the experience dynamic and engaging.

- **The Mirror Image:**
  - **Description:** In the Mirror Image position, both partners kneel facing each other, with their bodies mirroring each other's movements. This position allows for deep eye contact, synchronized movements, and a strong connection.
  - **Versatility and Adaptability:** The Mirror Image position is ideal for Gemini's dual nature, as it allows both partners to mirror each other's movements and adapt to each other's rhythms. The ability to synchronize and adjust the position to suit their needs makes it a perfect choice for Gemini, who thrives on variety and adaptability.
  - **Communication and Connection:** The Mirror Image position also encourages communication, as the partners can maintain eye contact and engage in verbal exchange. The mirroring of each other's movements creates a strong sense of connection and unity, catering to Gemini's love of intellectual and emotional engagement.

Enhancing Gemini's Energy Through Rituals and Practices

To fully harness Gemini's communicative energy in your sexual relationship, consider incorporating rituals and practices that emphasize communication, versatility, and the exploration of new ideas. These activities can help you align with Gemini's dynamic energy, making your sexual experiences more engaging, intellectually stimulating, and deeply satisfying.

- **Verbal Games:** Engage in verbal games that encourage communication and playfulness. This could include truth-or-dare, asking each other intimate questions, or playing a game of "Would You Rather?" tailored to your sexual preferences. These games can help partners explore their desires and boundaries in a fun, light-hearted way, catering to Gemini's love of conversation and intellectual stimulation.

- **Role Play and Fantasy Exploration:** Gemini loves to explore different roles and scenarios, so incorporating role play into your sexual relationship can be a great way to engage their curiosity and creativity. Whether it's trying out different characters, exploring fantasies, or switching roles, role play allows Gemini to express their dual nature and keep the experience fresh and exciting.

- **Spontaneous Encounters:** Gemini thrives on spontaneity and variety, so planning spontaneous sexual encounters can be a great way to keep things exciting. This might involve surprising your partner with an unplanned rendezvous, trying out a new location, or experimenting with a new position on the spur of the moment. Spontaneity adds an element of excitement and unpredictability, aligning with Gemini's dynamic energy.
- **Creative Communication:** Incorporate creative communication into your sexual relationship by exploring new ways to express your desires and fantasies. This could include writing love notes, sending playful texts, or engaging in sexting. Gemini will appreciate the opportunity to use their words and intellect to enhance the experience and deepen the connection.

Conclusion

Gemini's influence on sexuality brings a versatile, communicative energy that emphasizes curiosity, adaptability, and the exploration of new ideas. By incorporating the versatile and communicative positions outlined in this chapter, you can harness Gemini's dynamic energy to create sexual experiences that are engaging, intellectually stimulating, and deeply satisfying. Whether through the intimate exchange of the Conversationalist, the adaptable movement of the Pivot, or the playful interaction of the Whisper, Gemini's energy invites you to explore the full range of your desires, to communicate openly with your partner, and to keep the experience lively and engaging. Let Gemini guide you toward a more versatile, communicative, and dynamic sexual relationship, where every encounter is an opportunity to explore new possibilities, connect deeply, and enjoy the thrill of discovery.

Chapter 19: Cancer: The Nurturer

Cancer, the fourth sign of the zodiac, is ruled by the Moon, the celestial body associated with emotions, intuition, and the nurturing aspects of life. Known for their caring, protective nature, Cancers are the natural nurturers of the zodiac. In the realm of sexuality, Cancer seeks to create a deep emotional bond with their partner, prioritizing intimacy, security, and the emotional well-being of both. This chapter delves into Cancer's approach to sex, focusing on positions that emphasize protection, nurturing, and emotional connection. These positions are designed to cater to Cancer's need for closeness, tenderness, and the creation of a safe, loving environment where both partners can feel cared for and cherished.

The Cancer Lover: Protective, Intuitive, and Devoted

Cancer is a water sign, deeply connected to the emotional and intuitive realms. As a lover, Cancer is protective, devoted, and highly attuned to the needs and feelings of their partner. They thrive on creating a nurturing environment where both partners feel safe, loved, and emotionally connected. For Cancer, sex is not just a physical act; it's a way to express love, care, and deep emotional commitment.

- **Emotional Connection and Intuition:** Cancer is ruled by the Moon, which governs emotions, intuition, and the subconscious mind. This makes Cancer highly sensitive to the emotional needs of their partner. They are intuitive lovers, able to sense their partner's desires and respond with care and empathy. For Cancer, emotional connection is the foundation of a fulfilling sexual relationship.

- **Nurturing and Protection:** Cancer's protective nature extends to their sexual relationships, where they strive to create a safe and nurturing environment. They take pride in caring for their partner, ensuring that they feel loved, supported, and emotionally secure. Cancer's nurturing instincts make them gentle, attentive lovers who prioritize the well-being of their partner.

- **Devotion and Loyalty:** Cancer is deeply loyal and devoted to their partner, seeking to build a lasting, emotionally fulfilling relationship. They are not interested in casual flings or superficial connections; Cancer desires a deep, meaningful bond with someone they can trust and care for. In the bedroom, this translates to a focus on intimacy, tenderness, and the creation of a shared emotional experience.

Protective and Nurturing Positions for Cancer's Caring Nature

Certain sexual positions are particularly well-suited to channeling Cancer's nurturing, protective energy. These positions emphasize closeness, tenderness, and emotional connection, allowing Cancer to fully express their caring nature. They are designed to create a safe, loving environment where both partners can feel cherished, secure, and deeply connected.

- **The Cradle:**
    - **Description:** In the Cradle position, one partner lies on their back while the other partner lies on top, resting their head on their partner's chest. This position allows for gentle, slow movements and close physical contact.
    - **Nurturing and Protection:** The Cradle position is the epitome of nurturing and protection. The partner on the bottom cradles their partner in their arms, creating a sense of safety and security. The close physical contact and the ability to feel each other's heartbeat enhances the emotional connection, making it a deeply comforting and nurturing experience.
    - **Emotional Connection:** The Cradle position encourages a strong emotional bond, as it allows both partners to relax into each other's arms and enjoy the comfort of their connection. This position is perfect for moments when one or both partners need reassurance, care, and emotional support.
- **The Sheltering Spoon:**
    - **Description:** In the Sheltering Spoon position, both partners lie on their sides, with one partner spooning the other from behind. This position allows for gentle, rhythmic movements and close physical contact.
    - **Nurturing and Protection:** The Sheltering Spoon is a protective, nurturing position that allows Cancer to fully embrace their partner and create a sense of safety. The partner in front feels protected and cared for, while the partner behind provides warmth

and comfort through their embrace. This position is ideal for creating a sense of security and emotional connection.

- **Emotional Connection:** The Sheltering Spoon encourages emotional intimacy, as it allows both partners to feel the warmth of each other's bodies and the comfort of their connection. The gentle, rhythmic movements create a soothing, calming experience that enhances the emotional bond between partners.

- **The Protective Embrace:**
  - **Description:** In the Protective Embrace position, one partner sits on the bed with their back against the headboard, while the other partner sits between their legs, leaning back against their chest. This position allows for close physical contact and gentle, affectionate touch.
  - **Nurturing and Protection:** The Protective Embrace is a nurturing position that allows Cancer to envelop their partner in a protective embrace. The partner sitting behind can wrap their arms around their partner, creating a sense of safety and security. This position is perfect for moments when one partner needs comfort and reassurance.
  - **Emotional Connection:** The Protective Embrace encourages emotional connection through close physical contact and gentle touch. The position allows both partners to relax into each other's arms and enjoy the warmth and security of their connection. This is an ideal position for quiet, intimate moments where the focus is on emotional bonding.

- **The Heartfelt Hug:**
  - **Description:** In the Heartfelt Hug position, both partners kneel facing each other, with their bodies pressed close together and their arms wrapped around each other. This position allows for close physical contact, deep eye contact, and gentle, slow movements.
  - **Nurturing and Protection:** The Heartfelt Hug is a deeply nurturing position that allows Cancer to fully embrace their partner, creating a sense of safety and emotional security. The close physical contact and the ability to feel each other's heartbeat enhance the emotional connection, making it a deeply comforting and loving experience.

- ○ **Emotional Connection:** The Heartfelt Hug encourages emotional intimacy and connection through close physical contact and deep eye contact. The gentle, slow movements create a soothing, calming experience that strengthens the emotional bond between partners. This position is perfect for moments when both partners want to feel close and connected.
- **The Cocoon:**
  - ○ **Description:** In the Cocoon position, both partners lie on their sides facing each other, with their legs intertwined and their bodies pressed close together. This position allows for gentle, rhythmic movements and close physical contact.
  - ○ **Nurturing and Protection:** The Cocoon is a protective, nurturing position that allows Cancer to fully envelop their partner in a comforting embrace. The close physical contact creates a sense of security and warmth, making both partners feel safe and cared for. This position is ideal for creating a deep emotional connection and a sense of togetherness.
  - ○ **Emotional Connection:** The Cocoon encourages emotional intimacy and connection through close physical contact and the comforting feeling of being wrapped in each other's arms. The gentle, rhythmic movements create a soothing, calming experience that enhances the emotional bond between partners.

Enhancing Cancer's Energy Through Rituals and Practices

To fully harness Cancer's nurturing energy in your sexual relationship, consider incorporating rituals and practices that emphasize emotional connection, comfort, and the creation of a safe, loving environment. These activities can help you align with Cancer's caring energy, making your sexual experiences more emotionally fulfilling, intimate, and deeply satisfying.

- **Emotional Check-Ins:** Make a habit of regularly checking in with your partner about their emotional well-being and how they are feeling in your relationship. These emotional check-ins can help you stay attuned to each other's needs and ensure that both partners feel loved, supported, and emotionally secure. This practice aligns with Cancer's nurturing nature and helps create a strong emotional bond.

- **Creating a Safe Space:** Take the time to create a safe, comforting environment for your sexual encounters. This might include soft lighting, warm blankets, and soothing music that create a sense of security and relaxation. The goal is to create a space where both partners can feel safe, loved, and emotionally connected.
- **Cuddling and Touch:** Incorporate plenty of cuddling and gentle touch into your sexual relationship. Cuddling and touch are essential for Cancer's nurturing nature, as they help create a sense of warmth, comfort, and emotional security. Take the time to hold each other, stroke each other's hair, and enjoy the simple pleasure of being close.
- **Emotional Bonding Rituals:** Engage in rituals that strengthen your emotional bond, such as sharing your feelings, expressing your love and appreciation for each other, and engaging in activities that bring you closer together. These rituals help deepen your emotional connection and create a strong foundation of trust, love, and security.

Conclusion

Cancer's influence on sexuality brings a nurturing, protective energy that emphasizes emotional connection, comfort, and the creation of a safe, loving environment. By incorporating the protective and nurturing positions outlined in this chapter, you can harness Cancer's caring energy to create sexual experiences that are emotionally fulfilling, intimate, and deeply satisfying. Whether through the comforting embrace of the Cradle, the protective warmth of the Sheltering Spoon, or the deep connection of the Heartfelt Hug, Cancer's energy invites you to nurture, protect, and cherish your partner, creating a sexual relationship that is rooted in love, trust, and emotional security. Let Cancer guide you toward a more nurturing, emotionally connected, and loving sexual relationship, where every encounter is an opportunity to care for and cherish each other.

Chapter 20: Leo: The Performer

Leo, the fifth sign of the zodiac, is ruled by the Sun, the celestial body that represents vitality, self-expression, and the drive to shine brightly in the world. Known for their confidence, charisma, and dramatic flair, Leos are natural performers who love to be the center of attention. In the realm of sexuality, Leo brings passion, creativity, and a desire to impress and be admired. This chapter delves into Leo's approach to sex, focusing on positions that emphasize confidence, showmanship, and the ability to create a memorable, theatrical experience. These positions are designed to cater to Leo's need for attention, their love of the spotlight, and their desire to make every sexual encounter an unforgettable performance.

The Leo Lover: Confident, Passionate, and Charismatic

Leo is a fire sign, embodying the qualities of warmth, enthusiasm, and a zest for life. As a lover, Leo is confident, passionate, and always eager to impress their partner. They thrive on admiration and enjoy expressing their creativity and passion in the bedroom. For Leo, sex is an opportunity to shine, to showcase their skills, and to create a dynamic, exciting experience that both partners will remember.

- **Confidence and Charisma:** Leo is ruled by the Sun, symbolizing their innate confidence and charisma. They are natural leaders and love to take charge in their sexual relationships. Leo's confidence makes them bold and assertive lovers, unafraid to express their desires and to take the lead in creating a passionate, exciting encounter.
- **Passion and Drama:** Leos are known for their passion and love of drama, both in and out of the bedroom. They bring a sense of excitement and intensity to their sexual relationships, always striving to make each encounter more thrilling than the last. Leo enjoys creating an atmosphere of drama and anticipation, using their flair for the theatrical to heighten the experience.
- **Admiration and Attention:** Leo thrives on admiration and loves to be the center of attention. They enjoy knowing that their partner is captivated by them and will go to great lengths to impress and please. In the bedroom, Leo seeks positions that allow them to showcase their skills and to bask in their partner's admiration.

Show-Stopping and Confident Positions for Leo's Dramatic Flair

Certain sexual positions are particularly well-suited to channeling Leo's confident, show-stopping energy. These positions emphasize boldness, creativity, and the opportunity to shine in the spotlight, allowing Leo to fully express their dramatic flair. They are designed to create a dynamic, memorable experience that satisfies Leo's need for attention and their desire to impress.

- **The Royal Arch:**
    - **Description:** In the Royal Arch position, one partner lies on their back with their hips lifted into a bridge pose, while the other partner kneels between their legs. The partner in the bridge pose arches their back, creating a dramatic, elevated position that allows for deep penetration and an impressive visual display.
    - **Confidence and Charisma:** The Royal Arch is a bold, dramatic position that allows Leo to showcase their confidence and physical prowess. The arched back creates a powerful visual that is sure to impress, making it a perfect choice for a Leo lover who loves to be admired.
    - **Passion and Drama:** The elevated position of the Royal Arch adds a sense of drama and intensity to the encounter, heightening the overall experience. This position allows Leo to fully express their passion and to create a dynamic, show-stopping performance.
- **The Spotlight:**
    - **Description:** In the Spotlight position, one partner stands with their back against a wall, while the other partner kneels or crouches in front of them, providing oral stimulation. The standing partner can place one foot on a raised surface, such as a chair or bed, to create an even more commanding presence.
    - **Confidence and Charisma:** The Spotlight is a position that puts Leo front and center, allowing them to fully embrace their love of attention and admiration. The standing partner's commanding presence and the intense eye contact make this a powerful, confident position that aligns with Leo's need to be in control and admired.
    - **Passion and Drama:** The dramatic nature of the Spotlight position, combined with the intense focus on the standing partner, creates a sense of anticipation and excite-

ment. This position is perfect for Leo's flair for the theatrical and their desire to create a memorable, passionate experience.

- **The Throne:**
  - ◦ **Description:** In the Throne position, one partner sits on a chair or the edge of the bed, while the other partner straddles them, facing forward. The seated partner can lean back, placing their hands behind them for support, while the straddling partner takes control of the movements.
  - ◦ **Confidence and Charisma:** The Throne is a position that exudes power and confidence, making it ideal for a Leo lover who enjoys taking charge. The seated partner's relaxed posture and the commanding presence of the straddling partner create a dynamic, visually impressive experience.
  - ◦ **Passion and Drama:** The Throne position allows for deep penetration and intense eye contact, adding to the drama and passion of the encounter. This position is perfect for Leo's love of being in the spotlight and their desire to create a powerful, memorable experience.

- **The Lion's Prowl:**
  - ◦ **Description:** In the Lion's Prowl position, one partner is on all fours, while the other partner kneels behind them, taking control of the movements. The kneeling partner can vary the pace and intensity, creating a dynamic, animalistic experience.
  - ◦ **Confidence and Charisma:** The Lion's Prowl is a position that allows Leo to fully embrace their wild, confident nature. The dominant partner's control over the pace and intensity creates a powerful, commanding presence that aligns with Leo's need to be in charge.
  - ◦ **Passion and Drama:** The primal nature of the Lion's Prowl adds an element of raw, animalistic passion to the encounter, heightening the drama and intensity. This position is perfect for Leo's love of dramatic, powerful experiences that leave a lasting impression.

- **The Star Performer:**
  - ◦ **Description:** In the Star Performer position, one partner lies on their back with their legs spread wide, while the other partner kneels between their legs, taking full control

of the movements. The kneeling partner can vary the depth and rhythm, creating a dynamic, show-stopping experience.

- ◦ **Confidence and Charisma:** The Star Performer is a position that allows Leo to fully embrace their love of the spotlight. The kneeling partner's control over the pace and intensity, combined with the dramatic visual of the spread legs, creates a powerful, confident experience that satisfies Leo's need to be admired and in control.
- ◦ **Passion and Drama:** The Star Performer position is all about creating a dynamic, memorable experience that is both passionate and visually impressive. This position is perfect for Leo's flair for the dramatic and their desire to create a show-stopping performance that leaves both partners feeling exhilarated.

Enhancing Leo's Energy Through Rituals and Practices

To fully harness Leo's dramatic energy in your sexual relationship, consider incorporating rituals and practices that emphasize confidence, creativity, and the creation of a memorable, theatrical experience. These activities can help you align with Leo's charismatic energy, making your sexual experiences more dynamic, exciting, and deeply satisfying.

- **Performance Preparation:** Leos love to shine in the spotlight, so consider creating a pre-sex ritual that allows you to prepare mentally and physically for your "performance." This might include setting the stage with candles, music, and soft lighting, or even taking the time to groom and dress in a way that makes you feel confident and attractive. The goal is to create a sense of anticipation and excitement, making the experience feel special and memorable.
- **Role Play and Fantasy Exploration:** Leo loves to explore different roles and scenarios, so incorporating role play into your sexual relationship can be a great way to engage their creativity and flair for the dramatic. Whether it's trying out different characters, exploring fantasies, or setting up a scene, role play allows Leo to express their dynamic nature and to create a memorable, exciting experience.
- **Mirror Play:** Incorporate mirrors into your sexual encounters to enhance the visual experience and to allow Leo to see themselves in action. Mirrors can add a sense of drama and excitement, allowing both partners to fully appreciate the visual aspects of the experience. Leo

will enjoy the opportunity to admire themselves and their partner, enhancing the overall experience.

- **Praising and Admiration:** Leo thrives on admiration and praise, so be sure to express your appreciation for their efforts in the bedroom. Compliments, verbal affirmations, and expressions of admiration can help boost Leo's confidence and make them feel valued and appreciated. This practice aligns with Leo's need for attention and their desire to impress and please their partner.

Conclusion

Leo's influence on sexuality brings a confident, dramatic energy that emphasizes passion, creativity, and the desire to impress and be admired. By incorporating the show-stopping and confident positions outlined in this chapter, you can harness Leo's dynamic energy to create sexual experiences that are both exciting and deeply satisfying. Whether through the powerful visual of the Royal Arch, the commanding presence of the Spotlight, or the primal intensity of the Lion's Prowl, Leo's energy invites you to embrace your confidence, to shine in the spotlight, and to create a memorable, theatrical experience that leaves both partners feeling exhilarated and fulfilled. Let Leo guide you toward a more dynamic, confident, and exciting sexual relationship, where every encounter is an opportunity to perform, impress, and enjoy the thrill of the moment.

Chapter 21: Virgo: The Perfectionist

Virgo, the sixth sign of the zodiac, is ruled by Mercury, the planet of communication, intellect, and precision. Known for their meticulous nature, analytical mind, and attention to detail, Virgos approach life—and love—with a desire for perfection and a commitment to excellence. In the realm of sexuality, Virgo's perfectionist tendencies manifest as a focus on precision, technique, and the desire to create a flawless, deeply satisfying experience for both partners. This chapter delves into Virgo's approach to sex, focusing on positions that emphasize detail, precision, and the pursuit of perfection. These positions are designed to cater to Virgo's need for control, their analytical nature, and their desire to ensure that every aspect of the experience is executed flawlessly.

The Virgo Lover: Meticulous, Analytical, and Attentive

Virgo is an earth sign, grounded in practicality and deeply connected to the physical world. As a lover, Virgo is meticulous, analytical, and highly attentive to the needs and desires of their partner. They are not content with mediocrity; Virgo strives for perfection in everything they do, including their sexual relationships. For Virgo, sex is an opportunity to connect on a deep, intimate level while also showcasing their skills and attention to detail.

- **Precision and Technique:** Virgo is ruled by Mercury, making them naturally detail-oriented and focused on technique. In sexual relationships, this translates to a meticulous approach to pleasure, where every movement, touch, and action is carefully considered and executed with precision. Virgo takes pride in their ability to create a perfectly orchestrated experience that leaves their partner fully satisfied.

- **Analytical and Attentive:** Virgos are known for their analytical minds and their ability to observe and respond to the needs of others. In the bedroom, this means that Virgo is highly attuned to their partner's desires, preferences, and reactions. They use their keen observational skills to adjust and refine their approach, ensuring that every detail is just right.

- **Desire for Perfection:** Virgo is a perfectionist at heart, always striving to improve and perfect their skills. In sexual relationships, this manifests as a desire to continually enhance the experience, to learn and grow, and to ensure that every encounter is better than the last. Virgo is driven by a deep-seated desire to achieve excellence in all aspects of their sexual relationship.

Detail-Oriented and Precise Positions for Virgo's Meticulous Approach

Certain sexual positions are particularly well-suited to channeling Virgo's detail-oriented, precise energy. These positions emphasize control, technique, and the opportunity to fine-tune every aspect of the experience, allowing Virgo to fully express their meticulous nature. They are designed to create a perfectly orchestrated experience that satisfies Virgo's need for precision and their desire to ensure that every detail is just right.

- **The Precision Point:**
  - **Description:** In the Precision Point position, one partner lies on their back with their legs bent at the knees, while the other partner kneels between their legs, using their hands to guide the position and angle of penetration. This position allows for controlled, precise movements and deep penetration.
  - **Precision and Technique:** The Precision Point is ideal for Virgo's love of control and technique. The kneeling partner can carefully adjust the angle and depth of penetration, ensuring that every movement is perfectly executed. This position allows Virgo to showcase their attention to detail and their ability to create a flawless experience.
  - **Analytical and Attentive:** The Precision Point encourages Virgo's analytical nature, as the position allows for constant adjustment and fine-tuning based on their partner's responses. This ensures that the experience is perfectly tailored to their partner's desires, making it deeply satisfying for both.
- **The Methodical Embrace:**
  - **Description:** In the Methodical Embrace position, both partners lie on their sides, facing each other, with their legs intertwined and bodies pressed close together. This position allows for slow, controlled movements and deep emotional connection.
  - **Precision and Technique:** The Methodical Embrace is a position that allows Virgo to fully embrace their meticulous nature. The slow, deliberate movements encourage a focus on technique, ensuring that every touch and caress is perfectly timed and executed. This position is perfect for creating a deeply satisfying, detail-oriented experience.
  - **Analytical and Attentive:** The close physical contact and the ability to observe their partner's reactions make the Methodical Embrace ideal for Virgo's analytical approach.

The position allows for constant feedback and adjustment, ensuring that every detail is just right.

- **The Balanced Arch:**
  - **Description:** In the Balanced Arch position, one partner lies on their back with their hips lifted into a bridge pose, while the other partner kneels between their legs, holding their hips for support. This position allows for controlled, rhythmic movements and deep penetration.
  - **Precision and Technique:** The Balanced Arch is a position that requires precision and control, making it perfect for Virgo's meticulous approach. The kneeling partner can carefully control the pace and intensity of the movements, ensuring that every aspect of the experience is perfectly balanced and executed.
  - **Analytical and Attentive:** The Balanced Arch allows Virgo to focus on their partner's responses and to make adjustments as needed. The position encourages a methodical approach to pleasure, ensuring that every detail is carefully considered and optimized.
- **The Sculptor's Touch:**
  - **Description:** In the Sculptor's Touch position, one partner lies on their stomach with their legs slightly apart, while the other partner kneels behind them, using their hands to guide the position and movements. This position allows for deep penetration and controlled, deliberate movements.
  - **Precision and Technique:** The Sculptor's Touch is a position that allows Virgo to showcase their precision and technique. The kneeling partner can carefully guide the movements, using their hands to ensure that every touch and thrust is perfectly executed. This position is ideal for creating a finely tuned, detail-oriented experience.
  - **Analytical and Attentive:** The Sculptor's Touch encourages Virgo to focus on their partner's responses and to make adjustments as needed. The position allows for constant feedback and refinement, ensuring that every aspect of the experience is perfectly tailored to their partner's desires.

- **The Perfectionist's Glide:**
  - **Description:** In the Perfectionist's Glide position, both partners lie on their sides, with one partner slightly behind the other. The top partner's legs are intertwined with the bottom partner's, allowing for controlled, rhythmic movements and close physical contact.
  - **Precision and Technique:** The Perfectionist's Glide is a position that emphasizes control and precision, making it ideal for Virgo's meticulous nature. The slow, rhythmic movements allow Virgo to carefully adjust the pace and intensity, ensuring that every aspect of the experience is perfectly executed.
  - **Analytical and Attentive:** The Perfectionist's Glide allows Virgo to focus on their partner's responses and to make adjustments as needed. The position encourages a methodical approach to pleasure, ensuring that every detail is carefully considered and optimized.

Enhancing Virgo's Energy Through Rituals and Practices

To fully harness Virgo's meticulous energy in your sexual relationship, consider incorporating rituals and practices that emphasize precision, technique, and the pursuit of perfection. These activities can help you align with Virgo's detail-oriented energy, making your sexual experiences more refined, satisfying, and deeply fulfilling.

- **Mindful Breathing and Focus:** Virgo thrives on precision and control, so incorporating mindful breathing and focus into your sexual encounters can help enhance the experience. Focus on your breath, the rhythm of your movements, and the sensations in your body. This practice aligns with Virgo's meticulous nature and helps create a more refined, controlled experience.
- **Refinement Rituals:** Engage in rituals that allow you to refine and perfect your sexual technique. This might include studying new techniques, exploring different positions, or practicing communication with your partner to better understand their desires. The goal is to continually improve and refine your skills, aligning with Virgo's desire for perfection.

- **Creating a Clean, Organized Environment:** Virgo appreciates cleanliness and organization, so creating a clean, well-organized environment for your sexual encounters can help enhance the experience. Take the time to prepare your space, ensuring that everything is in order and that the environment is conducive to relaxation and pleasure. This practice aligns with Virgo's love of order and their desire for a refined, comfortable experience.
- **Detailed Communication:** Virgo thrives on clear, detailed communication, so make a habit of discussing your desires, preferences, and boundaries with your partner. This practice helps ensure that both partners are on the same page and that the experience is perfectly tailored to their needs and desires. Detailed communication aligns with Virgo's analytical nature and helps create a more satisfying, deeply connected experience.

Conclusion

Virgo's influence on sexuality brings a meticulous, detail-oriented energy that emphasizes precision, technique, and the pursuit of perfection. By incorporating the detail-oriented and precise positions outlined in this chapter, you can harness Virgo's meticulous energy to create sexual experiences that are refined, satisfying, and deeply fulfilling. Whether through the controlled movements of the Precision Point, the methodical approach of the Methodical Embrace, or the finely tuned balance of the Balanced Arch, Virgo's energy invites you to focus on the details, to refine your technique, and to create a perfectly orchestrated experience that leaves both partners fully satisfied. Let Virgo guide you toward a more refined, precise, and deeply connected sexual relationship, where every encounter is an opportunity to achieve excellence and to enjoy the satisfaction of a perfectly executed experience.

Chapter 22: Libra: The Diplomat

Libra, the seventh sign of the zodiac, is ruled by Venus, the planet of love, beauty, and harmony. Known for their strong sense of fairness, balance, and diplomacy, Libras are natural peacemakers who strive to create harmony in all aspects of their lives. In the realm of sexuality, Libra brings a desire for equilibrium, mutual pleasure, and a focus on creating a harmonious connection with their partner. This chapter delves into Libra's approach to sex, focusing on positions that emphasize balance, harmony, and the pursuit of mutual satisfaction. These positions are designed to cater to Libra's need for equilibrium, their love of beauty, and their desire to create a balanced, harmonious experience for both partners.

The Libra Lover: Harmonious, Fair, and Romantic

Libra is an air sign, associated with intellectualism, communication, and a strong desire for justice and fairness. As a lover, Libra is harmonious, fair, and deeply romantic. They seek to create a balanced and beautiful experience in the bedroom, where both partners feel valued, respected, and equally satisfied. For Libra, sex is not just about physical pleasure; it's about creating a harmonious connection that reflects their love of balance and their appreciation for beauty.

- **Balance and Equilibrium:** Libra is symbolized by the scales, representing their strong desire for balance and equilibrium in all things. In sexual relationships, this translates to a focus on ensuring that both partners are equally satisfied and that the experience is mutually enjoyable. Libra seeks to create a balanced, harmonious connection that leaves both partners feeling fulfilled.

- **Romance and Beauty:** Ruled by Venus, Libra has a deep appreciation for beauty and romance. They are naturally drawn to creating aesthetically pleasing environments and enjoy incorporating elements of beauty and elegance into their sexual experiences. For Libra, sex is an opportunity to express love, create a beautiful connection, and indulge in the pleasures of romance.

- **Fairness and Diplomacy:** Libra is known for their diplomatic nature and their desire for fairness. In the bedroom, this means that Libra is attentive to their partner's needs and desires, striving to create an experience that is equitable and satisfying for both. Libra is a considerate lover who values open communication and mutual respect.

Harmonious and Balanced Positions for Libra's Quest for Equilibrium

Certain sexual positions are particularly well-suited to channeling Libra's harmonious, balanced energy. These positions emphasize mutual pleasure, balance, and the creation of a beautiful, harmonious experience. They are designed to cater to Libra's need for equilibrium and their desire to ensure that both partners are equally satisfied.

- **The Mirror Reflection:**
    - **Description:** In the Mirror Reflection position, both partners lie on their sides, facing each other, with their bodies perfectly aligned and their legs intertwined. This position allows for deep eye contact, synchronized movements, and close physical contact.
    - **Balance and Equilibrium:** The Mirror Reflection is a position that emphasizes balance and harmony. The mirrored alignment of the partners' bodies creates a sense of equilibrium, allowing both to move in perfect synchrony. This position is ideal for Libra's desire for mutual satisfaction and their love of creating a balanced connection.
    - **Romance and Beauty:** The close physical contact and deep eye contact in the Mirror Reflection position enhance the romantic and intimate aspects of the encounter. Libra will appreciate the beauty of this position, as it allows for a deeply connected and aesthetically pleasing experience.
- **The Harmonious Arch:**
    - **Description:** In the Harmonious Arch position, one partner lies on their back with their legs bent at the knees, while the other partner kneels between their legs, leaning forward with their hands on either side of their partner's body. This position allows for controlled, balanced movements and deep penetration.
    - **Balance and Equilibrium:** The Harmonious Arch is a position that allows both partners to find a balanced rhythm that is mutually satisfying. The kneeling partner can adjust the depth and pace of penetration to ensure that both partners are equally engaged

and fulfilled. This position is perfect for Libra's quest for equilibrium and mutual pleasure.

- ◦ **Romance and Beauty:** The elegant, arched posture of the Harmonious Arch position adds an element of beauty and grace to the encounter. Libra will appreciate the romantic and visually pleasing aspects of this position, as it aligns with their love of creating a beautiful, harmonious experience.

- **The Diplomat's Embrace:**
  - ◦ **Description:** In the Diplomat's Embrace position, both partners sit facing each other, with their legs crossed and their bodies pressed close together. This position allows for deep eye contact, close physical contact, and synchronized movements.
  - ◦ **Balance and Equilibrium:** The Diplomat's Embrace is a position that emphasizes mutual engagement and balance. Both partners are equally involved in the experience, with each able to contribute to the rhythm and pace of the encounter. This position is ideal for Libra's desire to create a balanced, equitable connection.
  - ◦ **Romance and Beauty:** The Diplomat's Embrace is a deeply romantic position that allows for close physical contact and the exchange of loving words or kisses. Libra will appreciate the beauty and intimacy of this position, as it allows them to create a harmonious and romantic experience.

- **The Equal Exchange:**
  - ◦ **Description:** In the Equal Exchange position, one partner lies on their back with their legs spread wide, while the other partner lies on top, facing them. Both partners' bodies are aligned, allowing for deep penetration and synchronized movements.
  - ◦ **Balance and Equilibrium:** The Equal Exchange is a position that emphasizes mutual satisfaction and balance. Both partners are equally involved in the experience, with the ability to adjust the depth and rhythm to ensure that both are equally engaged and satisfied. This position is perfect for Libra's desire to create an equitable and balanced connection.
  - ◦ **Romance and Beauty:** The Equal Exchange position allows for deep eye contact and the exchange of loving touches, enhancing the romantic and intimate aspects of the en-

counter. Libra will appreciate the beauty and harmony of this position, as it aligns with their love of creating a balanced, mutually satisfying experience.

- **The Serene Balance:**
  - **Description:** In the Serene Balance position, both partners lie on their sides, with one partner slightly behind the other. The top partner's legs are intertwined with the bottom partner's, allowing for slow, controlled movements and close physical contact.
  - **Balance and Equilibrium:** The Serene Balance is a position that emphasizes harmony and balance. The intertwined legs and synchronized movements create a sense of equilibrium, allowing both partners to move together in perfect harmony. This position is ideal for Libra's quest for balance and their desire to create a serene, peaceful connection.
  - **Romance and Beauty:** The Serene Balance position allows for close physical contact and the exchange of loving touches, enhancing the romantic and intimate aspects of the encounter. Libra will appreciate the beauty and harmony of this position, as it aligns with their love of creating a peaceful, balanced experience.

Enhancing Libra's Energy Through Rituals and Practices

To fully harness Libra's harmonious energy in your sexual relationship, consider incorporating rituals and practices that emphasize balance, mutual pleasure, and the creation of a beautiful, harmonious experience. These activities can help you align with Libra's diplomatic energy, making your sexual experiences more balanced, satisfying, and deeply fulfilling.

- **Creating a Balanced Environment:** Libra thrives in environments that are aesthetically pleasing and harmonious. Take the time to create a beautiful, balanced environment for your sexual encounters by incorporating soft lighting, calming music, and soothing aromas. The goal is to create a space that feels peaceful, romantic, and conducive to mutual pleasure.
- **Mutual Massages:** Engage in mutual massages as part of your pre-sex ritual. Taking turns massaging each other allows both partners to relax, unwind, and feel equally cared for. This practice aligns with Libra's love of balance and mutual pleasure, helping to create a more harmonious and satisfying experience.

- **Open Communication:** Libra values fairness and open communication, so make a habit of discussing your desires, preferences, and boundaries with your partner. This practice ensures that both partners feel heard, respected, and equally satisfied, aligning with Libra's diplomatic nature and their desire to create a balanced, equitable connection.
- **Sharing Affirmations:** Incorporate the practice of sharing affirmations or words of appreciation during your sexual encounters. Expressing your admiration and love for each other helps to create a deeper emotional connection and reinforces the sense of balance and mutual respect that Libra values.

Conclusion

Libra's influence on sexuality brings a harmonious, balanced energy that emphasizes mutual pleasure, romance, and the creation of a beautiful, equitable experience. By incorporating the harmonious and balanced positions outlined in this chapter, you can harness Libra's diplomatic energy to create sexual experiences that are deeply satisfying, balanced, and romantically fulfilling. Whether through the mirrored alignment of the Mirror Reflection, the synchronized movements of the Harmonious Arch, or the equitable connection of the Equal Exchange, Libra's energy invites you to create a balanced, harmonious, and beautiful sexual relationship. Let Libra guide you toward a more balanced, romantic, and deeply connected sexual relationship, where every encounter is an opportunity to create harmony, mutual pleasure, and a lasting sense of equilibrium.

Chapter 23: Scorpio: The Intense Lover

Scorpio, the eighth sign of the zodiac, is ruled by Pluto, the planet of transformation, power, and rebirth. Known for their magnetic intensity, deep emotions, and unyielding passion, Scorpios are the most enigmatic and powerful lovers of the zodiac. In the realm of sexuality, Scorpio brings a level of depth, intensity, and connection that is unmatched. This chapter delves into Scorpio's approach to sex, focusing on positions that emphasize deep connection, passion, and the transformative power of intimacy. These positions are designed to cater to Scorpio's need for intensity, their desire to explore the depths of emotion, and their ability to create an experience that is both physically and emotionally overwhelming.

The Scorpio Lover: Intense, Passionate, and Transformative

Scorpio is a water sign, deeply connected to the emotional and subconscious realms. As a lover, Scorpio is intense, passionate, and driven by a desire to connect on a profound level. They are not interested in superficial encounters; for Scorpio, sex is a transformative experience that can reveal the deepest parts of the soul. Scorpio seeks to create a bond that is both powerful and lasting, making each encounter an unforgettable journey into the depths of emotion and desire.

- **Intensity and Passion:** Scorpio is ruled by Pluto, the planet of transformation, which gives them a deep and intense approach to life and love. In sexual relationships, this translates to a desire for passion that goes beyond the physical. Scorpio seeks to merge with their partner on every level—physically, emotionally, and spiritually. Their passion is all-consuming, making every encounter feel like a powerful and transformative experience.

- **Emotional Depth and Connection:** Scorpios are known for their emotional depth and their ability to connect with others on a profound level. They are highly intuitive and can sense the emotions and desires of their partner, allowing them to create an experience that is deeply satisfying for both. For Scorpio, sex is an opportunity to explore the depths of emotion, to uncover hidden desires, and to create a bond that is unbreakable.

- **Transformative Power:** Scorpio's connection to Pluto gives them the ability to transform themselves and their relationships through the power of intimacy. They see sex as a way to heal, grow, and evolve, both individually and as a couple. Scorpio's sexual experiences are often marked by a sense of renewal and rebirth, making each encounter a journey of transformation and discovery.

Deep and Passionate Positions for Scorpio's Magnetic Intensity

Certain sexual positions are particularly well-suited to channeling Scorpio's intense, passionate energy. These positions emphasize deep connection, emotional engagement, and the transformative power of intimacy. They are designed to create an experience that is both physically and emotionally overwhelming, satisfying Scorpio's need for intensity and their desire to connect on the deepest levels.

- **The Soul Merge:**
  - **Description:** In the Soul Merge position, both partners lie on their sides, facing each other, with their legs intertwined and their bodies pressed close together. This position allows for deep eye contact, synchronized breathing, and close physical contact.
  - **Intensity and Passion:** The Soul Merge is a position that allows Scorpio to fully express their desire for deep connection and intense passion. The close physical contact and deep eye contact create a powerful bond between partners, making the experience feel deeply intimate and transformative.
  - **Emotional Depth:** The Soul Merge encourages emotional vulnerability and openness, allowing both partners to connect on a profound level. This position is ideal for Scorpio's desire to explore the depths of emotion and to create a lasting, unbreakable bond.
- **The Deep Dive:**
  - **Description:** In the Deep Dive position, one partner lies on their back with their legs spread wide, while the other partner lies on top, maintaining deep eye contact and synchronized movements. This position allows for deep penetration and a slow, controlled pace.
  - **Intensity and Passion:** The Deep Dive is a position that emphasizes slow, deliberate movements and deep penetration, allowing Scorpio to fully immerse themselves in the

experience. The intense physical connection and deep eye contact make this position ideal for creating a powerful, transformative experience.

- **Emotional Depth:** The Deep Dive encourages emotional connection and intimacy, as it allows both partners to fully engage with each other's emotions and desires. The position is perfect for Scorpio's need for intensity and their desire to create a bond that is both powerful and enduring.

- **The Phoenix Rise:**
  - **Description:** In the Phoenix Rise position, one partner kneels with their back against the headboard or wall, while the other partner straddles them, facing forward. This position allows for close physical contact, deep penetration, and synchronized movements.
  - **Intensity and Passion:** The Phoenix Rise is a position that allows Scorpio to fully express their passionate, transformative energy. The close physical contact and the ability to maintain deep eye contact make this position ideal for creating a powerful, all-consuming experience.
  - **Transformative Power:** The Phoenix Rise is symbolic of Scorpio's ability to rise from the ashes and transform themselves through the power of intimacy. This position encourages both partners to explore their desires and emotions deeply, making it a perfect choice for a transformative, life-altering experience.

- **The Magnetic Lock:**
  - **Description:** In the Magnetic Lock position, both partners sit facing each other, with their legs intertwined and their bodies pressed close together. This position allows for deep penetration, close physical contact, and synchronized movements.
  - **Intensity and Passion:** The Magnetic Lock is a position that allows Scorpio to fully embrace their magnetic, intense nature. The close physical contact and the ability to maintain deep eye contact create a powerful connection between partners, making the experience feel both physically and emotionally overwhelming.
  - **Emotional Depth:** The Magnetic Lock encourages emotional connection and intimacy, as it allows both partners to fully engage with each other's emotions and desires.

This position is ideal for Scorpio's need for intensity and their desire to create a bond that is both deep and lasting.

- **The Scorpion's Sting:**
  - **Description:** In the Scorpion's Sting position, one partner lies on their back with their legs spread wide, while the other partner kneels between their legs, maintaining deep eye contact and slow, controlled movements.
  - **Intensity and Passion:** The Scorpion's Sting is a position that allows Scorpio to fully express their intense, passionate energy. The deep eye contact and slow, deliberate movements create a powerful, transformative experience that satisfies Scorpio's need for depth and intensity.
  - **Transformative Power:** The Scorpion's Sting is symbolic of Scorpio's ability to transform themselves and their relationships through the power of intimacy. This position encourages both partners to explore their desires and emotions deeply, making it a perfect choice for a life-altering experience.

Enhancing Scorpio's Energy Through Rituals and Practices

To fully harness Scorpio's intense energy in your sexual relationship, consider incorporating rituals and practices that emphasize emotional depth, passion, and the transformative power of intimacy. These activities can help you align with Scorpio's magnetic energy, making your sexual experiences more intense, satisfying, and deeply transformative.

- **Emotional Vulnerability:** Scorpio thrives on emotional depth and connection, so make a habit of exploring your emotions and desires with your partner. This might involve sharing your deepest fears, desires, and fantasies, or engaging in activities that encourage emotional vulnerability and openness. This practice aligns with Scorpio's desire for deep connection and their need for intensity.
- **Transformative Meditation:** Engage in meditation practices that focus on transformation and renewal before engaging in sexual activity. This might involve visualizing the release of old patterns, the shedding of emotional baggage, and the rebirth of your connection with

your partner. Transformative meditation aligns with Scorpio's ability to heal, grow, and evolve through the power of intimacy.

- **Creating a Sensual Environment:** Scorpio appreciates environments that are dark, mysterious, and sensual. Create a space that reflects this energy by incorporating candles, incense, and soft, luxurious fabrics. The goal is to create a space that feels intimate, mysterious, and conducive to deep emotional connection and passion.
- **Powerful Touch:** Incorporate touch as a way to deepen the connection between you and your partner. Slow, deliberate touches that focus on the most sensitive areas can help to create a powerful, intimate experience. This aligns with Scorpio's love of intensity and their desire to connect on a deep, emotional level.

Conclusion

Scorpio's influence on sexuality brings an intense, passionate energy that emphasizes deep connection, emotional depth, and the transformative power of intimacy. By incorporating the deep and passionate positions outlined in this chapter, you can harness Scorpio's magnetic energy to create sexual experiences that are intense, satisfying, and deeply transformative. Whether through the powerful connection of the Soul Merge, the symbolic rebirth of the Phoenix Rise, or the intense physical and emotional bond of the Magnetic Lock, Scorpio's energy invites you to explore the depths of your desires, to connect on the deepest levels, and to create a powerful, transformative experience that leaves both partners feeling profoundly connected and fulfilled. Let Scorpio guide you toward a more intense, passionate, and deeply connected sexual relationship, where every encounter is an opportunity to transform, heal, and grow together.

Chapter 24: Sagittarius: The Explorer

Sagittarius, the ninth sign of the zodiac, is ruled by Jupiter, the planet of expansion, adventure, and higher learning. Known for their love of freedom, exploration, and a thirst for new experiences, Sagittarians are the adventurers of the zodiac. In the realm of sexuality, Sagittarius brings an adventurous spirit, a desire for novelty, and an openness to explore new horizons. This chapter delves into Sagittarius' approach to sex, focusing on positions that emphasize adventure, expansiveness, and the thrill of exploration. These positions are designed to cater to Sagittarius' need for freedom, their love of spontaneity, and their desire to keep the experience fresh, exciting, and full of discovery.

The Sagittarius Lover: Adventurous, Open-Minded, and Free-Spirited

Sagittarius is a fire sign, embodying the qualities of enthusiasm, optimism, and a boundless sense of adventure. As a lover, Sagittarius is open-minded, adventurous, and always eager to explore new possibilities. They thrive on variety and spontaneity, seeking out experiences that push boundaries and offer a sense of freedom. For Sagittarius, sex is an opportunity to explore new terrains, both physically and emotionally, and to keep the experience vibrant, expansive, and full of excitement.

- **Love of Freedom and Exploration:** Sagittarius is ruled by Jupiter, the planet of expansion and exploration, making them natural adventurers who crave freedom and new experiences. In sexual relationships, this translates to a desire for variety and the willingness to explore different positions, techniques, and settings. Sagittarius seeks out experiences that are exciting, unconventional, and liberating.

- **Open-Mindedness and Curiosity:** Sagittarians are known for their open-mindedness and curiosity, both of which play a central role in their approach to sex. They are always eager to try new things, to push the boundaries, and to learn from each experience. For Sagittarius, sex is a journey of discovery, where they can explore their desires and expand their horizons.

- **Spontaneity and Enthusiasm:** Sagittarius is characterized by a spontaneous and enthusiastic approach to life, which extends to their sexual relationships. They enjoy taking risks, trying new things on the spur of the moment, and keeping the experience lively and unpredictable.

Sagittarius is driven by a desire to make every encounter an adventure, full of passion and excitement.

Adventurous and Expansive Positions for Sagittarius' Love of Freedom

Certain sexual positions are particularly well-suited to channeling Sagittarius' adventurous, expansive energy. These positions emphasize variety, spontaneity, and the thrill of exploration, allowing Sagittarius to fully express their love of freedom and their desire to keep the experience fresh and exciting. They are designed to create an experience that is both physically and emotionally expansive, satisfying Sagittarius' need for adventure and discovery.

- **The Wanderer's Embrace:**
  - **Description:** In the Wanderer's Embrace position, one partner stands with their back against a wall or sturdy surface, while the other partner lifts them slightly, supporting their weight with their arms wrapped around their waist. This position allows for deep penetration, close physical contact, and the ability to switch between different angles and movements.
  - **Adventurous and Expansive:** The Wanderer's Embrace is a position that embodies Sagittarius' love of adventure and variety. The standing orientation allows for flexibility and the ability to explore different angles and depths, making the experience dynamic and full of possibilities. This position is ideal for Sagittarius' desire to keep the experience exciting and unpredictable.
  - **Spontaneity and Enthusiasm:** The Wanderer's Embrace is a position that encourages spontaneity and quick transitions, allowing both partners to switch things up on the fly. Sagittarius will appreciate the freedom and flexibility of this position, as it aligns with their love of spontaneous, adventurous encounters.
- **The Open Horizon:**
  - **Description:** In the Open Horizon position, both partners lie on their sides, facing away from each other, with their legs intertwined. The top partner can use their legs to control the depth and angle of penetration, while both partners maintain a loose, relaxed posture.

- **Adventurous and Expansive:** The Open Horizon is a position that allows for expansive movement and the exploration of different sensations. The open, side-by-side orientation gives Sagittarius the freedom to explore different angles and rhythms, making the experience feel vast and open-ended. This position is perfect for Sagittarius' love of freedom and their desire to explore new possibilities.
  - **Spontaneity and Enthusiasm:** The Open Horizon encourages a relaxed, spontaneous approach to sex, allowing both partners to go with the flow and explore the experience without feeling constrained. Sagittarius will enjoy the sense of openness and the ability to experiment with different movements and angles.
- **The Trailblazer:**
  - **Description:** In the Trailblazer position, one partner kneels on the bed or floor, while the other partner straddles them from behind, facing the same direction. This position allows for deep penetration and the ability to switch between different speeds and rhythms.
  - **Adventurous and Expansive:** The Trailblazer is a position that embodies Sagittarius' adventurous spirit, allowing for deep, powerful movements and the exploration of new sensations. The kneeling orientation gives Sagittarius the ability to control the pace and intensity, making the experience feel dynamic and expansive.
  - **Spontaneity and Enthusiasm:** The Trailblazer encourages a playful, spontaneous approach to sex, with the ability to switch things up on the fly. Sagittarius will appreciate the freedom to experiment with different speeds and rhythms, as it aligns with their love of spontaneity and adventure.
- **The World Traveler:**
  - **Description:** In the World Traveler position, both partners stand facing each other, with one partner lifting the other's leg and wrapping it around their waist. This position allows for close physical contact, deep penetration, and the ability to explore different angles and depths.
  - **Adventurous and Expansive:** The World Traveler is a position that allows Sagittarius to fully embrace their love of exploration and variety. The standing orientation gives

both partners the freedom to move, switch angles, and explore different sensations, making the experience feel dynamic and expansive.

- ◦ **Spontaneity and Enthusiasm:** The World Traveler is a position that encourages spontaneity and quick transitions, allowing both partners to switch things up on the fly. Sagittarius will appreciate the freedom and flexibility of this position, as it aligns with their love of spontaneous, adventurous encounters.
- **The Skyward Stretch:**
  - ◦ **Description:** In the Skyward Stretch position, one partner lies on their back with their legs raised and spread wide, while the other partner stands or kneels between their legs, holding their ankles for support. This position allows for deep penetration and the ability to explore different angles and depths.
  - ◦ **Adventurous and Expansive:** The Skyward Stretch is a position that allows Sagittarius to fully embrace their love of adventure and exploration. The elevated leg position gives both partners the ability to explore different angles and depths, making the experience feel dynamic and expansive.
  - ◦ **Spontaneity and Enthusiasm:** The Skyward Stretch encourages a playful, spontaneous approach to sex, with the ability to switch things up on the fly. Sagittarius will enjoy the sense of freedom and the ability to experiment with different movements and angles.

Enhancing Sagittarius's Energy Through Rituals and Practices

To fully harness Sagittarius's adventurous energy in your sexual relationship, consider incorporating rituals and practices that emphasize exploration, spontaneity, and the thrill of discovery. These activities can help you align with Sagittarius's expansive energy, making your sexual experiences more exciting, dynamic, and deeply satisfying.

- **Exploring New Locations:** Sagittarius thrives on variety and exploration, so consider taking your sexual encounters to new and different locations. Whether it's a different room in the house, an outdoor setting, or a romantic getaway, changing your environment can add a sense of adventure and excitement to the experience. This practice aligns with Sagittarius's love of exploration and their desire to keep things fresh and exciting.

- **Trying New Techniques:** Sagittarius is always eager to learn and try new things, so incorporating new techniques and positions into your sexual repertoire can keep the experience dynamic and engaging. Experimenting with different rhythms, angles, and approaches allows both partners to explore new possibilities and discover what works best for them. This practice aligns with Sagittarius's open-mindedness and curiosity.
- **Spontaneous Encounters:** Sagittarius thrives on spontaneity, so planning spontaneous sexual encounters can add a sense of excitement and unpredictability to your relationship. This might involve surprising your partner with an unplanned rendezvous, trying out a new position on the spur of the moment, or exploring a new fantasy together. Spontaneity adds an element of excitement and unpredictability, aligning with Sagittarius's dynamic energy.
- **Travel-Inspired Play:** Incorporate elements of travel and exploration into your sexual experiences by incorporating themes, fantasies, or role-play scenarios inspired by different cultures, places, or adventures. Sagittarius will appreciate the opportunity to bring their love of travel and exploration into the bedroom, creating a sense of excitement and novelty.

Conclusion

Sagittarius's influence on sexuality brings an adventurous, expansive energy that emphasizes exploration, variety, and the thrill of discovery. By incorporating the adventurous and expansive positions outlined in this chapter, you can harness Sagittarius's love of freedom and their desire for new experiences to create sexual encounters that are dynamic, exciting, and deeply satisfying. Whether through the dynamic movements of the Wanderer's Embrace, the expansive exploration of the Open Horizon, or the spontaneous playfulness of the World Traveler, Sagittarius's energy invites you to explore new horizons, to keep the experience fresh and exciting, and to enjoy the thrill of discovery. Let Sagittarius guide you toward a more adventurous, free-spirited, and deeply connected sexual relationship, where every encounter is an opportunity to explore, expand, and enjoy the journey together.

Chapter 25: Capricorn: The Achiever

Capricorn, the tenth sign of the zodiac, is ruled by Saturn, the planet of discipline, structure, and ambition. Known for their determined nature, strong work ethic, and unwavering focus on achieving their goals, Capricorns approach life—and love—with a sense of purpose and dedication. In the realm of sexuality, Capricorn brings a disciplined, ambitious energy, striving to master every aspect of the experience and to ensure that both partners reach new heights of satisfaction. This chapter delves into Capricorn's approach to sex, focusing on positions that emphasize discipline, structure, and the pursuit of excellence. These positions are designed to cater to Capricorn's need for control, their ambition to achieve the best possible outcome, and their desire to create an experience that is both satisfying and deeply rewarding.

The Capricorn Lover: Ambitious, Disciplined, and Determined

Capricorn is an earth sign, grounded in practicality and deeply connected to the material world. As a lover, Capricorn is ambitious, disciplined, and highly focused on achieving their goals. They are not content with mediocrity; Capricorn strives for excellence in everything they do, including their sexual relationships. For Capricorn, sex is not just about physical pleasure; it's about mastering the experience, creating a deep connection, and achieving a sense of fulfillment that goes beyond the physical.

- **Ambition and Determination:** Capricorn is ruled by Saturn, the planet of discipline and structure, which gives them a strong sense of ambition and determination. In sexual relationships, this translates to a desire to achieve the highest levels of satisfaction, both for themselves and their partner. Capricorn is driven by a need to excel and to create an experience that is both powerful and deeply satisfying.
- **Discipline and Structure:** Capricorns are known for their disciplined nature and their ability to create structure in their lives. In the bedroom, this means that Capricorn is highly focused on technique, precision, and control. They take the time to understand their partner's needs and desires, ensuring that every aspect of the experience is carefully planned and executed.
- **Mastery and Achievement:** Capricorn is driven by a desire for mastery and achievement, both in their personal and professional lives. In sexual relationships, this manifests as a focus

on continual improvement, refinement, and the pursuit of excellence. Capricorn sees sex as an opportunity to grow, to learn, and to achieve new heights of satisfaction and connection.

Ambitious and Disciplined Positions for Capricorn's Determined Nature

Certain sexual positions are particularly well-suited to channeling Capricorn's ambitious, disciplined energy. These positions emphasize control, structure, and the pursuit of mastery, allowing Capricorn to fully express their determined nature. They are designed to create an experience that is both powerful and deeply satisfying, satisfying Capricorn's need for control and their desire to achieve the best possible outcome.

- **The Climber's Ascent:**
  - **Description:** In the Climber's Ascent position, one partner lies on their back with their legs bent at the knees, while the other partner kneels between their legs, holding their hips for support. This position allows for deep penetration, controlled movements, and the ability to gradually increase the intensity.
  - **Ambition and Determination:** The Climber's Ascent is a position that embodies Capricorn's ambition and determination. The gradual increase in intensity allows Capricorn to carefully control the experience, ensuring that both partners reach the peak of satisfaction together. This position is ideal for Capricorn's desire to achieve mastery and to create a powerful, rewarding experience.
  - **Discipline and Structure:** The controlled movements and the ability to maintain a steady pace make the Climber's Ascent perfect for Capricorn's disciplined nature. The position allows Capricorn to focus on technique and precision, ensuring that every aspect of the experience is perfectly executed.
- **The Summit:**
  - **Description:** In the Summit position, both partners kneel facing each other, with their bodies pressed close together and their arms wrapped around each other. This position allows for deep penetration, close physical contact, and synchronized movements.
  - **Ambition and Determination:** The Summit is a position that allows Capricorn to fully express their ambition and determination. The close physical contact and syn-

chronized movements create a powerful connection between partners, making the experience feel both intense and deeply satisfying. This position is ideal for Capricorn's desire to achieve new heights of satisfaction and connection.

- **Discipline and Structure:** The Summit encourages a disciplined approach to sex, with both partners working together to maintain a steady pace and rhythm. The position allows Capricorn to focus on structure and control, ensuring that the experience is perfectly balanced and deeply rewarding.

- **The Ladder to Success:**
  - **Description:** In the Ladder to Success position, one partner lies on their back with their legs raised and spread wide, while the other partner stands or kneels between their legs, holding their ankles for support. This position allows for deep penetration, controlled movements, and the ability to gradually increase the intensity.
  - **Ambition and Determination:** The Ladder to Success is a position that embodies Capricorn's drive to achieve and excel. The gradual increase in intensity and the ability to control the depth and angle of penetration make this position ideal for Capricorn's desire to create a powerful, satisfying experience.
  - **Discipline and Structure:** The Ladder to Success encourages a disciplined approach to sex, with Capricorn able to carefully control the pace and intensity of the experience. The position allows Capricorn to focus on precision and technique, ensuring that every aspect of the experience is perfectly executed.

- **The Architect's Design:**
  - **Description:** In the Architect's Design position, one partner lies on their side with their legs slightly bent, while the other partner lies behind them, spooning them closely. This position allows for slow, controlled movements and close physical contact.
  - **Ambition and Determination:** The Architect's Design is a position that allows Capricorn to fully express their ambition and determination. The close physical contact and the ability to control the pace and intensity make this position ideal for creating a deep, satisfying connection.
  - **Discipline and Structure:** The Architect's Design encourages a disciplined approach to sex, with Capricorn able to carefully control the rhythm and depth of the experience.

The position allows Capricorn to focus on structure and control, ensuring that the experience is perfectly balanced and deeply rewarding.

- **The Pinnacle:**
  - **Description:** In the Pinnacle position, one partner sits on a chair or the edge of the bed, while the other partner straddles them, facing forward. This position allows for deep penetration, close physical contact, and the ability to control the pace and intensity.
  - **Ambition and Determination:** The Pinnacle is a position that embodies Capricorn's desire to achieve new heights of satisfaction and connection. The close physical contact and the ability to control the pace and intensity make this position ideal for creating a powerful, rewarding experience.
  - **Discipline and Structure:** The Pinnacle encourages a disciplined approach to sex, with Capricorn able to carefully control the rhythm and depth of the experience. The position allows Capricorn to focus on structure and control, ensuring that every aspect of the experience is perfectly executed.

Enhancing Capricorn's Energy Through Rituals and Practices

To fully harness Capricorn's ambitious energy in your sexual relationship, consider incorporating rituals and practices that emphasize discipline, structure, and the pursuit of mastery. These activities can help you align with Capricorn's determined energy, making your sexual experiences more powerful, satisfying, and deeply rewarding.

- **Goal Setting:** Capricorn thrives on setting and achieving goals, so consider setting specific goals for your sexual relationship. This might involve exploring new techniques, improving communication, or experimenting with different positions. Setting goals allows Capricorn to channel their ambition and determination into the relationship, creating a sense of purpose and achievement.
- **Structured Routines:** Capricorn values discipline and structure, so consider establishing a structured routine for your sexual encounters. This might involve setting aside specific times for intimacy, creating a ritual that helps both partners relax and connect, or establishing a

set of practices that enhance the experience. Structured routines align with Capricorn's disciplined nature and help create a more focused, satisfying experience.

- **Practicing Precision:** Capricorn appreciates precision and technique, so consider incorporating practices that allow you to refine and perfect your sexual skills. This might involve studying new techniques, practicing communication with your partner, or focusing on specific aspects of the experience that you want to improve. Practicing precision allows Capricorn to channel their ambition and desire for mastery into the relationship.
- **Creating a Focused Environment:** Capricorn thrives in environments that are focused and free from distractions. Create a space that reflects this energy by eliminating distractions, incorporating calming elements, and ensuring that the environment is conducive to focus and connection. A focused environment aligns with Capricorn's disciplined nature and helps create a more powerful, satisfying experience.

Conclusion

Capricorn's influence on sexuality brings an ambitious, disciplined energy that emphasizes control, structure, and the pursuit of mastery. By incorporating the ambitious and disciplined positions outlined in this chapter, you can harness Capricorn's determined energy to create sexual experiences that are powerful, satisfying, and deeply rewarding. Whether through the controlled movements of the Climber's Ascent, the structured approach of the Architect's Design, or the ambitious drive of the Pinnacle, Capricorn's energy invites you to achieve new heights of satisfaction, to master every aspect of the experience, and to create a powerful, lasting connection with your partner. Let Capricorn guide you toward a more ambitious, disciplined, and deeply connected sexual relationship, where every encounter is an opportunity to achieve excellence and to enjoy the satisfaction of a perfectly executed experience.

Chapter 26: Aquarius: The Innovator

Aquarius, the eleventh sign of the zodiac, is ruled by Uranus, the planet of innovation, rebellion, and futuristic thinking. Known for their inventive spirit, intellectual curiosity, and desire to break free from convention, Aquarians are the visionaries of the zodiac. In the realm of sexuality, Aquarius brings a sense of adventure, a willingness to experiment, and a drive to explore new and unconventional approaches to intimacy. This chapter delves into Aquarius' approach to sex, focusing on positions that emphasize innovation, creativity, and the thrill of exploring uncharted territory. These positions are designed to cater to Aquarius' need for novelty, their inventive spirit, and their desire to keep the experience fresh, exciting, and ahead of the curve.

The Aquarius Lover: Innovative, Independent, and Experimental

Aquarius is an air sign, associated with intellect, communication, and a strong desire for freedom and individuality. As a lover, Aquarius is innovative, independent, and always eager to push boundaries. They thrive on intellectual stimulation and are often attracted to partners who share their curiosity and willingness to explore new ideas. For Aquarius, sex is not just about physical pleasure; it's about discovering new ways to connect, experimenting with unconventional approaches, and breaking free from the limitations of tradition.

- **Innovation and Creativity:** Aquarius is ruled by Uranus, the planet of innovation and change, which gives them a natural inclination toward creativity and experimentation. In sexual relationships, this translates to a desire to try new things, to explore unconventional positions and techniques, and to keep the experience dynamic and ever-evolving. Aquarius seeks to break free from routine and to create a sexual experience that is as unique and innovative as they are.

- **Independence and Freedom:** Aquarians value their independence and freedom, both in life and in love. They are not interested in conforming to societal norms or following the crowd; instead, they prefer to forge their own path and to explore new possibilities. In the bedroom, this means that Aquarius is open to trying new things, exploring different dynamics, and embracing a sense of spontaneity and freedom.

- **Experimental and Forward-Thinking:** Aquarius is always looking to the future, seeking out new ideas and approaches that challenge the status quo. In sexual relationships, this forward-thinking approach manifests as a desire to experiment with new techniques, to explore futuristic fantasies, and to push the boundaries of what is considered "normal." Aquarius is not afraid to step outside their comfort zone and to explore the unknown.

Unconventional and Futuristic Positions for Aquarius' Inventive Spirit

Certain sexual positions are particularly well-suited to channeling Aquarius' innovative, unconventional energy. These positions emphasize creativity, experimentation, and the thrill of exploring new possibilities, allowing Aquarius to fully express their inventive spirit. They are designed to create an experience that is both intellectually stimulating and physically exciting, satisfying Aquarius' need for novelty and their desire to stay ahead of the curve.

- **The Gravity Shift:**
  - **Description:** In the Gravity Shift position, one partner lies on their back with their legs raised and spread wide, while the other partner kneels between their legs, using their hands to support their partner's lower back and hips. This position allows for deep penetration and the ability to experiment with different angles and movements by shifting the partner's hips.
  - **Innovation and Creativity:** The Gravity Shift is a position that embodies Aquarius' love of innovation and experimentation. The ability to shift the angle and depth of penetration by adjusting the partner's hips allows for a dynamic, ever-changing experience that keeps both partners engaged and excited. This position is ideal for Aquarius' desire to explore new possibilities and to keep the experience fresh and unconventional.
  - **Independence and Freedom:** The Gravity Shift encourages a sense of freedom and spontaneity, allowing both partners to experiment with different movements and angles. Aquarius will appreciate the flexibility and creativity of this position, as it aligns with their love of independence and their desire to break free from routine.

- **The Futuristic Fusion:**
  - **Description:** In the Futuristic Fusion position, both partners sit facing each other, with their legs intertwined and their bodies pressed close together. This position allows for deep eye contact, synchronized movements, and the ability to experiment with different rhythms and angles.
  - **Innovation and Creativity:** The Futuristic Fusion is a position that allows Aquarius to fully express their inventive spirit. The close physical contact and the ability to experiment with different rhythms and angles make this position perfect for creating a dynamic, forward-thinking experience. Aquarius will enjoy the opportunity to explore new ways to connect and to push the boundaries of what is considered "normal."
  - **Experimental and Forward-Thinking:** The Futuristic Fusion encourages a sense of experimentation and exploration, allowing both partners to discover new ways to connect and to challenge the status quo. Aquarius will appreciate the innovative nature of this position, as it aligns with their love of forward-thinking ideas and their desire to stay ahead of the curve.
- **The Quantum Leap:**
  - **Description:** In the Quantum Leap position, one partner stands with their back against a wall or sturdy surface, while the other partner straddles them, wrapping their legs around their partner's waist. This position allows for deep penetration, close physical contact, and the ability to switch between different angles and movements.
  - **Innovation and Creativity:** The Quantum Leap is a position that embodies Aquarius' love of experimentation and innovation. The standing orientation and the ability to switch between different angles and depths make this position ideal for creating a dynamic, ever-changing experience. Aquarius will enjoy the thrill of exploring new possibilities and pushing the boundaries of what is possible.
  - **Independence and Freedom:** The Quantum Leap encourages a sense of freedom and spontaneity, allowing both partners to experiment with different movements and angles. Aquarius will appreciate the flexibility and creativity of this position, as it aligns with their love of independence and their desire to break free from routine.

- **The Electric Current:**
  - **Description:** In the Electric Current position, both partners lie on their sides, facing each other, with their legs intertwined and their bodies pressed close together. This position allows for deep penetration, synchronized movements, and the ability to experiment with different rhythms and angles.
  - **Innovation and Creativity:** The Electric Current is a position that allows Aquarius to fully express their inventive spirit. The close physical contact and the ability to experiment with different rhythms and angles make this position perfect for creating a dynamic, forward-thinking experience. Aquarius will enjoy the opportunity to explore new ways to connect and to push the boundaries of what is considered "normal."
  - **Experimental and Forward-Thinking:** The Electric Current encourages a sense of experimentation and exploration, allowing both partners to discover new ways to connect and to challenge the status quo. Aquarius will appreciate the innovative nature of this position, as it aligns with their love of forward-thinking ideas and their desire to stay ahead of the curve.
- **The Parallel Universe:**
  - **Description:** In the Parallel Universe position, one partner lies on their back with their legs raised and spread wide, while the other partner kneels between their legs, using their hands to support their partner's lower back and hips. This position allows for deep penetration and the ability to experiment with different angles and movements by shifting the partner's hips.
  - **Innovation and Creativity:** The Parallel Universe is a position that embodies Aquarius' love of innovation and experimentation. The ability to shift the angle and depth of penetration by adjusting the partner's hips allows for a dynamic, ever-changing experience that keeps both partners engaged and excited. This position is ideal for Aquarius' desire to explore new possibilities and to keep the experience fresh and unconventional.
  - **Independence and Freedom:** The Parallel Universe encourages a sense of freedom and spontaneity, allowing both partners to experiment with different movements and

angles. Aquarius will appreciate the flexibility and creativity of this position, as it aligns with their love of independence and their desire to break free from routine.

Enhancing Aquarius's Energy Through Rituals and Practices

To fully harness Aquarius's innovative energy in your sexual relationship, consider incorporating rituals and practices that emphasize creativity, experimentation, and the thrill of exploring new possibilities. These activities can help you align with Aquarius's inventive spirit, making your sexual experiences more dynamic, exciting, and deeply satisfying.

- **Exploring New Techniques:** Aquarius thrives on innovation and experimentation, so consider incorporating new techniques and positions into your sexual repertoire. Experimenting with different rhythms, angles, and approaches allows both partners to explore new possibilities and discover what works best for them. This practice aligns with Aquarius's love of creativity and their desire to stay ahead of the curve.
- **Futuristic Play:** Incorporate elements of futuristic play into your sexual experiences by exploring fantasies, role-play scenarios, or techniques that challenge the status quo. Aquarius will appreciate the opportunity to bring their love of innovation and forward-thinking ideas into the bedroom, creating a sense of excitement and novelty.
- **Spontaneous Exploration:** Aquarius thrives on spontaneity and the thrill of exploration, so consider planning spontaneous sexual encounters that incorporate new positions, techniques, or settings. This might involve surprising your partner with an unplanned rendezvous, trying out a new position on the spur of the moment, or exploring a new fantasy together. Spontaneity adds an element of excitement and unpredictability, aligning with Aquarius's dynamic energy.
- **Creating a High-Tech Environment:** Aquarius appreciates environments that are innovative and forward-thinking. Consider incorporating high-tech elements into your sexual environment, such as ambient lighting, music controlled by smart devices, or even virtual reality. Creating a space that reflects Aquarius's love of technology and innovation can enhance the overall experience and keep it exciting and fresh.

Conclusion

Aquarius's influence on sexuality brings an innovative, unconventional energy that emphasizes creativity, experimentation, and the thrill of exploring new possibilities. By incorporating the unconventional and futuristic positions outlined in this chapter, you can harness Aquarius's inventive spirit to create sexual experiences that are dynamic, exciting, and deeply satisfying. Whether through the innovative flexibility of the Gravity Shift, the synchronized experimentation of the Futuristic Fusion, or the thrilling dynamics of the Quantum Leap, Aquarius's energy invites you to push boundaries, explore the unconventional, and embrace the unknown in your sexual relationship. By channeling Aquarius's inventive spirit, you can transform your sexual experiences into a journey of discovery, where every encounter is an opportunity to break free from the ordinary and explore the extraordinary.

Aquarius encourages you to think outside the box, to experiment with new ideas, and to keep the experience vibrant and full of possibilities. Let Aquarius guide you toward a more innovative, adventurous, and deeply connected sexual relationship, where every encounter is an opportunity to explore, innovate, and stay ahead of the curve, ensuring that your connection remains as exciting and dynamic as the Aquarian spirit itself.

In embracing Aquarius's energy, you'll find that your sexual relationship can become a playground for innovation, where the exploration of new techniques, positions, and ideas leads to a deeper, more satisfying connection with your partner. The journey of sexual discovery becomes not just about physical pleasure but about intellectual stimulation, emotional bonding, and the joy of breaking free from convention to create something truly unique and fulfilling.

As you continue to explore the depths of Aquarius's innovative energy, remember that the key to a fulfilling sexual relationship lies in your willingness to experiment, to embrace the new, and to continually seek out the unknown. With Aquarius as your guide, your sexual relationship can become a thrilling, ever-evolving adventure that keeps both partners engaged, excited, and deeply connected for years to come.

Chapter 27: Pisces: The Dreamer

Pisces, the twelfth sign of the zodiac, is ruled by Neptune, the planet of dreams, intuition, and spirituality. Known for their deep empathy, mystical nature, and connection to the ethereal realms, Pisceans are the dreamers of the zodiac. In the realm of sexuality, Pisces brings a sense of fantasy, deep emotional connection, and a desire to transcend the physical and connect on a soul level. This chapter delves into Pisces' approach to sex, focusing on positions that emphasize empathy, emotional depth, and a mystical connection. These positions are designed to cater to Pisces' need for emotional intimacy, their love of the dreamy and ethereal, and their desire to create an experience that is both spiritually and physically fulfilling.

The Pisces Lover: Empathetic, Intuitive, and Mystical

Pisces is a water sign, deeply connected to the emotional and spiritual realms. As a lover, Pisces is empathetic, intuitive, and driven by a desire to create a deep emotional and spiritual bond with their partner. They are not just interested in physical pleasure; for Pisces, sex is an opportunity to connect on a soul level, to explore the depths of emotion, and to create a shared dream-like experience.

- **Empathy and Intuition:** Pisces is ruled by Neptune, the planet of dreams and intuition, which gives them a natural ability to sense and respond to the emotions and desires of their partner. In sexual relationships, this translates to a deep empathy and an intuitive understanding of what their partner needs, allowing Pisces to create an experience that is emotionally fulfilling and deeply connected.

- **Mystical and Dreamy:** Pisceans are known for their connection to the mystical and ethereal realms, and they bring this sense of fantasy and wonder into their sexual relationships. For Pisces, sex is not just a physical act; it is a spiritual experience that allows them to explore the mysteries of love, desire, and connection. They seek to create an experience that feels otherworldly, transcending the ordinary and touching the divine.

- **Emotional Depth and Connection:** Pisces is deeply emotional and seeks to create a profound connection with their partner. They are driven by a desire to merge with their partner on every level—emotionally, spiritually, and physically. For Pisces, sex is an opportunity to express love, to heal, and to create a bond that is unbreakable.

Ethereal and Empathetic Positions for Pisces' Mystical Approach

Certain sexual positions are particularly well-suited to channeling Pisces' ethereal, empathetic energy. These positions emphasize emotional connection, gentle movements, and the creation of a dream-like atmosphere, allowing Pisces to fully express their mystical nature. They are designed to create an experience that is both emotionally and spiritually fulfilling, satisfying Pisces' need for deep connection and their love of the ethereal and mystical.

- **The Mystic's Embrace:**
  - **Description:** In the Mystic's Embrace position, both partners lie on their sides, facing each other, with their legs intertwined and their bodies pressed close together. This position allows for gentle, rhythmic movements, deep eye contact, and close physical contact.
  - **Empathy and Intuition:** The Mystic's Embrace is a position that allows Pisces to fully express their deep empathy and intuition. The close physical contact and deep eye contact create a powerful emotional connection, making the experience feel intimate and spiritually fulfilling. This position is ideal for Pisces' desire to create a bond that is both emotionally and spiritually deep.
  - **Mystical and Dreamy:** The gentle, rhythmic movements and the close physical contact create a dream-like atmosphere, allowing Pisces to fully immerse themselves in the experience. The Mystic's Embrace is perfect for creating a mystical, otherworldly connection that feels both ethereal and deeply satisfying.
- **The Oceanic Flow:**
  - **Description:** In the Oceanic Flow position, one partner lies on their back with their legs bent at the knees, while the other partner lies on top, facing them. This position allows for slow, flowing movements and close physical contact, with both partners able to maintain deep eye contact and synchronized breathing.
  - **Empathy and Intuition:** The Oceanic Flow is a position that encourages a deep emotional connection and intuitive understanding between partners. The slow, flowing movements allow Pisces to fully attune to their partner's needs and desires, creating a harmonious and deeply connected experience.

- **Mystical and Dreamy:** The gentle, flowing movements of the Oceanic Flow create a sense of being carried by the waves of emotion, making the experience feel ethereal and otherworldly. This position is perfect for Pisces' love of the mystical and their desire to create a dream-like, spiritual connection.

- **The Soul Dive:**
  - **Description:** In the Soul Dive position, one partner lies on their back with their legs spread wide, while the other partner lies on top, maintaining deep eye contact and synchronized movements. This position allows for deep penetration, close physical contact, and the ability to fully merge with each other on an emotional and spiritual level.
  - **Empathy and Intuition:** The Soul Dive is a position that allows Pisces to fully immerse themselves in their partner's emotions and desires. The deep eye contact and synchronized movements create a powerful emotional connection, making the experience feel both intimate and spiritually transformative.
  - **Mystical and Dreamy:** The Soul Dive encourages a deep, soulful connection that transcends the physical and touches the divine. The position allows Pisces to fully express their mystical nature, creating an experience that feels like a journey into the depths of the soul.

- **The Dream Weaver:**
  - **Description:** In the Dream Weaver position, both partners lie on their sides, with one partner slightly behind the other, spooning them closely. This position allows for gentle, rhythmic movements, close physical contact, and the ability to fully merge with each other on an emotional and spiritual level.
  - **Empathy and Intuition:** The Dream Weaver is a position that encourages deep emotional intimacy and connection. The close physical contact and the gentle, rhythmic movements allow Pisces to fully attune to their partner's needs and desires, creating a harmonious and deeply connected experience.
  - **Mystical and Dreamy:** The Dream Weaver creates a sense of being wrapped in a cocoon of love and safety, making the experience feel ethereal and otherworldly. This position is perfect for Pisces' desire to create a mystical, dream-like connection that feels both emotionally and spiritually fulfilling.

- **The Ethereal Fusion:**
    - **Description:** In the Ethereal Fusion position, one partner sits with their back against a headboard or wall, while the other partner straddles them, facing forward. This position allows for deep penetration, close physical contact, and the ability to maintain deep eye contact and synchronized movements.
    - **Empathy and Intuition:** The Ethereal Fusion is a position that allows Pisces to fully merge with their partner on an emotional and spiritual level. The close physical contact and deep eye contact create a powerful emotional connection, making the experience feel both intimate and spiritually transformative.
    - **Mystical and Dreamy:** The Ethereal Fusion encourages a deep, soulful connection that transcends the physical and touches the divine. The position allows Pisces to fully express their mystical nature, creating an experience that feels like a journey into the depths of the soul.

Enhancing Pisces's Energy Through Rituals and Practices

To fully harness Pisces's ethereal energy in your sexual relationship, consider incorporating rituals and practices that emphasize emotional depth, empathy, and the creation of a mystical, dream-like atmosphere. These activities can help you align with Pisces's mystical spirit, making your sexual experiences more emotionally fulfilling, spiritually connected, and deeply satisfying.

- **Creating a Dreamy Environment:** Pisces thrives in environments that are soothing, mystical, and ethereal. Create a space that reflects this energy by incorporating soft lighting, candles, incense, and calming music. The goal is to create an environment that feels like a sanctuary, where both partners can fully relax and connect on a deep, spiritual level.
- **Meditative Touch:** Incorporate meditative touch into your sexual relationship by focusing on slow, deliberate movements that encourage relaxation and emotional connection. This practice allows Pisces to fully attune to their partner's needs and desires, creating a harmonious and deeply connected experience.
- **Shared Fantasies:** Pisces loves to explore the realms of fantasy and imagination, so consider incorporating shared fantasies or role-play into your sexual relationship. This practice allows

both partners to explore their deepest desires and to create a dream-like experience that feels both exciting and deeply fulfilling.

- **Emotional Intimacy Rituals:** Engage in rituals that strengthen your emotional bond, such as sharing your feelings, expressing your love and appreciation for each other, and engaging in activities that bring you closer together. These rituals help deepen your emotional connection and create a strong foundation of trust, love, and spiritual intimacy.

Conclusion

Pisces's influence on sexuality brings an ethereal, empathetic energy that emphasizes emotional depth, spiritual connection, and the creation of a mystical, dream-like experience. By incorporating the ethereal and empathetic positions outlined in this chapter, you can harness Pisces's mystical energy to create sexual experiences that are emotionally fulfilling, spiritually connected, and deeply satisfying. Whether through the gentle rhythms of the Mystic's Embrace, the soulful connection of the Soul Dive, or the dream-like atmosphere of the Dream Weaver, Pisces's energy invites you to explore the depths of emotion, to connect on a soul level, and to create an experience that transcends the physical and touches the divine. Let Pisces guide you toward a more ethereal, emotionally connected, and spiritually fulfilling sexual relationship, where every encounter is an opportunity to dream, to connect, and to explore the mystical realms of love and desire.

Part 4: Celestial Bodies and Their Influence

Chapter 28: Stars: Guiding Lights in Sexual Exploration

The stars have been humanity's guiding lights for millennia, serving as both navigational aids and sources of mythological inspiration. The constellations that grace our night sky are not just random patterns of stars; they are storied symbols, each with its own rich tapestry of mythology, culture, and meaning. In the realm of sexuality, these celestial formations can inspire positions that evoke the mysteries of the cosmos, bringing the ancient stories of the stars into the intimate dance between lovers. This chapter delves into sexual positions inspired by constellations and their mythological tales, creating an experience that is as imaginative as it is passionate. These positions are designed to invoke the spirit of the stars, offering a celestial guide to exploring deeper connections, passion, and the mystical allure of the night sky.

The Celestial Lover: Inspired, Imaginative, and Connected to the Cosmos

Throughout history, the stars have been seen as symbols of fate, destiny, and the divine. As lovers, those who draw inspiration from the stars seek to connect with something greater than themselves, using the stories and symbolism of the constellations to guide their intimate experiences. This approach to sexuality is imaginative, deeply connected to the cosmos, and filled with a sense of wonder and reverence for the mysteries of the universe.

- **Mythological Inspiration:** Each constellation carries with it a story from ancient mythology, often filled with themes of love, passion, tragedy, and triumph. By invoking these stories, lovers can tap into the rich symbolism of the stars, bringing a sense of depth and meaning to their intimate encounters.
- **Connection to the Cosmos:** For those who feel a deep connection to the stars, sexuality becomes an extension of their cosmic journey—a way to explore the mysteries of the universe through the lens of human connection. This celestial approach to intimacy is about more than just physical pleasure; it's about aligning with the rhythms of the cosmos and connecting with the universal forces that shape our lives.
- **Imaginative and Symbolic:** The positions inspired by the constellations are not just about physical alignment; they are also about invoking the symbolic power of the stars. Each posi-

tion tells a story, invites reflection, and encourages a deeper exploration of the themes that have shaped human understanding of love and desire for millennia.

Positions Inspired by Constellations and Their Mythological Stories

These sexual positions are inspired by some of the most famous constellations and their associated mythological tales. Each position is designed to evoke the spirit of the stars, offering a unique way to explore the connection between mythology, the cosmos, and intimate relationships.

- **The Andromeda Chain:**
  - **Description:** Inspired by the constellation Andromeda, which represents the mythological princess chained to a rock as a sacrifice to the sea monster Cetus. In this position, one partner lies on their back with their arms stretched above their head, mimicking the pose of Andromeda. The other partner kneels between their legs, gently holding their wrists to create a sense of gentle restraint and deep connection.
  - **Mythological Inspiration:** The story of Andromeda is one of sacrifice, rescue, and ultimate union. This position symbolizes the vulnerability and trust required in a deep relationship, as well as the power of love to overcome obstacles. The Andromeda Chain is perfect for lovers who wish to explore themes of surrender, trust, and the transformative power of love.
  - **Connection to the Cosmos:** The Andromeda Chain aligns lovers with the stars that represent Andromeda, inviting them to reflect on the themes of rescue and redemption that this myth represents. This position encourages a deep emotional connection, as well as an exploration of the balance between vulnerability and strength.
- **The Orion's Hunt:**
  - **Description:** Inspired by Orion, the great hunter of Greek mythology, this position involves one partner on all fours, representing Orion's readiness for the hunt. The other partner stands or kneels behind them, guiding the movement in a steady, rhythmic pace. The position allows for deep penetration and a powerful, controlled pace.
  - **Mythological Inspiration:** Orion's story is one of pursuit, strength, and the thrill of the chase. This position embodies the dynamic energy of the hunt, with one partner

leading the way and the other following with determination. The Orion's Hunt is ideal for lovers who want to explore themes of power, pursuit, and the primal aspects of desire.

- **Connection to the Cosmos:** Aligning with the stars of Orion, this position invokes the spirit of the hunter, encouraging lovers to embrace their instincts and to pursue their desires with passion and intent. The Orion's Hunt connects lovers with the powerful energy of this mighty constellation, making their encounter feel both primal and empowering.

- **The Cassiopeia Throne:**
  - **Description:** Cassiopeia, the queen who boasted of her beauty, is represented in the stars by a distinctive "W" shape. In this position, one partner sits on a chair or the edge of the bed, representing the throne of Cassiopeia. The other partner straddles them, facing forward, with their legs wrapped around their partner's waist. This position allows for deep penetration, close physical contact, and the ability to maintain deep eye contact.
  - **Mythological Inspiration:** The story of Cassiopeia is one of pride, beauty, and the consequences of vanity. This position symbolizes the power and grace of the queen, as well as the importance of balance and harmony in relationships. The Cassiopeia Throne is perfect for lovers who want to explore themes of power, beauty, and the dynamic interplay between dominance and submission.
  - **Connection to the Cosmos:** The Cassiopeia Throne aligns lovers with the stars that represent this regal figure, encouraging them to reflect on the qualities of leadership, beauty, and balance. This position enhances the emotional and physical connection between partners, making their encounter feel both regal and intimate.

- **The Pegasus Flight:**
  - **Description:** Inspired by Pegasus, the winged horse of Greek mythology, this position involves one partner lying on their back with their legs raised and spread wide, representing the wings of Pegasus. The other partner kneels between their legs, holding their ankles to guide the movement. This position allows for deep penetration and the ability to explore different angles.

- **Mythological Inspiration:** Pegasus represents freedom, flight, and the pursuit of the impossible. This position embodies the spirit of adventure and the desire to transcend earthly limitations. The Pegasus Flight is ideal for lovers who want to explore themes of freedom, exploration, and the boundless potential of their connection.
  - **Connection to the Cosmos:** The Pegasus Flight aligns lovers with the stars that represent this mythical creature, inviting them to soar to new heights in their relationship. This position encourages a sense of freedom and exploration, making the experience feel expansive and liberating.
- **The Lyra Harmony:**
  - **Description:** Inspired by Lyra, the harp of Orpheus, this position involves one partner lying on their side, representing the strings of the harp. The other partner lies behind them, spooning closely and moving in a slow, rhythmic pace. This position allows for gentle, harmonious movements and close physical contact.
  - **Mythological Inspiration:** Lyra represents the power of music, harmony, and the soul's connection to the divine. This position embodies the gentle, harmonious flow of music, creating a soothing and deeply connected experience. The Lyra Harmony is perfect for lovers who want to explore themes of unity, tranquility, and the spiritual aspects of their connection.
  - **Connection to the Cosmos:** The Lyra Harmony aligns lovers with the stars that represent this celestial harp, encouraging them to move in harmony and to connect with the deeper rhythms of their relationship. This position enhances emotional and spiritual connection, making the experience feel both peaceful and deeply fulfilling.

Enhancing the Celestial Connection Through Rituals and Practices

To fully harness the energy of the stars in your sexual relationship, consider incorporating rituals and practices that emphasize connection to the cosmos, the power of myth, and the symbolic meaning of the constellations. These activities can help you align with the celestial energies, making your sexual experiences more imaginative, meaningful, and deeply connected.

- **Star-Gazing Rituals:** Before engaging in intimacy, spend time together under the night sky, identifying constellations and reflecting on their mythological meanings. This practice helps create a sense of connection to the cosmos and sets the stage for a celestial-inspired encounter. It aligns your energy with the stars, making the experience feel more magical and connected to the greater universe.
- **Storytelling and Mythology:** Share stories from mythology that inspire you, discussing the themes and lessons they offer. This practice not only enhances your connection to each other but also deepens your understanding of the constellations and their symbolic meanings. It adds a layer of depth and meaning to your intimate encounters, making them more resonant and meaningful.
- **Celestial Music and Atmosphere:** Create a celestial atmosphere by incorporating music inspired by the stars or mythology. Choose calming, ethereal melodies that enhance the dream-like quality of your encounter. The right music can help you tap into the mystical energy of the stars, making your experience feel more transcendent and connected to the cosmos.
- **Reflecting on the Night Sky:** After your encounter, spend time reflecting on the night sky, considering how the constellations and their stories have influenced your connection. This practice reinforces your bond and helps you integrate the lessons and energies of the stars into your relationship. It's a way to close the experience with a sense of reverence and gratitude for the guidance of the cosmos.

Conclusion

The stars have guided humanity for millennia, offering not only physical navigation but also a map of our inner worlds through their mythological stories. By incorporating positions inspired by constellations and their associated myths, you can bring the magic of the cosmos into your intimate life, creating a unique and meaningful connection that transcends the ordinary. Each constellation tells a story of love, power, adventure, and transformation, and by aligning with these celestial patterns, you invite these energies into your relationship.

Whether through the empowering stance of The Andromeda Chain, the primal pursuit of The Orion's Hunt, or the harmonious flow of The Lyra Harmony, these positions offer a way to explore the depths of your connection while drawing inspiration from the stars. They encourage you to see your relationship not just as a series of physical encounters, but as a cosmic journey—a shared adventure that mirrors the grand tales written in the heavens.

As you continue to explore these positions, let the stars be your guide, helping you to navigate the complexities of love, passion, and connection. By embracing the mythological stories and symbolic meanings of the constellations, you can transform your sexual relationship into a celestial dance—a harmonious, adventurous, and deeply fulfilling exploration of both body and soul.

With each encounter, allow the energy of the stars to illuminate your path, guiding you toward deeper understanding, greater intimacy, and a profound connection that resonates with the timeless rhythms of the universe. In doing so, you'll not only enhance your relationship but also align yourself with the eternal dance of the cosmos, where love and desire are written in the stars.

Let the constellations be your guiding lights in sexual exploration, and may your journey through the heavens bring you closer to the divine mysteries of love and intimacy.

Chapter 29: Asteroids: Adding Depth to Intimacy

Astrology is a vast and intricate system, and while the planets are often the primary focus, the asteroids offer a rich layer of complexity that can add significant depth to our understanding of relationships and intimacy. Among these celestial bodies, asteroids like Chiron and Eros play particularly important roles in shaping sexual dynamics, helping us explore themes of healing, desire, and the deeper emotional currents that influence our connections. This chapter delves into the influence of these significant asteroids, examining how they add nuance to sexual relationships and how their energies can be harnessed to deepen intimacy and understanding between partners.

The Role of Asteroids in Astrology

Asteroids are smaller celestial bodies that orbit the Sun, much like planets, but they are often overlooked in mainstream astrology. However, these bodies hold powerful symbolic meanings that can greatly influence various aspects of life, including sexuality. While there are thousands of asteroids, a select few, such as Chiron and Eros, are particularly relevant when it comes to exploring the intricacies of intimate relationships.

- **Chiron: The Wounded Healer:** Chiron is known as the "wounded healer" in astrology, representing our deepest wounds and the potential for healing through understanding and compassion. In the context of sexual relationships, Chiron can highlight areas where past hurts or insecurities may affect intimacy, while also pointing the way toward healing and deeper connection.
- **Eros: The God of Desire:** Eros, named after the Greek god of love and desire, is the asteroid most closely associated with sexual attraction, passion, and the expression of erotic energy. Eros reveals where and how we experience intense desire, as well as how we express our sexuality and pursue our passions in relationships.
- **Other Significant Asteroids:** While Chiron and Eros are among the most influential, other asteroids, such as Juno (associated with marriage and commitment), Psyche (representing the soul's journey), and Vesta (symbolizing sacred sexuality and devotion), also contribute to the richness of our sexual and relational dynamics. These asteroids can provide additional insights into the deeper layers of our intimate connections.

Chiron: Healing Through Intimacy

Chiron's influence in astrology is deeply tied to themes of wounding, healing, and the transformative power of vulnerability. In sexual dynamics, Chiron often highlights areas where individuals may feel insecure or wounded, but it also offers the potential for profound healing through intimacy and connection.

- **Understanding Chiron in Your Chart:** In a birth chart, Chiron's placement reveals where you may carry deep-seated wounds related to your sense of self-worth, sexuality, or emotional intimacy. These wounds can manifest as insecurities or fears that hinder your ability to fully engage in a sexual relationship. However, Chiron also represents the ability to heal these wounds through self-awareness, compassion, and the loving support of a partner.
- **Healing Through Vulnerability:** Chiron's energy encourages us to embrace vulnerability as a path to healing. In a sexual relationship, this might involve sharing your deepest fears or insecurities with your partner, creating a safe space where both partners can be open and honest about their emotional needs. This process of mutual vulnerability can lead to a deeper, more compassionate connection, where both partners support each other's healing journeys.
- **Chiron-Inspired Positions:** To align with Chiron's healing energy, consider engaging in positions that encourage deep emotional connection and gentle, nurturing touch. Positions that allow for close physical contact, eye contact, and a slow, deliberate pace can help create a sense of safety and trust, fostering an environment where healing can take place.
- **The Wounded Healer:**
  - **Description:** In this position, one partner lies on their back with their arms stretched above their head, symbolizing surrender and vulnerability. The other partner lies on top, maintaining deep eye contact and a slow, gentle rhythm. This position encourages emotional openness and deep connection, aligning with Chiron's energy of healing through vulnerability.
  - **Healing Potential:** The Wounded Healer position is perfect for partners who want to explore and heal emotional wounds together. The deep physical and emotional connection in this position allows both partners to feel supported and understood, creating a space where healing can naturally occur.

Eros: Embracing Passion and Desire

Eros is the asteroid of passion, eroticism, and intense desire. Named after the Greek god of love, Eros reveals where we experience the most potent and magnetic attractions in our lives. Eros's energy is all about the thrill of the chase, the intensity of sexual connection, and the powerful pull of desire that can drive us to pursue our deepest passions.

- **Understanding Eros in Your Chart:** Eros's placement in a birth chart indicates where and how you experience the most intense forms of desire and sexual attraction. It highlights the areas of life where you are most likely to experience a powerful pull toward others, as well as how you express your own sexual energy. Eros is also associated with the creative force of life itself, linking sexuality with creativity and the pursuit of pleasure.
- **Embracing Erotic Energy:** Eros encourages us to embrace our passions fully and to explore the depths of our desires without fear or shame. In a sexual relationship, this might involve exploring fantasies, engaging in playful experimentation, or simply allowing yourself to fully experience the pleasure of the moment. Eros's energy is about being present with your desires and sharing that passionate energy with your partner.
- **Eros-Inspired Positions:** To align with Eros's passionate energy, consider engaging in positions that emphasize intensity, deep penetration, and the thrill of exploration. Positions that allow for a sense of adventure, playfulness, and spontaneity can help you tap into the raw, magnetic energy of Eros.
- **The Arrow of Eros:**
  - **Description:** In this position, one partner kneels with their back against a headboard or wall, representing the bow of Eros. The other partner straddles them, facing forward, with their legs wrapped around their partner's waist. This position allows for deep penetration, close physical contact, and the ability to maintain intense eye contact.
  - **Passionate Connection:** The Arrow of Eros is ideal for lovers who want to explore the full intensity of their desire. The close physical contact and deep penetration create a powerful connection, allowing both partners to fully embrace their erotic energy and passion.

Integrating Chiron and Eros into Sexual Exploration

By understanding the roles of Chiron and Eros in your astrological chart, you can gain deeper insights into your sexual dynamics and how to navigate the complexities of desire, intimacy, and healing. Integrating these asteroids into your sexual exploration allows you to approach intimacy with a greater sense of awareness, compassion, and passion.

- **Balancing Healing and Passion:** Chiron and Eros represent two sides of the same coin—healing and passion. While Chiron encourages you to address and heal emotional wounds, Eros invites you to fully embrace your desires and passions. Balancing these energies in your relationship can lead to a more fulfilling and holistic experience of intimacy, where both emotional connection and physical pleasure are honored.
- **Asteroid Rituals:** To fully align with the energies of Chiron and Eros, consider incorporating rituals that honor these asteroids. For Chiron, this might involve creating a healing space with calming elements, such as candles, soft music, and comforting textures, where you can focus on emotional connection and vulnerability. For Eros, consider creating a more sensual atmosphere with passionate colors, intoxicating scents, and playful elements that invite exploration and the celebration of desire.
- **Exploring Asteroid Influence Together:** Engage in conversations with your partner about how Chiron and Eros influence your relationship. Discuss your individual placements of these asteroids and how they manifest in your intimacy. This shared exploration can deepen your understanding of each other and create a stronger, more connected relationship.

Conclusion

Asteroids like Chiron and Eros add profound depth to our understanding of sexual dynamics, offering insights into the healing potential of intimacy and the powerful pull of desire. By exploring the influence of these celestial bodies, you can enrich your sexual relationships with a deeper sense of connection, passion, and understanding. Whether through the healing energy of Chiron or the passionate drive of Eros, these asteroids guide you toward a more nuanced and fulfilling experience of intimacy—one that honors both the emotional and physical aspects of love.

As you continue to explore the impact of these asteroids in your life, allow their energies to guide you toward a deeper understanding of yourself and your partner. By integrating the lessons of Chiron and Eros, you can create a sexual relationship that is not only physically satisfying but also emotionally healing and spiritually enriching. Let these celestial bodies add depth to your intimacy, guiding you toward a more profound and meaningful connection.

Chapter 30: Comets: Brief and Intense Encounters

Comets, with their dazzling beauty and fleeting presence, have long fascinated humanity. These celestial travelers, composed of ice, dust, and cosmic material, blaze across the sky in brief yet unforgettable displays of light. In astrology, comets are often seen as harbingers of change, bringing sudden bursts of energy, transformation, and intensity. Their presence is rare and short-lived, but their impact is profound. This chapter explores how the energy of comets can inspire brief, intense sexual encounters that are filled with passion, urgency, and a sense of the extraordinary. These positions are designed to capture the fleeting, powerful energy of comets, offering moments of explosive connection that, though short, are deeply memorable.

The Symbolism of Comets in Astrology

Comets are symbolic of sudden change, intensity, and the unpredictable nature of life. In astrology, they are often associated with moments of transformation, disruption, and the arrival of something new and unexpected. Just as comets streak across the sky in a burst of light before disappearing, the energy they bring into our lives is similarly brief but powerful. In the context of sexual relationships, this comet energy can be harnessed to create encounters that are intense, passionate, and filled with a sense of urgency.

- **Intensity and Urgency:** Comets are known for their intense and sudden appearances, often taking the observer by surprise. In sexual dynamics, this energy translates into encounters that are marked by a sense of urgency and passion—moments that demand to be experienced fully, without hesitation or restraint.
- **Transformation and Impact:** The arrival of a comet is often seen as a catalyst for change, bringing new perspectives and transformative experiences. In intimacy, comet-inspired encounters can be moments of profound connection, where the intensity of the experience leaves a lasting impact on both partners.
- **Fleeting Yet Memorable:** Just as comets are only visible for a short time, these encounters are brief but unforgettable. They are moments of pure, unbridled passion that, while not lasting, leave a lasting impression on the heart and soul.

Positions Inspired by the Intensity of Comets

The following positions are designed to capture the essence of a comet's energy—brief, intense, and unforgettable. These positions emphasize quick, passionate encounters that are filled with intensity and a sense of immediacy, allowing partners to fully embrace the moment and the powerful connection that comes with it.

- **The Comet's Tail:**
  - **Description:** In the Comet's Tail position, one partner stands with their back against a wall, while the other partner straddles them, wrapping their legs around their partner's waist. This position allows for deep penetration, close physical contact, and quick, intense movements.
  - **Intensity and Urgency:** The Comet's Tail is a position that embodies the urgency and intensity of a comet's energy. The standing orientation and the ability to move quickly and passionately make this position perfect for lovers who want to experience a brief but powerful connection.
  - **Transformation and Impact:** The close physical contact and the intense, fast-paced movements create a transformative experience that leaves both partners feeling deeply connected and energized. The Comet's Tail is ideal for moments when passion strikes suddenly, and there's a need to embrace it fully.
- **The Celestial Flash:**
  - **Description:** In the Celestial Flash position, one partner lies on their back with their legs raised and spread wide, while the other partner kneels between their legs. This position allows for deep penetration and fast, rhythmic movements, creating a sense of intensity and urgency.
  - **Intensity and Urgency:** The Celestial Flash is a position that captures the sudden, explosive energy of a comet. The fast, rhythmic movements create a powerful connection that is both brief and intensely satisfying, making it perfect for moments of spontaneous passion.

- ◦ **Fleeting Yet Memorable:** Like a flash of light across the sky, the Celestial Flash is a position that is brief but unforgettable. It's ideal for lovers who want to create a moment of intense passion that, while short-lived, leaves a lasting impression.
- **The Streaking Flame:**
  - ◦ **Description:** In the Streaking Flame position, both partners stand, facing each other, with one partner lifting the other's leg and wrapping it around their waist. This position allows for deep penetration, close physical contact, and quick, passionate movements.
  - ◦ **Intensity and Urgency:** The Streaking Flame is a position that embodies the fiery intensity of a comet as it streaks across the sky. The standing orientation and the ability to move quickly and intensely make this position perfect for lovers who want to experience a brief but powerful connection.
  - ◦ **Transformation and Impact:** The Streaking Flame creates a transformative experience that leaves both partners feeling deeply connected and energized. It's a position that captures the fleeting yet impactful nature of a comet's energy, making the encounter memorable and profound.
- **The Meteor Shower:**
  - ◦ **Description:** In the Meteor Shower position, one partner kneels on the bed or floor, while the other partner straddles them from behind, facing the same direction. This position allows for deep penetration and quick, rhythmic movements, creating a sense of intensity and urgency.
  - ◦ **Intensity and Urgency:** The Meteor Shower is a position that captures the explosive energy of a meteor shower, with quick, intense movements that create a powerful connection. It's perfect for moments when passion strikes suddenly, and there's a need to embrace it fully.
  - ◦ **Fleeting Yet Memorable:** Like the sudden burst of meteors across the sky, the Meteor Shower is a position that is brief but unforgettable. It's ideal for lovers who want to create a moment of intense passion that leaves a lasting impression.

- **The Cosmic Collision:**
  - **Description:** In the Cosmic Collision position, one partner lies on their back with their legs spread wide, while the other partner kneels between their legs, holding their ankles for support. This position allows for deep penetration and fast, intense movements, creating a sense of urgency and connection.
  - **Intensity and Urgency:** The Cosmic Collision is a position that embodies the powerful, sudden impact of a comet's collision. The fast, intense movements create a brief but powerful connection that is both deeply satisfying and transformative.
  - **Transformation and Impact:** The Cosmic Collision creates an experience that is intense and unforgettable, capturing the fleeting yet impactful nature of a comet's energy. It's perfect for lovers who want to embrace the moment fully and experience a powerful, transformative connection.

Enhancing the Comet Energy Through Rituals and Practices

To fully harness the energy of comets in your sexual relationship, consider incorporating rituals and practices that emphasize intensity, urgency, and the fleeting nature of these encounters. These activities can help you align with the powerful energy of comets, making your sexual experiences more intense, passionate, and deeply memorable.

- **Spontaneous Encounters:** Comet energy is all about spontaneity and seizing the moment. Consider planning spontaneous sexual encounters that embrace the urgency and intensity of comet-inspired positions. This might involve surprising your partner with an unplanned rendezvous or trying out a new position on the spur of the moment. Spontaneity adds an element of excitement and unpredictability, aligning with the dynamic energy of comets.
- **Creating a Charged Atmosphere:** To capture the intensity of comet energy, create an atmosphere that is charged with passion and urgency. This might involve dim lighting, fast-paced music, and a focus on creating an environment that encourages quick, intense connections. The right atmosphere can help you tap into the powerful, fleeting energy of comets, making your encounters feel more intense and memorable.

- **Embracing the Moment:** Comet-inspired encounters are about embracing the moment fully and without hesitation. Practice being fully present during these moments of intensity, allowing yourself to be swept up in the passion and energy of the encounter. This practice helps you align with the comet's energy and makes the experience feel more profound and impactful.

Conclusion

Comets, with their brief yet intense presence, offer a powerful metaphor for the fleeting but unforgettable moments of passion that can define a sexual relationship. By incorporating positions that capture the energy of comets, you can create encounters that are filled with intensity, urgency, and a sense of the extraordinary. Whether through the explosive movements of the Meteor Shower, the fiery intensity of the Streaking Flame, or the transformative impact of the Cosmic Collision, these positions offer a way to embrace the fleeting yet powerful energy of comets in your intimate life.

As you explore these comet-inspired positions, let the energy of the cosmos guide you toward a deeper understanding of the intensity and passion that can arise in brief encounters. By aligning with the energy of comets, you can create moments of connection that, though short-lived, leave a lasting impression on both you and your partner. Embrace the brief but powerful impact of comets, and let their energy infuse your relationship with intensity, passion, and unforgettable memories.

Chapter 31: Meteor Showers: Passionate Bursts of Energy

Meteor showers are some of the most spectacular celestial events, where the night sky is illuminated by a cascade of shooting stars. These brief, intense bursts of light have captivated human imagination for centuries, symbolizing passion, energy, and the sudden, fleeting nature of life's most powerful moments. In astrology and spirituality, meteor showers are often associated with intense bursts of energy, rapid transformations, and moments of heightened passion. This chapter explores how to harness the energy of meteor showers for intense sexual experiences, creating encounters that are as exhilarating and unforgettable as the celestial phenomenon itself.

The Symbolism of Meteor Showers in Astrology

Meteor showers occur when Earth passes through the debris left by comets, resulting in a cascade of meteors that light up the sky. In astrology, meteor showers are symbolic of sudden, powerful energy that can bring about rapid changes and intense experiences. These celestial events are associated with moments of clarity, inspiration, and heightened passion, offering an opportunity to tap into the dynamic energy of the cosmos.

- **Passion and Intensity:** Meteor showers represent the sudden and intense bursts of energy that can ignite passion and drive rapid transformation. In the context of sexual relationships, this energy can be harnessed to create moments of powerful connection, where the intensity of the experience leaves both partners feeling energized and deeply satisfied.
- **Transformation and Release:** Meteor showers are also symbolic of the transformative power of passion. Just as the meteors burn brightly as they enter the Earth's atmosphere, the energy of a meteor shower can be used to release pent-up emotions, ignite desire, and transform the dynamic between partners. This transformative energy can lead to deeper emotional connections and a renewed sense of intimacy.
- **Brief but Impactful:** Like the meteors that streak across the sky, the energy of a meteor shower is brief but impactful. These moments of intense passion are not meant to last forever,

but their effects can be long-lasting, creating memories that linger long after the encounter has ended.

Positions Inspired by the Energy of Meteor Showers

The following positions are designed to capture the essence of a meteor shower—brief, intense, and powerful. These positions emphasize quick, passionate encounters that are filled with energy and a sense of immediacy, allowing partners to fully embrace the moment and the powerful connection that comes with it.

- **The Shooting Star:**
  - **Description:** In the Shooting Star position, one partner stands with their back against a wall, while the other partner kneels or crouches in front of them, providing intense oral stimulation. This position allows for quick, focused movements and a deep connection between partners.
  - **Passion and Intensity:** The Shooting Star is a position that embodies the sudden, intense energy of a meteor shower. The standing orientation and the ability to focus on one partner's pleasure make this position perfect for creating a brief but powerful connection that is deeply satisfying.
  - **Transformation and Release:** The Shooting Star allows for the release of built-up tension and desire, creating a moment of pure, focused passion that can transform the energy between partners. It's ideal for moments when one partner wants to give and the other wants to receive in a powerful, impactful way.
- **The Meteor Strike:**
  - **Description:** In the Meteor Strike position, one partner lies on their back with their legs bent at the knees, while the other partner straddles them, facing forward. This position allows for deep penetration and quick, rhythmic movements, creating a sense of intensity and urgency.
  - **Passion and Intensity:** The Meteor Strike is a position that captures the explosive energy of a meteor hitting the Earth's atmosphere. The quick, rhythmic movements and

deep penetration create a powerful connection that is both brief and intensely satisfying.

- **Brief but Impactful:** Like a meteor streaking across the sky, the Meteor Strike is a position that is brief but unforgettable. It's ideal for lovers who want to create a moment of intense passion that leaves a lasting impression.

- **The Cosmic Cascade:**
  - **Description:** In the Cosmic Cascade position, both partners kneel facing each other, with their bodies pressed close together and their arms wrapped around each other. This position allows for synchronized movements and a deep, emotional connection.
  - **Passion and Intensity:** The Cosmic Cascade is a position that embodies the cascading energy of a meteor shower, with synchronized movements that create a powerful, shared experience. The close physical contact and the ability to move together in harmony make this position ideal for lovers who want to experience a deep connection and intense passion.
  - **Transformation and Release:** The Cosmic Cascade allows for the release of pent-up emotions and the transformation of the energy between partners. It's a position that encourages deep emotional connection, making the encounter feel both intense and spiritually fulfilling.

- **The Celestial Impact:**
  - **Description:** In the Celestial Impact position, one partner stands with their back against a sturdy surface, while the other partner stands or kneels in front, providing deep, rhythmic penetration. This position allows for intense physical connection and quick, powerful movements.
  - **Passion and Intensity:** The Celestial Impact is a position that captures the sudden, powerful impact of a meteor hitting the Earth. The standing orientation and the ability to move quickly and intensely make this position perfect for lovers who want to experience a brief but powerful connection.
  - **Brief but Impactful:** Like a meteor shower, the Celestial Impact is a position that is brief but leaves a lasting impression. It's ideal for moments of intense passion that transform the energy between partners and create lasting memories.

- **The Starburst:**
  - **Description:** In the Starburst position, one partner lies on their back with their legs raised and spread wide, while the other partner kneels between their legs, holding their hips for support. This position allows for deep penetration and quick, intense movements, creating a sense of urgency and connection.
  - **Passion and Intensity:** The Starburst is a position that embodies the explosive energy of a meteor shower, with quick, intense movements that create a powerful connection. It's perfect for lovers who want to embrace the moment fully and experience a brief but powerful encounter.
  - **Transformation and Release:** The Starburst creates an experience that is intense and transformative, capturing the fleeting yet impactful nature of a meteor shower. It's ideal for moments when passion strikes suddenly and there's a need to embrace it fully.

Enhancing the Meteor Shower Energy Through Rituals and Practices

To fully harness the energy of meteor showers in your sexual relationship, consider incorporating rituals and practices that emphasize intensity, passion, and the fleeting nature of these encounters. These activities can help you align with the powerful energy of meteor showers, making your sexual experiences more intense, passionate, and deeply memorable.

- **Embracing Spontaneity:** Meteor showers are all about the unexpected and the fleeting. To align with this energy, consider embracing spontaneity in your sexual encounters. This might involve surprising your partner with an unplanned rendezvous, trying out a new position on the spur of the moment, or simply allowing the moment to guide your actions. Spontaneity adds an element of excitement and unpredictability, aligning with the dynamic energy of meteor showers.
- **Creating a High-Energy Atmosphere:** To capture the intensity of meteor showers, create an atmosphere that is charged with passion and energy. This might involve dim lighting, fast-paced music, and a focus on creating an environment that encourages quick, intense connections. The right atmosphere can help you tap into the powerful, fleeting energy of meteor showers, making your encounters feel more intense and memorable.

- **Focusing on the Moment:** Meteor showers are brief but intense, and the key to harnessing this energy is to focus fully on the moment. Practice being fully present during these moments of intensity, allowing yourself to be swept up in the passion and energy of the encounter. This practice helps you align with the meteor shower's energy and makes the experience feel more profound and impactful.

Conclusion

Meteor showers, with their brief yet powerful displays of light, offer a compelling metaphor for the intense, passionate moments that can define a sexual relationship. By incorporating positions that capture the energy of meteor showers, you can create encounters that are filled with intensity, urgency, and a sense of the extraordinary. Whether through the explosive movements of the Starburst, the cascading energy of the Cosmic Cascade, or the powerful impact of the Celestial Impact, these positions offer a way to embrace the fleeting yet powerful energy of meteor showers in your intimate life.

As you explore these meteor shower-inspired positions, let the energy of the cosmos guide you toward a deeper understanding of the intensity and passion that can arise in brief encounters. By aligning with the energy of meteor showers, you can create moments of connection that, though short-lived, leave a lasting impression on both you and your partner. Embrace the brief but powerful impact of meteor showers, and let their energy infuse your relationship with intensity, passion, and unforgettable memories.

Chapter 32: Eclipses: Shadow and Light in Sexuality

Eclipses are among the most awe-inspiring celestial events, where the interplay of shadow and light creates a powerful spectacle in the sky. In astrology, eclipses are often associated with transformation, revelation, and the unveiling of hidden truths. They symbolize moments when the ordinary is obscured, and deeper layers of reality are revealed, offering opportunities for profound insight and change. In the realm of sexuality, eclipses inspire a delicate dance between concealment and revelation, where the interplay of shadow and light can deepen intimacy and create a more dynamic, powerful connection. This chapter explores how to harness the energy of eclipses in sexual experiences, with positions that emphasize the balance between what is hidden and what is revealed, creating encounters that are as transformative as the celestial events themselves.

The Symbolism of Eclipses in Astrology

In astrology, eclipses—whether solar or lunar—are seen as times of significant change and transformation. They represent moments when the normal order is disrupted, and hidden aspects of the self or the world are brought to light. Eclipses can be times of revelation, where what was once in shadow comes into full view, or times of concealment, where the light is temporarily obscured, allowing for introspection and reflection.

- **Concealment and Revelation:** Eclipses symbolize the dynamic interplay between what is hidden and what is revealed. In sexual dynamics, this can translate into exploring the balance between intimacy and mystery, where moments of deep connection are contrasted with moments of playful concealment or surprise.

- **Transformation and Insight:** Eclipses are often associated with transformation, bringing about changes in perspective and understanding. In the context of a sexual relationship, eclipse-inspired encounters can be moments of profound insight, where deeper layers of emotion, desire, and connection are explored and revealed.

- **Duality and Balance:** Eclipses highlight the duality of light and shadow, creating a balance between opposing forces. This theme of duality can be reflected in sexual encounters that emphasize the balance between giving and receiving, dominance and submission, or the interplay between power and vulnerability.

Positions Inspired by the Energy of Eclipses

The following positions are designed to capture the essence of an eclipse—the interplay of shadow and light, concealment and revelation. These positions emphasize the balance between intimacy and mystery, creating encounters that are both dynamic and transformative.

- **The Solar Veil:**
  - **Description:** In the Solar Veil position, one partner stands with their back against a wall, while the other partner kneels in front of them, using a blindfold or scarf to partially obscure their partner's vision. This position allows for deep oral stimulation and emphasizes the contrast between what is hidden and what is revealed.
  - **Concealment and Revelation:** The Solar Veil is a position that embodies the balance between concealment and revelation. The use of a blindfold heightens the senses and creates a sense of mystery, while the intense physical connection ensures that the moment is deeply intimate and satisfying.
  - **Transformation and Insight:** The Solar Veil encourages partners to explore the power of mystery and the heightened sensations that come with it. This position is ideal for lovers who want to deepen their connection through the interplay of shadow and light, creating a transformative experience that reveals new layers of intimacy.
- **The Lunar Eclipse:**
  - **Description:** In the Lunar Eclipse position, both partners lie on their sides, facing each other, with their bodies partially obscured by a soft, flowing fabric or sheet. This position allows for gentle, rhythmic movements and close physical contact, with the fabric adding an element of concealment and mystery.
  - **Concealment and Revelation:** The Lunar Eclipse is a position that captures the subtle interplay of shadow and light, where parts of the body are hidden, and others are revealed. The use of fabric adds a layer of mystery, allowing partners to explore each other's bodies in a way that is both intimate and playful.

- ◦ **Duality and Balance:** The Lunar Eclipse encourages a balanced, harmonious connection, where the rhythm of the movements and the gentle concealment of the fabric create a sense of unity and balance. This position is perfect for lovers who want to explore the duality of intimacy, where what is hidden is just as important as what is revealed.
- **The Shadow Embrace:**
  - ◦ **Description:** In the Shadow Embrace position, one partner sits with their back against a headboard or wall, while the other partner straddles them, facing away. This position allows for deep penetration and close physical contact, with the straddling partner partially concealing their face and chest, adding an element of mystery.
  - ◦ **Concealment and Revelation:** The Shadow Embrace is a position that emphasizes the power of concealment, where one partner's body is partially hidden, heightening the sense of anticipation and discovery. The close physical contact ensures that the connection remains intimate and deeply satisfying.
  - ◦ **Transformation and Insight:** The Shadow Embrace allows partners to explore the balance between concealment and revelation, where the gradual unveiling of the body mirrors the process of emotional discovery and connection. This position is ideal for lovers who want to deepen their understanding of each other through the interplay of shadow and light.
- **The Eclipse Kiss:**
  - ◦ **Description:** In the Eclipse Kiss position, both partners sit facing each other, with their legs intertwined and their bodies pressed close together. One partner uses their hands to gently obscure the other's face, creating a sense of mystery and anticipation before leaning in for a deep, passionate kiss.
  - ◦ **Concealment and Revelation:** The Eclipse Kiss is a position that captures the moment of revelation that follows concealment. The use of the hands to obscure the face adds an element of playfulness and mystery, while the kiss that follows is intense and deeply satisfying.
  - ◦ **Duality and Balance:** The Eclipse Kiss encourages a balanced, intimate connection, where the act of concealment heightens the sense of revelation. This position is perfect

for lovers who want to explore the duality of passion, where moments of anticipation lead to moments of deep connection.

- **The Total Eclipse:**
    - **Description:** In the Total Eclipse position, one partner lies on their back with their legs raised and spread wide, while the other partner kneels between their legs, using a blindfold to obscure their partner's vision. This position allows for deep penetration and quick, intense movements, creating a sense of urgency and connection.
    - **Concealment and Revelation:** The Total Eclipse is a position that embodies the full eclipse, where one partner's vision is completely obscured, heightening the other senses and creating a powerful connection. The intense physical connection that follows the concealment makes the experience both transformative and deeply satisfying.
    - **Transformation and Insight:** The Total Eclipse allows partners to explore the power of complete concealment and the heightened sensations that come with it. This position is ideal for lovers who want to experience a powerful, transformative connection that reveals new layers of intimacy.

Enhancing the Eclipse Energy Through Rituals and Practices

To fully harness the energy of eclipses in your sexual relationship, consider incorporating rituals and practices that emphasize the balance between concealment and revelation, shadow and light. These activities can help you align with the powerful energy of eclipses, making your sexual experiences more dynamic, transformative, and deeply connected.

- **Creating an Eclipse-Inspired Atmosphere:** To capture the energy of an eclipse, create an atmosphere that emphasizes the interplay of shadow and light. This might involve using dim lighting, candles, or shadow play to create a sense of mystery and anticipation. The right atmosphere can help you tap into the transformative energy of an eclipse, making your encounters feel more profound and connected.
- **Embracing Mystery and Playfulness:** Eclipses are about the unexpected and the hidden. To align with this energy, consider incorporating elements of mystery and playfulness into your sexual encounters. This might involve using blindfolds, soft fabrics, or playful touches

to create a sense of anticipation and discovery. Embracing mystery can add an element of excitement and unpredictability, aligning with the dynamic energy of eclipses.

- **Focusing on the Balance of Power:** Eclipses highlight the balance between opposing forces, such as light and shadow, concealment and revelation. To align with this energy, consider exploring the balance of power in your sexual relationship. This might involve experimenting with different dynamics, such as dominance and submission, or simply being mindful of the give-and-take that occurs in intimate encounters. Focusing on balance can help you create a more harmonious and fulfilling connection.

Conclusion

Eclipses, with their dramatic interplay of shadow and light, offer a powerful metaphor for the dynamic balance between concealment and revelation in sexual relationships. By incorporating positions that capture the energy of eclipses, you can create encounters that are filled with intensity, mystery, and transformation. Whether through the playful concealment of the Solar Veil, the gentle balance of the Lunar Eclipse, or the powerful connection of the Total Eclipse, these positions offer a way to embrace the duality of shadow and light in your intimate life.

As you explore these eclipse-inspired positions, let the energy of the cosmos guide you toward a deeper understanding of the balance between intimacy and mystery, passion and playfulness. By aligning with the energy of eclipses, you can create moments of connection that are both transformative and deeply satisfying. Embrace the dynamic interplay of shadow and light, and let the energy of eclipses infuse your relationship with depth, passion, and a profound sense of connection.

Chapter 33: Solar Flares: Sudden Surges of Passion

Solar flares are powerful bursts of radiation that erupt from the surface of the Sun, sending waves of energy across the solar system. These intense explosions are among the most energetic events in the cosmos, capable of disrupting communications on Earth and illuminating the night sky with auroras. In astrology and spirituality, solar flares are symbolic of sudden surges of energy, passion, and transformation. They represent moments when energy is released explosively, creating opportunities for powerful change and intense experiences. This chapter explores how to harness the explosive energy of solar flares in sexual experiences, with positions that emphasize high-intensity, dynamic encounters that mirror the sudden, powerful surges of these cosmic phenomena.

The Symbolism of Solar Flares in Astrology

In astrology, solar flares are associated with sudden, intense bursts of energy that can lead to rapid changes and transformations. They are often seen as catalysts for action, driving individuals to break free from old patterns and embrace new, more dynamic ways of being. In the context of sexuality, the energy of solar flares can inspire encounters that are filled with passion, urgency, and an overwhelming sense of connection.

- **Sudden Surges of Passion:** Solar flares represent the sudden release of pent-up energy, creating moments of intense passion and connection. In sexual dynamics, this energy translates into high-intensity encounters where the focus is on fully experiencing the moment and embracing the powerful connection between partners.
- **Transformation and Release:** Just as solar flares can disrupt the status quo, the energy they symbolize can be used to break through barriers in a relationship, releasing old tensions and reigniting passion. These encounters can be moments of transformation, where the intensity of the experience leads to deeper emotional and physical connections.
- **Dynamic and Unpredictable:** Solar flares are unpredictable, often occurring without warning. This unpredictability adds an element of excitement and spontaneity to sexual encounters inspired by their energy, encouraging partners to embrace the unknown and fully engage with the present moment.

Positions Inspired by the Energy of Solar Flares

The following positions are designed to capture the essence of a solar flare—sudden, intense, and powerful. These positions emphasize high-energy, dynamic encounters that are filled with passion and urgency, allowing partners to fully immerse themselves in the explosive energy of the moment.

- **The Solar Burst:**
    - **Description:** In the Solar Burst position, one partner stands with their back against a wall, while the other partner lifts them slightly, supporting their weight with their arms and legs wrapped around their partner's waist. This position allows for deep penetration, close physical contact, and intense, rhythmic movements.
    - **Sudden Surges of Passion:** The Solar Burst is a position that embodies the explosive energy of a solar flare. The standing orientation and the ability to move quickly and powerfully make this position perfect for creating a brief but intense connection that leaves both partners breathless.
    - **Transformation and Release:** The Solar Burst allows for the release of pent-up energy and passion, creating a moment of pure, focused intensity that can transform the energy between partners. It's ideal for moments when passion strikes suddenly, and there's a need to embrace it fully.
- **The Flare's Embrace:**
    - **Description:** In the Flare's Embrace position, both partners lie on their sides, facing each other, with their legs intertwined and their bodies pressed close together. This position allows for deep penetration, synchronized movements, and close physical contact.
    - **Sudden Surges of Passion:** The Flare's Embrace is a position that captures the sudden, overwhelming energy of a solar flare. The close physical contact and synchronized movements create a powerful connection that is both intense and deeply satisfying.
    - **Dynamic and Unpredictable:** The Flare's Embrace encourages a dynamic, spontaneous connection, where both partners are fully engaged with the present moment. This position is ideal for lovers who want to experience the full intensity of their connection in a way that feels both powerful and unpredictable.

- **The Radiant Spiral:**
  - **Description:** In the Radiant Spiral position, one partner sits on a chair or the edge of the bed, while the other partner straddles them, facing forward. This position allows for deep penetration, close physical contact, and the ability to move in a spiral or circular motion, creating a sense of dynamic energy and flow.
  - **Sudden Surges of Passion:** The Radiant Spiral is a position that embodies the swirling, dynamic energy of a solar flare. The circular motion and deep physical connection create a powerful, intense experience that mirrors the explosive nature of a flare.
  - **Transformation and Release:** The Radiant Spiral allows partners to explore the release of pent-up energy in a controlled yet dynamic way, creating a transformative experience that can deepen the connection between them. It's perfect for moments when both partners want to embrace the intensity of their connection fully.
- **The Solar Impact:**
  - **Description:** In the Solar Impact position, one partner lies on their back with their legs raised and spread wide, while the other partner kneels between their legs, holding their hips for support. This position allows for deep penetration and quick, powerful movements, creating a sense of urgency and connection.
  - **Sudden Surges of Passion:** The Solar Impact is a position that captures the explosive energy of a solar flare, with quick, intense movements that create a powerful connection. It's perfect for lovers who want to embrace the moment fully and experience a brief but powerful encounter.
  - **Dynamic and Unpredictable:** The Solar Impact encourages a dynamic, intense connection, where both partners are fully engaged with the present moment. This position is ideal for moments of spontaneous passion that leave a lasting impression.
- **The Flare's Peak:**
  - **Description:** In the Flare's Peak position, one partner stands behind the other, both facing the same direction. The partner in front bends forward slightly, while the part-

ner behind holds their hips, allowing for deep penetration and fast, rhythmic movements.

- ◦ **Sudden Surges of Passion:** The Flare's Peak is a position that embodies the peak intensity of a solar flare, with fast, rhythmic movements that create a powerful connection. It's perfect for moments of intense passion that demand to be fully experienced.
- ◦ **Transformation and Release:** The Flare's Peak allows for the release of pent-up energy in a way that feels both powerful and transformative, creating a deep, lasting connection between partners. It's ideal for lovers who want to embrace the full intensity of their connection in a brief but powerful encounter.

Enhancing the Solar Flare Energy Through Rituals and Practices

To fully harness the energy of solar flares in your sexual relationship, consider incorporating rituals and practices that emphasize intensity, passion, and the dynamic, unpredictable nature of these encounters. These activities can help you align with the powerful energy of solar flares, making your sexual experiences more intense, passionate, and deeply connected.

- **Embracing Spontaneity and Intensity:** Solar flares are sudden and unpredictable, and to align with this energy, consider embracing spontaneity in your sexual encounters. This might involve surprising your partner with an unplanned, intense rendezvous or allowing the moment to guide your actions. Embracing spontaneity and intensity can add an element of excitement and unpredictability to your relationship, aligning with the dynamic energy of solar flares.
- **Creating a High-Energy Atmosphere:** To capture the explosive energy of solar flares, create an atmosphere that is charged with passion and intensity. This might involve using bright, dynamic lighting, energizing music, and a focus on creating an environment that encourages quick, powerful connections. The right atmosphere can help you tap into the powerful, sudden energy of solar flares, making your encounters feel more intense and memorable.
- **Focusing on the Present Moment:** Solar flares are brief but powerful, and the key to harnessing this energy is to focus fully on the present moment. Practice being fully present during these moments of intensity, allowing yourself to be swept up in the passion and energy of

the encounter. This practice helps you align with the solar flare's energy and makes the experience feel more profound and impactful.

Conclusion

Solar flares, with their sudden and powerful surges of energy, offer a compelling metaphor for the intense, passionate moments that can define a sexual relationship. By incorporating positions that capture the energy of solar flares, you can create encounters that are filled with intensity, urgency, and a sense of the extraordinary. Whether through the explosive movements of the Solar Burst, the dynamic energy of the Radiant Spiral, or the powerful connection of the Flare's Peak, these positions offer a way to embrace the dynamic, unpredictable energy of solar flares in your intimate life.

As you explore these solar flare-inspired positions, let the energy of the cosmos guide you toward a deeper understanding of the intensity and passion that can arise in brief, powerful encounters. By aligning with the energy of solar flares, you can create moments of connection that, though short-lived, leave a lasting impression on both you and your partner. Embrace the sudden surges of passion that solar flares symbolize, and let their energy infuse your relationship with intensity, excitement, and unforgettable memories.

Part 5: Integrating Astrology and Sexual Exploration

Chapter 34: Aligning Sexual Energy with Moon Phases

Timing sexual activities with the moon's phases for optimal intimacy.

The moon has been a symbol of mystery, emotion, and transformation across cultures and time. Its phases, from new to full and back again, reflect a natural cycle of growth, culmination, and renewal that influences everything from tides to human emotions. In astrology, the moon governs our inner world—our emotions, instincts, and subconscious. By aligning sexual energy with the phases of the moon, couples can tap into the natural rhythms of the cosmos, enhancing intimacy, connection, and overall satisfaction. This chapter explores how to time sexual activities with the moon's phases for optimal intimacy, harnessing the unique energies of each phase to deepen emotional and physical bonds.

The Significance of the Moon in Astrology

In astrology, the moon represents the emotional self, governing our instincts, habits, and unconscious reactions. It is closely tied to our sense of security, nurturing, and how we express and receive love. The moon's phases—new, waxing, full, and waning—each carry distinct energies that can be harnessed to enhance different aspects of life, including sexuality and intimacy.

- **New Moon:** The new moon marks the beginning of the lunar cycle, a time for setting intentions, new beginnings, and introspection. It's a period of quiet energy, ideal for intimate, reflective encounters that focus on emotional connection and setting the stage for growth in the relationship.
- **Waxing Moon:** As the moon grows from new to full, its energy is expansive, building towards culmination. The waxing phase is a time for action, exploration, and development. In sexual relationships, this phase is ideal for experimentation, trying new things, and nurturing the growth of intimacy and passion.
- **Full Moon:** The full moon represents the peak of the lunar cycle, a time of heightened emotions, energy, and clarity. It's associated with culmination, celebration, and the full expression of desires. Sexual activities during the full moon are often intense, passionate, and deeply fulfilling, as the energy of the full moon amplifies emotional and physical connections.

- **Waning Moon:** As the moon wanes from full to new, its energy is introspective, focusing on release, reflection, and closure. The waning phase is a time for letting go, healing, and deepening emotional bonds. In sexual relationships, this phase is ideal for slow, nurturing encounters that emphasize emotional connection and the release of any built-up tension or stress.

Timing Sexual Activities with the Moon Phases

By aligning sexual activities with the phases of the moon, couples can enhance their intimacy and connection by tapping into the natural rhythms of the lunar cycle. Each phase offers unique energies that can be harnessed to create more fulfilling and dynamic sexual experiences.

- **New Moon: Setting Intentions and Emotional Intimacy**
  - **Energy Focus:** The new moon is a time of new beginnings, introspection, and setting intentions. It's a quiet, reflective phase that is ideal for intimate, emotionally focused sexual encounters.
  - **Ideal Activities:** During the new moon, consider engaging in slow, intimate activities that focus on emotional connection, such as cuddling, gentle massages, and eye-gazing. This phase is also a good time to set intentions for your sexual relationship, discussing desires, goals, and what you want to cultivate together.
  - **Positions:** Positions that emphasize closeness and emotional intimacy, such as spooning or the Lotus position (where partners sit facing each other with legs intertwined), are ideal for the new moon phase. These positions encourage deep emotional connection and a sense of safety and security.
- **Waxing Moon: Building Passion and Exploration**
  - **Energy Focus:** As the moon waxes, its energy is expansive and growth-oriented. This phase is ideal for building passion, exploring new sexual activities, and nurturing the growth of intimacy.
  - **Ideal Activities:** During the waxing moon, consider trying new positions, experimenting with fantasies, or exploring new forms of intimacy, such as tantric practices or role-playing. This phase is about building and expanding your sexual connection.

- ◦ **Positions:** Positions that allow for exploration and experimentation, such as the Standing Lover (where one partner stands while the other wraps their legs around their waist) or the Cowgirl position, are ideal for the waxing moon. These positions encourage a sense of adventure and growth in the relationship.
- **Full Moon: Celebrating Passion and Connection**
  - ◦ **Energy Focus:** The full moon is a time of heightened energy, emotions, and clarity. It's associated with the full expression of desires, making it ideal for passionate, celebratory sexual encounters.
  - ◦ **Ideal Activities:** During the full moon, embrace the heightened energy by engaging in passionate, intense sexual activities. This is a time to fully express your desires and celebrate your connection. Consider activities that involve deep penetration, intense eye contact, and synchronized movements to maximize the connection.
  - ◦ **Positions:** Positions that allow for deep, intense connection, such as the Missionary position (with deep eye contact) or the Doggy Style position (for powerful thrusts), are ideal for the full moon. These positions help amplify the emotional and physical intensity of the encounter.
- **Waning Moon: Reflecting and Releasing**
  - ◦ **Energy Focus:** As the moon wanes, its energy is introspective and focused on release and healing. This phase is ideal for nurturing, reflective sexual encounters that emphasize emotional connection and letting go of tension.
  - ◦ **Ideal Activities:** During the waning moon, focus on slow, nurturing activities that promote relaxation and emotional bonding. Consider incorporating elements of massage, gentle touch, and extended foreplay to create a calming, healing atmosphere. This is also a good time for emotional conversations that deepen your connection.
  - ◦ **Positions:** Positions that emphasize relaxation and emotional intimacy, such as spooning (with one partner behind the other) or the Yab Yum position (where one partner sits cross-legged and the other sits on their lap, facing them), are ideal for the waning moon. These positions encourage a sense of comfort and emotional closeness.

Rituals to Enhance Moon-Phase-Aligned Sexuality

To fully harness the energy of the moon phases in your sexual relationship, consider incorporating rituals that align with each phase's unique energy. These rituals can enhance your connection, deepen your understanding of each other, and create a more fulfilling sexual experience.

- **New Moon Intention Setting:** During the new moon, take time to set intentions for your sexual relationship. Write down what you want to cultivate together, whether it's deeper emotional intimacy, more frequent sexual encounters, or the exploration of new fantasies. Share your intentions with each other and discuss how you can work together to achieve them.
- **Waxing Moon Exploration Ritual:** During the waxing moon, create a ritual that encourages exploration and growth in your sexual relationship. This could involve trying a new sexual activity, reading a book on sexual techniques together, or attending a workshop on intimacy. The goal is to embrace the energy of growth and expansion in your relationship.
- **Full Moon Celebration:** During the full moon, celebrate your connection with a ritual that honors your passion and love for each other. This could involve a special date night, a romantic bath together, or simply dedicating time to fully express your desires. The full moon is a time to celebrate what you've built together and to fully enjoy each other's company.
- **Waning Moon Release Ritual:** During the waning moon, create a ritual that focuses on release and healing. This could involve a calming meditation together, a shared massage, or a conversation about any tensions or challenges in your relationship. The goal is to let go of anything that no longer serves your connection, creating space for renewal and growth.

Conclusion

The moon's phases offer a natural rhythm that can be harnessed to enhance sexual intimacy and connection. By aligning sexual activities with the moon's phases, couples can tap into the unique energies of each phase, creating encounters that are more fulfilling, dynamic, and deeply connected. Whether through the introspection of the new moon, the exploration of the waxing moon, the celebration of the full moon, or the release of the waning moon, the moon's energy can guide you toward a more intimate and harmonious sexual relationship.

As you explore the practice of aligning sexual energy with the moon phases, let the cycles of the moon guide you toward deeper emotional and physical connections with your partner. By embracing the natural rhythms of the cosmos, you can create a sexual relationship that is not only physically satisfying but also spiritually and emotionally fulfilling. Let the moon be your guide in the dance of intimacy, and allow its phases to illuminate the path to deeper connection and love.

Chapter 36: Harnessing Celestial Events for Sexual Magic

Rituals and practices to enhance sexual experiences during celestial events

Celestial events—such as eclipses, meteor showers, planetary alignments, and solstices—have long been regarded as powerful moments of transformation, energy shifts, and heightened spiritual activity. These cosmic occurrences are believed to open portals of energy, influencing everything from our emotions to our relationships. By aligning sexual experiences with these potent celestial events, couples can tap into the enhanced energy of the cosmos, using it to deepen their connection, amplify their passion, and create moments of profound intimacy. This chapter explores how to harness the power of celestial events for sexual magic, offering rituals and practices designed to make the most of these extraordinary moments.

The Power of Celestial Events in Astrology

In astrology, celestial events are seen as times when the veil between the earthly and the cosmic is thinner, allowing for greater access to spiritual insights, emotional clarity, and transformative energies. These events can act as catalysts for change, bringing about new beginnings, deep emotional releases, or significant shifts in perspective. When incorporated into sexual experiences, the heightened energy of celestial events can lead to more intense, meaningful, and spiritually fulfilling encounters.

- **Eclipses:** Eclipses are powerful events that represent transformation, revelation, and the unveiling of hidden truths. They are times of sudden change and profound insight, making them ideal for rituals that focus on revealing deeper aspects of the self, enhancing intimacy, and transforming sexual dynamics.
- **Meteor Showers:** Meteor showers are associated with bursts of energy, inspiration, and rapid shifts in consciousness. They symbolize moments of heightened passion and creativity, making them perfect for spontaneous, high-energy sexual encounters that embrace the fleeting yet intense nature of these celestial events.

- **Planetary Alignments:** When planets align, their combined energies create powerful influences that can amplify certain aspects of life, including relationships and sexuality. These alignments are ideal times for rituals that focus on balancing energies, enhancing connection, and exploring the synergy between partners.
- **Solstices and Equinoxes:** The solstices and equinoxes mark the turning points of the year, representing the balance between light and dark, the changing of seasons, and cycles of growth and rest. These events are ideal for rituals that align sexual energy with the natural rhythms of the earth, creating a deeper connection with nature and the cosmos.

Rituals and Practices for Harnessing Celestial Events

To fully harness the power of celestial events in your sexual relationship, consider incorporating rituals and practices that align with the specific energies of these cosmic occurrences. Each event offers a unique opportunity to enhance sexual magic, deepen intimacy, and create transformative experiences.

- **Eclipse Ritual: Unveiling the Hidden Self**
  - **Purpose:** Eclipses are times of revelation and transformation, making them ideal for rituals that focus on uncovering hidden desires, deepening emotional intimacy, and transforming sexual dynamics.
  - **Ritual:** Begin by creating a sacred space, using candles, incense, and symbols that resonate with the energy of the eclipse. Sit facing each other and take turns sharing something that you've kept hidden—this could be a desire, a fear, or an aspect of your sexuality that you want to explore. As you share, maintain eye contact and hold hands, creating a sense of trust and connection. After the sharing, engage in a sexual encounter that focuses on exploring these newly revealed aspects of yourselves, using the energy of the eclipse to transform and deepen your connection.
- **Meteor Shower Ritual: Embracing Passion and Spontaneity**
  - **Purpose:** Meteor showers symbolize bursts of energy and inspiration, making them ideal for rituals that focus on spontaneity, passion, and creative sexual expression.

- **Ritual:** On the night of a meteor shower, find a private outdoor space where you can watch the meteors together. As you observe the meteors, allow their energy to inspire you. Let the spontaneity of the meteor shower guide your actions, whether it's engaging in a passionate kiss, dancing under the stars, or exploring a spontaneous sexual encounter. The key is to embrace the fleeting, intense energy of the meteor shower, allowing it to fuel your passion and creativity.

- **Planetary Alignment Ritual: Harmonizing Energies**
  - **Purpose:** Planetary alignments are powerful times for balancing energies and enhancing the synergy between partners, making them ideal for rituals that focus on creating harmony and deepening connection.
  - **Ritual:** Begin by identifying the specific planets involved in the alignment and their associated energies. For example, a Venus-Mars alignment might focus on balancing love and desire, while a Jupiter-Saturn alignment could emphasize growth and discipline. Create a ritual space that reflects these energies, using colors, symbols, and objects associated with the planets. Sit facing each other and perform a guided meditation that focuses on harmonizing your energies, visualizing the planetary alignment as a source of balance and connection. After the meditation, engage in a sexual encounter that embodies the balanced energies you've cultivated, allowing the planetary alignment to enhance your connection.

- **Solstice and Equinox Ritual: Aligning with Nature's Rhythms**
  - **Purpose:** The solstices and equinoxes mark the changing of seasons and the balance between light and dark, making them ideal for rituals that align sexual energy with the natural rhythms of the earth.
  - **Ritual:** On the night of the solstice or equinox, create a ritual space that reflects the energies of the season. For the summer solstice, focus on themes of light, warmth, and abundance, using candles, flowers, and bright colors. For the winter solstice, emphasize introspection, warmth, and coziness, using soft lighting, blankets, and warm drinks. Begin the ritual by reflecting on the themes of the season and how they relate to your relationship. Engage in a sexual encounter that aligns with these themes, whether it's celebrating the light and passion of summer or embracing the warmth and intimacy of

winter. Allow the natural rhythms of the earth to guide your connection, deepening your bond with each other and the cosmos.

Enhancing Celestial Magic Through Intentions and Symbols

To further enhance the power of celestial events in your sexual relationship, consider incorporating intentions and symbols that resonate with the specific energies of the event. These elements can add depth and meaning to your rituals, making them more impactful and spiritually fulfilling.

- **Setting Intentions:** Before each ritual, take time to set specific intentions that align with the energy of the celestial event. For example, during an eclipse, you might set an intention to reveal and heal hidden aspects of your relationship. During a meteor shower, your intention might be to embrace spontaneity and passion. Clearly stating your intentions helps to focus the energy of the ritual and guides the outcome.
- **Incorporating Symbols:** Use symbols that resonate with the energy of the celestial event to enhance the ritual. For example, you might use a sun or moon symbol during a solstice ritual, or planetary symbols during a planetary alignment ritual. These symbols can be incorporated into your ritual space, worn as jewelry, or used as focal points during meditation, helping to anchor the energy of the event.
- **Meditation and Visualization:** Incorporating meditation and visualization into your rituals can help you connect more deeply with the energy of the celestial event. For example, during a solar flare ritual, you might visualize the intense, explosive energy of the flare igniting your passion and fueling your connection. During an eclipse ritual, you might meditate on the balance between shadow and light, visualizing the unveiling of hidden truths in your relationship.

Conclusion

Celestial events offer powerful opportunities to enhance sexual magic, deepen intimacy, and create transformative experiences. By aligning your sexual practices with the energies of these cosmic occurrences, you can tap into the heightened energy of the cosmos, using it to fuel your passion, deepen your connection, and explore new dimensions of your relationship. Whether through the transformative energy of an eclipse, the spontaneous passion of a meteor shower, the harmonious synergy of a planetary alignment, or the natural rhythms of a solstice or equinox, celestial events provide a rich source of inspiration for sexual magic.

As you explore the rituals and practices outlined in this chapter, let the energy of the cosmos guide you toward deeper understanding, greater intimacy, and a more fulfilling sexual relationship. By embracing the power of celestial events, you can create moments of connection that are not only physically satisfying but also spiritually and emotionally transformative. Let the stars, planets, and cosmic rhythms be your guides in the dance of intimacy, and allow their energies to illuminate the path to deeper connection, passion, and love.

Chapter 37: Planetary Retrogrades: Navigating Sexual Challenges

Understanding the impact of retrogrades on sexual relationships and how to overcome challenges.

Planetary retrogrades are often associated with disruptions, delays, and the resurfacing of unresolved issues. When a planet goes into retrograde, it appears to move backward in its orbit from our perspective on Earth, symbolizing a reversal of energy that can bring challenges, reflection, and a need for re-evaluation. In astrology, retrogrades are times when the normal flow of energy is disrupted, requiring us to slow down, reconsider, and address underlying issues. In the context of sexual relationships, retrogrades can bring about challenges such as miscommunication, emotional distance, and unresolved tensions. However, these periods also offer opportunities for growth, healing, and deeper connection. This chapter explores how to navigate sexual challenges during planetary retrogrades, offering insights and strategies for overcoming obstacles and strengthening relationships.

The Significance of Retrogrades in Astrology

In astrology, retrogrades are viewed as periods of introspection, revision, and re-evaluation. Each planet governs different aspects of life, and when a planet goes into retrograde, the areas it influences are often affected, leading to challenges that require attention and adjustment.

- **Mercury Retrograde:** Mercury governs communication, technology, and travel. During Mercury retrograde, miscommunications, misunderstandings, and technical issues are common, making it a challenging time for clear communication in relationships. Sexual relationships may suffer from misunderstandings, misaligned desires, or the resurfacing of old arguments.
- **Venus Retrograde:** Venus rules love, beauty, and relationships. During Venus retrograde, issues related to love, self-worth, and intimacy often come to the forefront. This period can

bring up unresolved tensions in sexual relationships, leading to feelings of insecurity, dissatisfaction, or emotional distance.

- **Mars Retrograde:** Mars is associated with passion, desire, and action. During Mars retrograde, sexual energy may feel stifled or misdirected, leading to frustrations, conflicts, or a lack of motivation in sexual relationships. This period may also bring up issues related to anger, aggression, or power dynamics.
- **Other Planetary Retrogrades:** While Mercury, Venus, and Mars retrogrades tend to have the most immediate impact on sexual relationships, other planetary retrogrades, such as Jupiter (expansion), Saturn (structure), Uranus (change), Neptune (illusion), and Pluto (transformation), can also influence sexual dynamics, particularly in terms of long-term growth, stability, and transformation.

Navigating Sexual Challenges During Retrogrades

While retrogrades can bring challenges to sexual relationships, they also offer opportunities for growth and healing. By understanding the specific energies of each retrograde and adopting strategies to navigate these challenges, couples can use retrograde periods as opportunities to strengthen their connection and deepen their intimacy.

- **Mercury Retrograde: Enhancing Communication**
  - **Challenges:** During Mercury retrograde, miscommunications and misunderstandings are common, which can lead to conflicts, frustration, and emotional distance in sexual relationships. This period may also bring up unresolved issues from the past, requiring careful communication and patience.
  - **Strategies:** To navigate the challenges of Mercury retrograde, focus on enhancing communication in your relationship. Take extra care to articulate your desires, needs, and concerns clearly, and practice active listening to ensure that your partner feels heard and understood. This is also a good time to revisit and resolve any past misunderstandings or conflicts, using the retrograde energy to bring closure and clarity. Consider scheduling regular check-ins with your partner to discuss how you're feeling and to address any issues that arise. Engaging in activities that promote communication, such as

writing love letters or sharing your thoughts in a journal, can also help bridge any gaps that Mercury retrograde may create.

- **Venus Retrograde: Re-Evaluating Love and Intimacy**
  - **Challenges:** Venus retrograde often brings up issues related to love, self-worth, and intimacy, which can lead to feelings of insecurity, dissatisfaction, or emotional distance in sexual relationships. This period may also cause couples to question their connection or revisit unresolved tensions.
  - **Strategies:** During Venus retrograde, focus on re-evaluating your relationship and addressing any underlying issues that may be affecting your intimacy. Take time to reflect on what you truly value in your relationship and how you can cultivate a deeper sense of love and connection. This is also a good time to work on self-love and self-worth, as feelings of insecurity may arise during this period. Consider engaging in activities that promote emotional intimacy, such as cuddling, sharing your feelings, or practicing vulnerability with your partner. Venus retrograde is also an ideal time for couples to revisit their sexual relationship, exploring new ways to connect and enhance intimacy. Use this period to experiment with different forms of touch, explore each other's desires, and communicate openly about what you both need to feel satisfied and connected.
- **Mars Retrograde: Managing Passion and Conflict**
  - **Challenges:** Mars retrograde can lead to a decrease in sexual energy, frustrations, conflicts, and issues related to power dynamics in relationships. This period may also bring up unresolved anger or aggression, leading to tension or disagreements.
  - **Strategies:** To navigate the challenges of Mars retrograde, focus on managing your sexual energy and addressing any conflicts that arise in your relationship. Take time to explore new ways to express passion and desire, such as engaging in slow, sensual activities that build anticipation and connection. This is also a good time to address any underlying tensions or power dynamics in your relationship, using the retrograde energy to bring about resolution and balance. Consider practicing relaxation techniques, such as deep breathing or meditation, to help manage any frustrations or anger that may arise. Engaging in physical activities, such as exercise or outdoor adventures, can also help release pent-up energy and reduce tension.

- **Jupiter and Saturn Retrograde: Re-Evaluating Growth and Stability**
  - **Challenges:** Jupiter retrograde can bring about a re-evaluation of personal growth, expansion, and beliefs, while Saturn retrograde often focuses on structure, discipline, and long-term stability. In sexual relationships, these retrogrades may lead to questions about the direction of the relationship, challenges in maintaining stability, or a need to revisit long-term goals.
  - **Strategies:** During Jupiter and Saturn retrogrades, focus on re-evaluating the direction of your relationship and how you can cultivate growth and stability. Take time to reflect on your shared goals and how you can work together to achieve them. This is also a good time to address any areas of the relationship that may feel stagnant or in need of attention, using the retrograde energy to bring about positive change. Consider engaging in activities that promote personal and relational growth, such as learning new skills together, exploring spiritual practices, or setting long-term goals for your relationship. Use this period to strengthen the foundation of your relationship, ensuring that it is built on mutual respect, trust, and shared values.
- **Uranus, Neptune, and Pluto Retrograde: Embracing Change and Transformation**
  - **Challenges:** Uranus retrograde often brings about unexpected changes, Neptune retrograde can reveal illusions and bring clarity, and Pluto retrograde focuses on transformation and the release of old patterns. In sexual relationships, these retrogrades may lead to significant shifts, challenges in adapting to change, or a need to confront deep-seated issues.
  - **Strategies:** During Uranus, Neptune, and Pluto retrogrades, focus on embracing change and transformation in your relationship. Take time to reflect on any patterns or behaviors that may be holding you back, and use the retrograde energy to release what no longer serves you. This is also a good time to explore new ways of connecting with your partner, embracing the changes that these retrogrades may bring. Consider engaging in activities that promote transformation and healing, such as exploring new sexual practices, engaging in deep emotional conversations, or practicing forgiveness and letting go of past hurts. Use this period to create a stronger, more resilient relationship that can adapt to change and embrace growth.

Rituals to Navigate Retrogrades in Sexual Relationships

To further enhance your ability to navigate the challenges of retrogrades in your sexual relationship, consider incorporating rituals that align with the specific energies of each retrograde. These rituals can help you stay grounded, connected, and focused during these potentially disruptive periods.

- **Mercury Retrograde Communication Ritual:** Create a ritual that focuses on enhancing communication during Mercury retrograde. This could involve lighting a blue or purple candle (colors associated with communication) and sitting down with your partner to share your thoughts, feelings, and concerns. Use this time to listen to each other without interruption, ensuring that both of you feel heard and understood. Consider writing down any important decisions or agreements to avoid misunderstandings.
- **Venus Retrograde Love and Intimacy Ritual:** During Venus retrograde, create a ritual that focuses on re-evaluating and deepening your love and intimacy. This could involve taking a ritual bath together, using rose petals and essential oils associated with love, such as rose or jasmine. Spend time reflecting on what you love about each other and how you can enhance your connection. Consider exchanging small tokens of love or writing love letters to each other as a way to reaffirm your commitment.
- **Mars Retrograde Passion and Conflict Resolution Ritual:** Create a ritual that focuses on managing passion and resolving conflicts during Mars retrograde. This could involve lighting a red or orange candle (colors associated with passion and energy) and engaging in a physical activity together, such as dancing or exercising, to release any built-up tension. Afterward, sit down together to discuss any conflicts or frustrations, using the energy of the ritual to bring about resolution and balance.
- **Jupiter and Saturn Retrograde Growth and Stability Ritual:** During Jupiter and Saturn retrogrades, create a ritual that focuses on re-evaluating growth and stability in your relationship. This could involve setting up an altar with symbols of growth, such as plants or crystals, and sitting down together to discuss your long-term goals and aspirations as a couple. Use this time to reflect on the areas of your relationship that may need attention or improvement and set intentions for how you can work together to achieve greater stability and growth. Con-

sider creating a shared vision board or writing down your goals and placing them on the altar as a reminder of your commitment to each other.

- **Uranus, Neptune, and Pluto Retrograde Transformation Ritual:** During Uranus, Neptune, and Pluto retrogrades, create a ritual that focuses on embracing change and transformation in your relationship. Begin by setting up a space that feels sacred and safe, using symbols of transformation such as butterflies, snakes, or phoenix imagery. Light a candle and sit together, holding hands, as you discuss any significant changes or challenges that have arisen during the retrograde period. Reflect on how these changes have impacted your relationship and what you can do to adapt and grow together. Consider engaging in a symbolic act of release, such as writing down old patterns or beliefs that no longer serve you and burning the paper, or creating a piece of art together that represents your journey of transformation.
- **Conclusion**

Planetary retrogrades, while often challenging and disruptive, also offer valuable opportunities for growth, reflection, and transformation in sexual relationships. By understanding the specific energies and challenges associated with each retrograde, couples can navigate these periods with greater awareness and intention. Retrogrades invite us to slow down, reassess, and address underlying issues, making them powerful times for deepening emotional connections, enhancing communication, and transforming sexual dynamics.

Whether through the careful communication needed during Mercury retrograde, the re-evaluation of love and intimacy during Venus retrograde, or the management of passion and conflict during Mars retrograde, these periods offer unique opportunities to strengthen your relationship. By incorporating rituals and practices that align with the energy of each retrograde, you can turn challenges into opportunities for growth and transformation.

As you continue to explore the impact of retrogrades on your sexual relationship, remember that these periods are not just about overcoming obstacles—they are also about embracing the lessons that each retrograde brings. By approaching retrogrades with an open heart and a willingness to grow, you can navigate these challenges together, emerging with a stronger, more resilient connection.

Ultimately, planetary retrogrades remind us that relationships, like all aspects of life, are subject to cycles of growth, change, and renewal. By aligning with these cycles and using them to your advantage, you can create a sexual relationship that is not only resilient in the face of challenges but also rich with depth, intimacy, and mutual understanding. Let the energy of the retrogrades guide you on your journey of connection and transformation, helping you to navigate the highs and lows of your relationship with grace, love, and a deep sense of partnership.

Chapter 38: Astrological Synastry: Compatibility in the Bedroom

Analyzing astrological charts for sexual compatibility and harmonious connections.

Astrological synastry is the study of how two individuals' astrological charts interact and influence one another. In the realm of relationships, synastry provides valuable insights into the dynamics of love, attraction, and compatibility. When it comes to sexual relationships, synastry can reveal the potential for passion, intimacy, and harmonious connections, as well as areas where challenges may arise. By analyzing the positions of key planets, aspects, and houses in both partners' charts, couples can gain a deeper understanding of their sexual compatibility and how to navigate their relationship's complexities. This chapter delves into the art of astrological synastry, focusing on how to assess sexual compatibility and create harmonious connections in the bedroom.

Understanding Synastry in Astrology

Synastry is the comparison of two astrological charts to determine how the energies of each person interact and influence one another. In sexual relationships, synastry can reveal the underlying dynamics that contribute to attraction, passion, and emotional connection. Key factors to consider in synastry include the positions of Venus, Mars, the Moon, and the Sun, as well as aspects between these planets and other significant points in the chart.

- **Venus and Mars:** Venus represents love, beauty, and attraction, while Mars governs passion, desire, and sexual energy. The interaction between Venus and Mars in synastry is crucial for understanding sexual compatibility. Harmonious aspects between these planets, such as trines or sextiles, indicate a natural flow of attraction and desire, while challenging aspects, such as squares or oppositions, may suggest tension or conflicting desires.

- **The Moon:** The Moon represents emotions, instincts, and the need for security in relationships. In synastry, the Moon's position reveals how emotionally connected partners feel with each other and how their emotional needs are met within the relationship. Harmonious

Moon aspects suggest emotional compatibility and a deep sense of comfort, while challenging aspects may indicate emotional disconnects or misunderstandings.

- **The Sun:** The Sun represents the core identity and vitality of an individual. In synastry, the Sun's position and aspects reveal how well partners align on fundamental levels, such as shared values, goals, and life direction. Harmonious Sun aspects suggest a strong, supportive connection, while challenging aspects may highlight areas of conflict or differing priorities.
- **Houses:** The houses where planets fall in a partner's chart can provide insights into how different areas of life are affected by the relationship. For example, if one partner's Venus falls in the other partner's 5th house of romance and creativity, this indicates a strong attraction and a playful, passionate connection. If Mars falls in the 8th house, it suggests a deep, transformative sexual connection.

Key Aspects and Configurations for Sexual Compatibility

Certain aspects and configurations in synastry are particularly important for assessing sexual compatibility and the potential for a harmonious connection in the bedroom. Understanding these aspects can help couples navigate their relationship with greater awareness and intention.

- **Venus-Mars Aspects:** The interaction between Venus and Mars in synastry is a key indicator of sexual chemistry. Harmonious aspects, such as trines and sextiles, suggest a natural flow of attraction and a strong sexual connection. These aspects indicate that partners are likely to find each other physically appealing and share similar desires in the bedroom. Challenging aspects, such as squares and oppositions, may indicate sexual tension or conflicting desires, but they can also add excitement and intensity to the relationship if managed well.
- **Moon-Venus Aspects:** The Moon and Venus in synastry reveal how well partners meet each other's emotional and sensual needs. Harmonious aspects between these planets suggest a deep emotional connection and a shared appreciation for sensual pleasures. Partners with strong Moon-Venus aspects are likely to feel comfortable and nurtured by each other, creating a foundation for a fulfilling sexual relationship.
- **Mars-Pluto Aspects:** Mars and Pluto aspects in synastry are associated with intense sexual attraction and transformative experiences. These aspects can create a powerful, magnetic con-

nection that draws partners together on a deep, primal level. However, Mars-Pluto aspects can also bring challenges related to power dynamics, control, and intense emotions, requiring conscious effort to maintain balance and harmony.

- **Sun-Moon Aspects:** The interaction between the Sun and Moon in synastry reveals the potential for emotional and physical harmony in the relationship. Harmonious Sun-Moon aspects, such as conjunctions, trines, or sextiles, suggest a strong emotional bond and a natural understanding of each other's needs. These aspects indicate that partners are likely to feel emotionally and physically in sync, contributing to a harmonious sexual connection.
- **Venus-Neptune Aspects:** Venus-Neptune aspects in synastry are associated with romantic idealism, spiritual connection, and a sense of transcendence in the relationship. These aspects can create a dreamy, magical atmosphere in the bedroom, where partners feel deeply connected on a spiritual and emotional level. However, Venus-Neptune aspects can also bring challenges related to unrealistic expectations or illusions, requiring a balance between fantasy and reality.

Interpreting Synastry in Sexual Relationships

When interpreting synastry for sexual compatibility, it's essential to consider the overall context of the charts and how the various aspects interact with each other. A holistic approach to synastry involves looking at the broader picture, including how each partner's individual chart influences the relationship and how the synastry aspects contribute to the dynamics of the connection.

- **Overlaying Charts:** One of the first steps in synastry analysis is overlaying the two charts to see where the planets of one partner fall in the houses of the other. This overlay reveals how each partner influences different areas of the other's life, including love, intimacy, and sexuality. For example, if one partner's Venus falls in the other partner's 7th house of partnership, this indicates a strong attraction and a desire for a committed relationship.
- **Aspect Patterns:** In addition to individual aspects, consider the overall pattern of aspects in the synastry chart. A predominance of harmonious aspects suggests an easy, flowing connection, while a mix of harmonious and challenging aspects indicates a relationship with both strengths and areas for growth. Challenging aspects are not necessarily negative; they can add

excitement, depth, and opportunities for personal growth if approached with awareness and mutual respect.

- **Balancing Energies:** Synastry also involves understanding how to balance the energies between partners. For example, if one partner has a strong Mars influence and the other has a strong Venus influence, the relationship may involve balancing assertiveness and receptivity. Recognizing these dynamics can help partners navigate their differences and create a more harmonious connection.

- **Addressing Challenges:** Every relationship has its challenges, and synastry can help identify potential areas of conflict or misunderstanding. By understanding the astrological influences at play, couples can address these challenges with greater awareness and compassion. For example, if there are challenging aspects between Mars and Saturn, this may indicate difficulties in expressing sexual desire or managing sexual tension. Understanding this can help partners communicate openly and find ways to overcome these obstacles together.

Enhancing Sexual Compatibility Through Astrology

Astrological synastry offers valuable insights into sexual compatibility, but it also provides tools for enhancing and deepening the connection between partners. By using astrology as a guide, couples can work together to create a more fulfilling and harmonious sexual relationship.

- **Communication:** Open and honest communication is essential for navigating the complexities of sexual compatibility. By discussing each partner's astrological influences, desires, and needs, couples can create a deeper understanding of each other and address any potential challenges with empathy and clarity.

- **Astrological Timing:** Understanding the influence of transits and progressions in the synastry chart can help couples navigate changes and challenges in their sexual relationship. For example, a challenging transit to Venus or Mars may indicate a temporary period of tension or dissatisfaction. By being aware of these influences, couples can approach these periods with patience and understanding, knowing that the energy will eventually shift.

- **Rituals and Practices:** Incorporating astrological rituals and practices into the relationship can enhance sexual compatibility and deepen the connection. For example, couples might use the energy of a specific planetary transit to focus on a particular aspect of their relationship, such as enhancing passion during a Mars transit or deepening emotional intimacy during a Moon transit. Rituals that align with the astrological influences at play can help couples harness the energy of the cosmos to support their relationship.

Conclusion

Astrological synastry is a powerful tool for understanding sexual compatibility and creating harmonious connections in the bedroom. By analyzing the positions of key planets, aspects, and houses in both partners' charts, couples can gain valuable insights into the dynamics of their relationship, including areas of strength and potential challenges. Synastry offers a roadmap for navigating the complexities of sexual relationships, helping partners create a deeper, more fulfilling connection.

As you explore the art of synastry in your sexual relationship, remember that astrology is a tool for growth, understanding, and connection. By using synastry to guide your relationship, you can deepen your intimacy, enhance your sexual compatibility, and navigate challenges with greater awareness and compassion. Let the wisdom of the stars illuminate your path to a more harmonious and passionate connection in the bedroom, helping you and your partner create a relationship that is truly aligned with the cosmos.

Chapter 39: Transits and Progressions: Evolving Sexual Dynamics

How planetary movements influence the evolution of sexual relationships over time

Astrology is not a static discipline; it reflects the dynamic and ever-changing nature of life. As planets move through the zodiac, they form transits that interact with our natal charts, triggering events, shifts in consciousness, and changes in various areas of life, including relationships. Progressions, which are symbolic movements of the planets over time, also play a crucial role in shaping our evolving experiences. In the context of sexual relationships, both transits and progressions can significantly influence the dynamics between partners, affecting everything from sexual desire and intimacy to communication and emotional connection. This chapter explores how these planetary movements influence the evolution of sexual dynamics over time and how couples can navigate these changes to foster a deeper, more fulfilling relationship.

Understanding Transits and Progressions in Astrology

In astrology, transits refer to the current positions of the planets as they move through the sky and how these positions interact with the planets and points in our natal charts. Transits can trigger significant events, shifts in perspective, and changes in various aspects of life, including relationships and sexuality. Progressions, on the other hand, are symbolic movements of the planets over time, representing the inner growth and development of an individual. Progressions offer insight into how our personal experiences and relationships evolve as we mature.

- **Transits:** Transits occur when a planet in its current position forms an aspect to a planet or point in our natal chart. These interactions can bring about changes, challenges, or opportunities in the area of life governed by the affected planet or house. For example, a transit of Venus to Mars might ignite passion or bring issues of desire and compatibility to the forefront of a relationship.
- **Progressions:** Progressions are calculated by advancing the planets a day for each year of life, creating a symbolic chart that reflects the inner development of an individual over time. Progressions reveal how our needs, desires, and approaches to relationships evolve as we grow. For example, a progressed Venus moving into a new sign or house can signify a shift in how we express love and seek pleasure, influencing the dynamics of our sexual relationships.

Key Transits and Their Influence on Sexual Dynamics

Certain transits have a particularly strong impact on sexual relationships, influencing everything from desire and passion to communication and emotional intimacy. Understanding these transits can help couples navigate changes and challenges in their relationship with greater awareness and intention.

- **Venus Transits:** Venus transits influence love, attraction, and sensuality in relationships. When Venus transits a personal planet, such as the Sun, Moon, or Mars, it can enhance feelings of affection, increase sexual desire, and create opportunities for deeper emotional connection. A Venus transit to Mars, for example, can ignite passion and enhance sexual chemistry, while a Venus transit to Saturn might bring up issues related to commitment or self-worth.

- **Mars Transits:** Mars transits affect sexual energy, desire, and assertiveness. When Mars transits a personal planet or point in the chart, it can increase libido, create sexual tension, or bring issues related to power dynamics to the surface. A Mars transit to Venus can spark intense attraction and desire, while a Mars transit to Pluto might trigger deep, transformative experiences in the sexual relationship.

- **Pluto Transits:** Pluto transits are associated with deep transformation, power, and intensity. These transits often bring about profound changes in relationships, challenging partners to confront hidden desires, fears, and power dynamics. A Pluto transit to Venus or Mars can lead to a period of intense sexual exploration, uncovering deep-seated issues and transforming the way partners connect on a physical and emotional level.

- **Saturn Transits:** Saturn transits are known for bringing structure, discipline, and sometimes challenges or restrictions. In the context of sexual relationships, Saturn transits can highlight issues related to commitment, responsibility, and long-term goals. A Saturn transit to Venus might bring up concerns about emotional security and self-worth, while a Saturn transit to Mars could require a reevaluation of sexual desires and the dynamics of power and control in the relationship.

- **Neptune Transits:** Neptune transits are associated with dreams, illusions, and spirituality. These transits can create a sense of idealism or confusion in relationships, blurring the lines between reality and fantasy. A Neptune transit to Venus might inspire a romantic, almost otherworldly connection, but it could also lead to unrealistic expectations or disillusionment if not grounded in reality.

- **Uranus Transits:** Uranus transits bring sudden changes, excitement, and a desire for freedom and experimentation. These transits can shake up established dynamics in a relationship, encouraging partners to explore new ways of connecting and expressing their sexuality. A Uranus transit to Venus or Mars might lead to unexpected attractions, a desire for more spontaneity, or a shift in sexual preferences.

Progressions and the Evolution of Sexual Dynamics

While transits often bring about external events and changes, progressions reflect the internal growth and evolution of an individual over time. In the context of sexual relationships, progressions can signify shifts in how we express love, desire, and intimacy as we mature.

- **Progressed Venus:** The progression of Venus through different signs and houses can reveal how our approach to love, relationships, and pleasure evolves over time. For example, a progressed Venus moving into a more assertive sign like Aries might indicate a period where one becomes more confident and proactive in pursuing love and sexual connections. If Venus progresses into the 7th house of partnership, it could signify a time when relationships take on greater importance, potentially leading to a deeper commitment or a focus on finding balance and harmony in partnerships.
- **Progressed Mars:** The progression of Mars can indicate changes in how we assert ourselves, pursue our desires, and express our sexual energy. A progressed Mars moving into a new sign or house might reflect a shift in how one experiences and expresses passion. For instance, a progression of Mars into a more sensual sign like Taurus might lead to a greater focus on physical pleasure and the enjoyment of sensual experiences.
- **Progressed Moon:** The progressed Moon reflects the evolution of our emotional needs and how we seek comfort and security. As the Moon progresses through different signs and houses, it can influence how we connect emotionally with our partners and how our needs for intimacy and nurturing evolve. A progressed Moon moving into the 8th house, associated

with deep emotional bonds and sexual intimacy, might indicate a period of increased focus on the emotional and transformative aspects of sexual relationships.

- **Progressed Sun:** The progressed Sun represents the development of our core identity and life direction. As the Sun progresses through different signs and houses, it can reveal shifts in our sense of self and how we approach relationships and sexuality. A progressed Sun moving into a sign known for its emphasis on relationships, such as Libra, might indicate a period where partnership and connection become central to one's identity and life path.

Navigating Changes and Challenges in Sexual Relationships

As transits and progressions influence the dynamics of sexual relationships, they can bring about periods of growth, challenge, and transformation. By understanding these influences, couples can navigate changes with greater awareness and work together to strengthen their connection.

- **Embracing Change:** Both transits and progressions can bring about significant changes in a relationship. Whether it's a shift in sexual desire, a reevaluation of relationship goals, or a transformative experience that deepens intimacy, it's important to approach these changes with an open mind and a willingness to adapt. Embracing change can lead to new levels of connection and fulfillment in the relationship.
- **Communication:** Open and honest communication is key to navigating the challenges that may arise during significant transits or progressions. By discussing the shifts that each partner is experiencing and how they are affecting the relationship, couples can work together to find solutions and maintain a strong connection. Regular check-ins can help ensure that both partners feel supported and understood during times of change.
- **Rituals and Practices:** Incorporating rituals and practices that align with the current transits or progressions can help couples navigate these periods with greater intention. For example, during a Pluto transit, a ritual focused on transformation and letting go of old patterns can help facilitate growth and healing in the relationship. During a Venus progression, rituals that emphasize love, beauty, and connection can help deepen intimacy and strengthen the bond between partners.

• **Seeking Guidance:** For couples experiencing significant challenges or changes in their relationship, seeking guidance from a professional astrologer or relationship counselor can provide valuable insights and support. Understanding the astrological influences at play can help couples gain perspective and develop strategies for navigating these periods with greater ease and understanding.

Conclusion

Transits and progressions are powerful tools for understanding the evolving dynamics of sexual relationships. By recognizing the influence of planetary movements on desire, intimacy, and connection, couples can navigate changes and challenges with greater awareness and intention. Whether through the excitement of a Uranus transit, the deep transformation of a Pluto progression, or the re-evaluation of love during a Venus retrograde, these astrological influences offer opportunities for growth, healing, and deeper connection.

As you explore the impact of transits and progressions on your sexual relationship, remember that these periods are not just about navigating challenges—they are also about embracing the potential for transformation and growth. By working together to understand and harness the energy of these planetary movements, you and your partner can create a relationship that is resilient, dynamic, and deeply fulfilling. Let the wisdom of astrology guide you on your journey of connection, helping you navigate the ever-evolving landscape of your sexual relationship with grace, love, and mutual understanding.

Chapter 40: Healing Sexual Energy with Astrology

Using astrology to address and heal sexual traumas and blockages.

Sexual energy is a powerful force that influences our emotional, physical, and spiritual well-being. However, this energy can become blocked or distorted due to past traumas, unresolved emotional wounds, or negative experiences. Healing sexual energy is essential for cultivating a healthy, fulfilling relationship with oneself and others. Astrology offers a unique and insightful approach to understanding and addressing sexual traumas and blockages. By analyzing key astrological factors, individuals can gain deeper insights into the root causes of their challenges, identify healing pathways, and work toward reclaiming their sexual vitality and empowerment. This chapter explores how astrology can be used to address and heal sexual traumas and blockages, offering practical guidance for using astrological tools in the healing process.

The Role of Astrology in Healing Sexual Energy

Astrology provides a holistic framework for understanding the complex interplay of energies that shape our sexual experiences and identities. By examining the positions of key planets, aspects, and houses in the natal chart, individuals can gain insights into the underlying causes of sexual traumas, blockages, and challenges. Astrology can also reveal the potential for healing and transformation, guiding individuals toward practices and approaches that support their journey toward wholeness and empowerment.

- **Key Planets and Asteroids:** Certain planets and asteroids are particularly relevant when addressing sexual energy and healing. These include Venus (love and attraction), Mars (desire and passion), Pluto (transformation and power), Chiron (the wounded healer), and Eros (sexual desire and eroticism). The positions and aspects of these celestial bodies can provide valuable insights into the dynamics of sexual energy, including areas where healing is needed.

- **Houses of Healing:** The 8th house, associated with sexuality, transformation, and shared resources, is a critical area of the chart to examine when addressing sexual traumas and blockages. The 12th house, which governs the subconscious, hidden fears, and karmic patterns, is also important in understanding deep-seated issues that may affect sexual energy. Additionally, the 4th house (emotional foundations) and the 7th house (relationships and partnerships) can offer insights into how early life experiences and relationships impact sexual dynamics.
- **Aspects and Patterns:** The aspects between key planets, particularly challenging ones (such as squares and oppositions), can reveal areas of conflict, tension, or unresolved trauma that may be affecting sexual energy. Conversely, harmonious aspects (such as trines and sextiles) can highlight strengths and areas where healing energy can flow more easily. Patterns such as grand trines, T-squares, and stelliums can also provide insights into the dynamics of sexual energy and the potential for healing.

Identifying Sexual Traumas and Blockages in the Natal Chart

The natal chart serves as a map of an individual's potential experiences, challenges, and growth opportunities. When it comes to sexual energy, certain configurations and placements can indicate areas where trauma or blockages may be present. By identifying these factors, individuals can gain a clearer understanding of the root causes of their challenges and begin the healing process.

- **Pluto in the 8th House or Challenging Aspects to Pluto:** Pluto represents deep transformation, power, and control. When Pluto is in the 8th house or forms challenging aspects (such as squares or oppositions) to personal planets (like the Sun, Moon, Venus, or Mars), it can indicate experiences related to power struggles, sexual trauma, or control issues. These placements may suggest a need to heal wounds related to trust, intimacy, and personal power.
- **Chiron in the 8th House or Aspecting Venus/Mars:** Chiron, known as the "wounded healer," represents areas of deep wounding and the potential for profound healing. When Chiron is in the 8th house or forms aspects to Venus or Mars, it may indicate sexual wounds

or traumas that need to be addressed. These placements suggest that healing sexual energy requires confronting and transforming past wounds, often through therapeutic or spiritual practices.

- **Saturn in the 5th, 7th, or 8th House:** Saturn represents limitations, restrictions, and lessons learned through discipline and perseverance. When Saturn is in the 5th house (associated with pleasure and creativity), the 7th house (relationships), or the 8th house, it may indicate blockages or fears related to sexual expression and intimacy. These placements suggest that overcoming sexual blockages involves working through fears, insecurities, and self-imposed limitations.
- **Venus Retrograde or Challenging Aspects to Venus:** Venus governs love, attraction, and sensuality. A retrograde Venus in the natal chart or challenging aspects to Venus (such as squares or oppositions) may indicate difficulties in expressing or receiving love, unresolved issues related to self-worth, or past experiences that have led to distrust or fear of intimacy. Healing these issues often involves rebuilding a positive relationship with oneself and learning to open up to love and affection.

Healing Practices Using Astrology

Once sexual traumas and blockages have been identified in the natal chart, individuals can use astrology as a tool for healing and transformation. The following practices are designed to help individuals work with their astrological influences to heal sexual energy and reclaim their sense of empowerment and wholeness.

- **Astrological Journaling:** Keeping a journal that tracks the transits and progressions of key planets, particularly those related to sexual energy (such as Venus, Mars, Pluto, and Chiron), can help individuals gain insight into the timing and nature of their healing process. Journaling about emotions, experiences, and shifts in energy during significant transits can provide clarity and guidance on how to address and heal sexual traumas.
- **Chiron Healing Rituals:** For individuals with significant Chiron placements related to sexual energy, rituals that focus on healing and transformation can be particularly effective. This might involve meditative practices that connect with Chiron's energy, visualizations that fo-

cus on releasing pain and embracing healing, or using crystals, herbs, or symbols associated with healing and transformation.

- **Venus and Mars Balancing Practices:** For those with challenging aspects to Venus or Mars, practices that focus on balancing feminine and masculine energies can be helpful. This might include engaging in activities that nurture self-love and sensuality (Venus), such as taking a ritual bath, practicing self-care, or exploring creative expression. For Mars, activities that channel assertiveness and passion in healthy ways, such as physical exercise, martial arts, or dance, can help restore balance and vitality to sexual energy.

- **Pluto Transformation Work:** For individuals dealing with deep-seated sexual traumas related to Pluto, transformative practices that focus on reclaiming power and releasing control can be essential. This might involve working with a therapist who specializes in trauma, engaging in shadow work to confront and integrate darker aspects of the psyche, or participating in rituals that symbolize rebirth and renewal.

- **Lunar Healing Practices:** The Moon's phases offer a natural rhythm for healing sexual energy. New Moons are ideal for setting intentions for healing and transformation, while Full Moons can be used to release old patterns and emotions that no longer serve you. Waning Moons are a time for introspection and letting go, while Waxing Moons are perfect for nurturing new growth and positive change. Aligning healing practices with the lunar cycle can enhance their effectiveness and bring a sense of natural flow to the healing process.

Creating a Safe Space for Healing

Healing sexual energy requires creating a safe, supportive environment where individuals can explore their wounds, emotions, and desires without fear of judgment. Whether working with a therapist, a partner, or independently, it's important to cultivate an atmosphere of trust, respect, and compassion.

- **Therapeutic Support:** For those dealing with deep-seated sexual traumas, working with a therapist who specializes in sexual healing can be invaluable. A skilled therapist can provide guidance, support, and tools for processing and healing trauma, helping individuals reclaim their sense of power and agency.

- **Partner Support:** In relationships, partners can play a crucial role in supporting each other's healing journey. Open communication, patience, and empathy are essential when navigating sexual healing together. Partners can also engage in healing practices together, such as couples' therapy, shared rituals, or practices that focus on building trust, intimacy, and emotional connection.
- **Self-Compassion:** Healing sexual energy is a deeply personal journey that requires self-compassion and self-acceptance. It's important to approach the healing process with kindness and patience, allowing yourself the time and space to heal at your own pace. Practicing mindfulness, meditation, and self-care can help cultivate self-compassion and support the healing journey.

Conclusion

Healing sexual energy with astrology offers a powerful, holistic approach to addressing and transforming sexual traumas and blockages. By understanding the astrological influences at play and engaging in practices that support healing and empowerment, individuals can reclaim their sexual vitality and cultivate a deeper, more fulfilling relationship with themselves and others.

As you explore the use of astrology in healing sexual energy, remember that this journey is one of self-discovery, growth, and transformation. By embracing the wisdom of the stars and the healing power within yourself, you can navigate the complexities of sexual energy with grace, courage, and a renewed sense of wholeness. Let astrology be your guide on this transformative journey, helping you heal, grow, and embrace your true, empowered self.

Part 6: Practical Applications and Advanced Techniques

Chapter 41: Combining Yoga and Sexual Astrology

Integrating yoga poses with sexual positions for enhanced intimacy and flexibility.

Yoga, a practice that harmonizes the body, mind, and spirit, has long been celebrated for its ability to enhance physical flexibility, mental clarity, and emotional balance. When combined with the insights of sexual astrology, yoga can be a powerful tool for deepening intimacy, enhancing sexual experiences, and improving flexibility in both body and relationships. This chapter explores how to integrate yoga poses with sexual positions, using the principles of sexual astrology to align these practices with your unique astrological energies. By combining yoga and sexual astrology, couples can create a more harmonious, fulfilling, and connected sexual relationship.

The Synergy of Yoga and Sexual Astrology

Yoga and astrology are both ancient practices that offer pathways to greater self-awareness, balance, and harmony. When these practices are combined, they create a holistic approach to sexual intimacy that honors the physical, emotional, and spiritual aspects of the relationship.

- **Yoga for Flexibility and Connection:** Yoga's focus on stretching, breathing, and mindfulness can help improve physical flexibility, enhance body awareness, and promote a deeper connection with one's partner. Certain yoga poses can be adapted into sexual positions, allowing couples to explore new dimensions of intimacy while benefiting from the physical and mental effects of yoga.

- **Astrological Insights for Personalized Practice:** Sexual astrology provides insights into how planetary influences shape your sexual desires, needs, and compatibility. By understanding these influences, couples can tailor their yoga and sexual practices to align with their unique astrological energies, creating a more personalized and effective approach to intimacy.

- **Mindfulness and Presence:** Both yoga and astrology emphasize the importance of mindfulness and being present in the moment. Integrating these practices into sexual intimacy encourages couples to connect more deeply, communicate more effectively, and experience greater pleasure and satisfaction.

Key Yoga Poses for Enhanced Sexual Intimacy

The following yoga poses are particularly effective for enhancing flexibility, strength, and connection in sexual relationships. These poses can be adapted into sexual positions or used as part of a pre- or post-sexual practice to promote relaxation, increase physical comfort, and deepen emotional intimacy.

- **Cat-Cow Pose (Marjaryasana-Bitilasana):**
  - **Benefits:** Cat-Cow Pose is a gentle, flowing movement that stretches the spine, opens the hips, and promotes flexibility in the back and pelvis. This pose also helps synchronize breath with movement, enhancing mindfulness and relaxation.
  - **Integration:** Cat-Cow can be adapted into a sexual position by incorporating the movements into a partnered experience. For example, one partner can take on the Cat-Cow position while the other mirrors the movements, creating a rhythmic, synchronized connection. This position is particularly effective for warming up the body and increasing awareness of each other's movements.
- **Downward-Facing Dog (Adho Mukha Svanasana):**
  - **Benefits:** Downward-Facing Dog is a foundational yoga pose that stretches the entire body, particularly the hamstrings, calves, and spine. This pose also strengthens the arms and shoulders while promoting circulation and energy flow.
  - **Integration:** Downward-Facing Dog can be adapted into a sexual position by having one partner take on the pose while the other partner engages from behind. This position allows for deep penetration while maintaining the stretch and alignment benefits of the yoga pose. It can also be a powerful way to enhance the connection between physical strength and sexual energy.
- **Child's Pose (Balasana):**
  - **Benefits:** Child's Pose is a restful, grounding pose that stretches the lower back, hips, and thighs. It promotes relaxation, introspection, and emotional release, making it an ideal pose for connecting with one's inner self and partner.
  - **Integration:** Child's Pose can be used as a pre- or post-sexual practice to promote relaxation and emotional connection. Partners can practice Child's Pose side by side, fo-

cusing on deep breathing and emotional attunement. This pose can also be integrated into a sexual position by adapting it into a kneeling position with one partner leaning forward while the other supports and embraces from behind.

- **Bridge Pose (Setu Bandhasana):**
  - **Benefits:** Bridge Pose strengthens the back, glutes, and hamstrings while opening the chest and hips. This pose also promotes stability, grounding, and energy flow through the spine, making it ideal for enhancing sexual energy and connection.
  - **Integration:** Bridge Pose can be adapted into a sexual position by having one partner take on the pose while the other partner engages from above. This position allows for deep penetration while maintaining the stretch and strength benefits of the yoga pose. It can also be a way to explore power dynamics and mutual support within the relationship.

- **Lotus Pose (Padmasana):**
  - **Benefits:** Lotus Pose is a seated meditation pose that promotes grounding, stability, and spiritual connection. It opens the hips, stretches the knees and ankles, and encourages deep breathing and mindfulness.
  - **Integration:** Lotus Pose can be adapted into a sexual position by having both partners sit facing each other with their legs intertwined. This position, often called the "Yab-Yum" position, allows for deep emotional and physical connection, as partners maintain close eye contact, synchronize their breath, and engage in gentle, rhythmic movements. This position is ideal for exploring tantra or deepening the spiritual connection within the relationship.

- **Cobra Pose (Bhujangasana):**
  - **Benefits:** Cobra Pose strengthens the spine, opens the chest, and increases flexibility in the back and shoulders. It also promotes energy flow and enhances confidence and vitality, making it an excellent pose for boosting sexual energy.
  - **Integration:** Cobra Pose can be adapted into a sexual position by having one partner take on the pose while the other engages from behind or above. This position allows for deep penetration while maintaining the stretch and strength benefits of the yoga pose. It can also be a way to explore themes of power and surrender within the relationship.

Tailoring Yoga and Sexual Practices to Astrological Energies

By understanding your unique astrological influences, you can tailor your yoga and sexual practices to align with your specific needs, desires, and strengths. The following guidelines offer suggestions for integrating yoga and sexual astrology based on key astrological factors.

- **Fire Signs (Aries, Leo, Sagittarius):**
    - **Energy:** Fire signs are associated with passion, spontaneity, and dynamic energy. These signs thrive on excitement, movement, and exploration.
    - **Yoga Integration:** Fire signs may benefit from incorporating dynamic, energetic yoga poses that enhance strength, flexibility, and stamina. Consider integrating poses like Downward-Facing Dog, Cobra, and Bridge into your sexual practice to channel fiery energy and enhance physical connection. Fire signs may also enjoy exploring more adventurous sexual positions that align with their desire for spontaneity and excitement.
- **Earth Signs (Taurus, Virgo, Capricorn):**
    - **Energy:** Earth signs are associated with stability, sensuality, and grounding. These signs value physical pleasure, comfort, and connection to the body.
    - **Yoga Integration:** Earth signs may benefit from incorporating grounding, stabilizing yoga poses that enhance relaxation and sensuality. Consider integrating poses like Child's Pose, Lotus, and Bridge into your sexual practice to deepen physical connection and promote relaxation. Earth signs may also enjoy exploring slow, sensual sexual positions that align with their desire for tactile pleasure and connection.
- **Air Signs (Gemini, Libra, Aquarius):**
    - **Energy:** Air signs are associated with communication, intellectual stimulation, and adaptability. These signs value mental connection, creativity, and variety.
    - **Yoga Integration:** Air signs may benefit from incorporating fluid, creative yoga poses that enhance flexibility, balance, and mental clarity. Consider integrating poses like Cat-Cow, Lotus, and Downward-Facing Dog into your sexual practice to promote flexibility and mental connection. Air signs may also enjoy exploring playful, communicative sexual positions that align with their desire for variety and mental stimulation.
- **Water Signs (Cancer, Scorpio, Pisces):**

- ◦ **Energy:** Water signs are associated with emotion, intuition, and depth. These signs value emotional connection, intimacy, and spiritual connection.
- ◦ **Yoga Integration:** Water signs may benefit from incorporating flowing, introspective yoga poses that enhance emotional connection, intuition, and fluidity. Consider integrating poses like Cobra, Child's Pose, and Lotus into your sexual practice to deepen emotional intimacy and promote spiritual connection. Water signs may also enjoy exploring intimate, emotionally connected sexual positions that align with their desire for deep, soulful connection.

Creating a Yoga-Sexual Astrology Practice

To fully integrate yoga and sexual astrology into your relationship, consider creating a regular practice that incorporates both elements. This practice can be customized to your unique needs, desires, and astrological influences, allowing you to explore new dimensions of intimacy and connection.

- **Daily or Weekly Yoga Routine:** Establish a regular yoga routine that incorporates poses designed to enhance flexibility, strength, and relaxation. This routine can be practiced alone or with your partner, depending on your preferences and goals. Consider aligning your routine with the lunar cycle or other astrological events to enhance its effectiveness and connection to your astrological energies.
- **Pre- or Post-Sexual Yoga Practice:** Incorporate yoga into your pre- or post-sexual routine to enhance relaxation, connection, and flexibility. Pre-sexual yoga can help warm up the body, increase awareness, and set the stage for a more connected, fulfilling experience. Post-sexual yoga can help promote relaxation, emotional connection, and physical recovery.
- **Astrological Meditation and Visualization:** Incorporate astrological meditation and visualization into your yoga and sexual practice to align your energies with the planets and signs that influence your relationship. For example, during a Venus transit, you might visualize the energy of love and connection flowing through your body as you practice yoga or engage in sexual intimacy. During a Mars transit, you might focus on channeling passion and desire through your movements and breath.

- **Astrological-Themed Yoga Sessions:** Design yoga sessions that focus on specific astrological themes relevant to your relationship. For example, during a Venus retrograde, you could create a session that emphasizes poses and practices to reconnect with love and intimacy, focusing on heart-opening poses like Cobra and Bridge. During a Mars transit, you might design a session that channels assertiveness and passion through poses like Warrior or Downward-Facing Dog. Tailoring your yoga sessions to astrological themes can help you align more deeply with the cosmic energies at play and enhance your connection with your partner.

- **Couples Yoga and Tantric Practices:** Incorporate couples yoga and tantric practices into your routine to deepen physical and emotional intimacy. Tantric practices emphasize the connection between sexuality and spirituality, using breath, movement, and mindfulness to create a deeper bond between partners. Poses like Lotus, where partners sit facing each other and synchronize their breath, or supported Bridge pose, where one partner supports the other in a backbend, can enhance both physical connection and spiritual unity.

- **Lunar and Planetary Rituals:** Integrate yoga with lunar and planetary rituals to harness the power of celestial events in your sexual relationship. For example, on a Full Moon night, you might perform a yoga session focused on releasing old patterns and embracing new possibilities, followed by a ritual that honors the energy of the Moon. Similarly, during significant planetary transits, you might create rituals that align your sexual energy with the transformative power of the planets, using yoga as a foundation for these practices.

- **Mindful Breathing and Partner Synchronization:** Incorporate mindful breathing and partner synchronization into your yoga and sexual practices to enhance connection and awareness. Practicing synchronized breathing during yoga poses or sexual intimacy can help partners attune to each other's rhythms, creating a deeper sense of unity and presence. Breathing exercises, such as deep belly breathing or alternate nostril breathing, can also help calm the mind, reduce stress, and prepare the body for a more connected and fulfilling experience.

Conclusion

Combining yoga and sexual astrology offers a holistic approach to enhancing intimacy, flexibility, and connection in relationships. By integrating the physical, emotional, and spiritual benefits of yoga with the personalized insights of sexual astrology, couples can create a practice that deepens their bond, enhances their sexual experiences, and aligns with their unique astrological energies.

As you explore the integration of yoga and sexual astrology in your relationship, remember that this practice is not just about physical poses or astrological charts—it's about creating a deeper connection with yourself, your partner, and the cosmic energies that influence your lives. By approaching this practice with mindfulness, intention, and an open heart, you can transform your sexual relationship into a source of profound joy, growth, and spiritual fulfillment. Let the wisdom of yoga and astrology guide you on this journey, helping you cultivate a relationship that is flexible, harmonious, and deeply connected.

Chapter 42: Tantric Practices and Astrological Alignments

Deepening sexual experiences through Tantric practices aligned with astrological insights.

Tantra, an ancient spiritual practice, weaves together the physical, emotional, and spiritual aspects of sexuality, transforming intimate encounters into profound experiences of connection and enlightenment. When combined with the insights of astrology, Tantra offers a unique path to deepening sexual experiences by aligning practices with the cosmic energies influencing each individual and relationship. This chapter explores how to integrate Tantric practices with astrological alignments, providing a roadmap for using these powerful tools to enhance intimacy, deepen emotional bonds, and elevate sexual experiences to new levels of spiritual awareness.

The Foundations of Tantra

Tantra, originating from ancient Indian spiritual traditions, views sexuality as a sacred act that can lead to spiritual awakening and greater self-awareness. Unlike approaches that focus solely on physical pleasure, Tantra emphasizes the union of body, mind, and spirit, encouraging practitioners to explore sexuality as a path to personal and relational growth.

- **Energy Awareness:** Central to Tantra is the concept of energy, particularly sexual energy, as a potent force that can be harnessed for spiritual growth. Practitioners learn to cultivate and direct this energy through breathwork, meditation, and conscious touch, enhancing both physical pleasure and spiritual connection.
- **Sacred Union:** Tantra views sexual union as a sacred act, a merging of energies that reflects the divine union of masculine and feminine principles. Through Tantric practices, partners can experience deeper levels of intimacy, connection, and spiritual harmony.
- **Mindfulness and Presence:** Tantra emphasizes the importance of mindfulness and being fully present in each moment. This heightened awareness allows practitioners to connect more deeply with their own bodies, their partner, and the divine, transforming sexual encounters into meditative experiences of unity and bliss.

Integrating Astrology with Tantric Practices

Astrology provides a personalized framework for understanding how cosmic energies influence sexual dynamics, desires, and potentials. By aligning Tantric practices with astrological insights, couples can create a more harmonious and spiritually fulfilling sexual relationship.

- **Personalized Tantra:** By understanding each partner's astrological chart, couples can tailor Tantric practices to align with their unique energies. For example, a person with a strong Venus influence might benefit from practices that emphasize love and sensuality, while someone with prominent Mars energy might be drawn to more dynamic, passionate practices.
- **Timing and Celestial Events:** Astrological transits, progressions, and celestial events like Full Moons, eclipses, and planetary alignments can be powerful times for deepening Tantric practices. Aligning Tantric rituals with these cosmic events can amplify their effectiveness, creating opportunities for profound spiritual and sexual experiences.
- **Elemental Balance:** Astrology divides the zodiac into four elements—fire, earth, air, and water—each associated with different qualities and energies. By incorporating the principles of these elements into Tantric practices, couples can create a more balanced and harmonious sexual experience. For example, fire signs might focus on passionate, dynamic practices, while water signs might explore more fluid, emotionally connected practices.

Key Tantric Practices Aligned with Astrological Energies

The following Tantric practices can be aligned with astrological insights to deepen sexual experiences, enhance intimacy, and promote spiritual growth.

- **Breathwork and Pranayama:** Breathwork is a foundational practice in both Tantra and many spiritual traditions, used to cultivate and direct energy throughout the body. In Tantric practices, breathwork can enhance sexual energy, deepen connection, and promote mindfulness.
  - **Astrological Alignment:** Tailor breathwork practices to align with the dominant astrological energies. For instance, during a Mars transit, focus on energizing breath tech-

niques like Bhastrika (bellows breath) to stoke the inner fire and enhance passion. During a Venus transit, practice deep, calming breaths to cultivate love and relaxation.

- **Eye Gazing:** Eye gazing, or "soul gazing," is a Tantric practice where partners sit facing each other and maintain eye contact for an extended period. This practice fosters deep emotional connection, vulnerability, and intimacy.
    - **Astrological Alignment:** Align eye gazing sessions with lunar phases or specific transits that emphasize emotional connection, such as a Full Moon or a Moon-Venus transit. These times are particularly conducive to exploring deep emotional bonds and experiencing heightened sensitivity and connection.
- **Sacred Touch and Sensual Massage:** Tantric touch and sensual massage are practices that use conscious, mindful touch to explore and enhance the body's sensitivity and energy flow. These practices help partners connect more deeply with their own bodies and with each other, promoting relaxation, trust, and intimacy.
    - **Astrological Alignment:** Integrate sacred touch and massage practices with the astrological elements. For example, during an earth sign transit, focus on grounding, nurturing touch that connects with the physical body. During a water sign transit, explore fluid, soothing touch that enhances emotional connection and trust.
- **Yab-Yum Position:** The Yab-Yum position is a classic Tantric posture where one partner sits cross-legged while the other sits on their lap, facing them, with legs wrapped around the partner's waist. This position facilitates close physical contact, synchronized breathing, and energy exchange, creating a powerful experience of unity and connection.
    - **Astrological Alignment:** Practice Yab-Yum during significant planetary alignments, such as a conjunction or opposition involving Venus, Mars, or the Moon. These alignments can amplify the energy of the practice, deepening the emotional and spiritual connection between partners.
- **Chakra Activation:** Tantra often involves working with the chakras, or energy centers in the body, to balance and enhance energy flow. Specific Tantric practices focus on activating and harmonizing the chakras, particularly those associated with sexuality, such as the sacral (Svadhisthana) and root (Muladhara) chakras.

○ **Astrological Alignment:** Align chakra activation practices with the transits of planets associated with specific chakras. For example, during a Mars transit, focus on activating the root chakra to enhance vitality and sexual energy. During a Neptune transit, work on the third eye (Ajna) chakra to enhance intuition and spiritual connection.

Rituals and Practices for Tantric Astrology

To fully integrate Tantric practices with astrological alignments, consider creating rituals that incorporate both elements. These rituals can be tailored to specific astrological events, transits, or personal goals, enhancing their effectiveness and deepening the connection between partners.

- **Lunar Tantric Rituals:** The Moon's phases are deeply connected to emotions, intuition, and the feminine energy. Create Tantric rituals aligned with the lunar cycle to enhance emotional intimacy and spiritual connection. For example, during a New Moon, set intentions for your sexual relationship, focusing on new beginnings and growth. During a Full Moon, practice Tantric rituals that celebrate and amplify the emotional and spiritual connection between partners.
- **Planetary Tantra Sessions:** Align your Tantric practices with the energies of specific planetary transits. For instance, during a Venus retrograde, focus on healing practices that address issues of love, self-worth, and intimacy. During a Mars transit, engage in dynamic, passionate practices that channel the planet's assertive, fiery energy.
- **Seasonal Tantric Rituals:** Incorporate the changing seasons and astrological signs into your Tantric practices. For example, during the spring equinox, which corresponds with Aries (a fire sign), practice Tantric rituals that celebrate renewal, vitality, and passion. During the autumn equinox, aligned with Libra (an air sign), focus on balance, harmony, and communication in your relationship.
- **Astrological Meditation:** Enhance your Tantric practices with guided meditations that focus on astrological energies. For example, meditate on the qualities of Venus—love, beauty, and connection—during a Venus transit, or visualize the transformative energy of Pluto to facilitate deep emotional healing and sexual renewal.

Enhancing the Tantric Experience with Astrology

To maximize the benefits of combining Tantra and astrology, it's essential to approach these practices with mindfulness, intention, and openness. The following tips can help you and your partner deepen your Tantric experience and align it with your astrological energies.

- **Mindful Awareness:** Approach each practice with a deep sense of mindfulness and presence. Whether it's a simple breathing exercise or a complex ritual, being fully present enhances the effectiveness of the practice and deepens the connection between partners.
- **Communication:** Open and honest communication is key to successful Tantric practices. Discuss your astrological insights, desires, and intentions with your partner before engaging in Tantric rituals, ensuring that both partners are aligned and comfortable with the practices.
- **Personalization:** Tailor your practices to your unique astrological influences and relationship dynamics. Consider each partner's astrological chart, including their sun sign, moon sign, Venus, Mars, and rising sign, to create a practice that resonates with your specific energies.
- **Patience and Compassion:** Tantra and astrology are both complex practices that require patience, compassion, and ongoing exploration. Allow yourself and your partner the time and space to explore these practices at your own pace, being gentle and compassionate with each other as you navigate this journey of deepening connection and spiritual growth.

Conclusion

Tantric practices and astrological alignments offer a profound and transformative approach to sexual intimacy, combining the spiritual depth of Tantra with the personalized insights of astrology. By integrating these practices, couples can enhance their connection, deepen their sexual experiences, and align their relationship with the cosmic energies that influence their lives.

As you explore the intersection of Tantra and astrology in your relationship, remember that this journey is about more than just physical pleasure—it's about cultivating a deeper connection with yourself, your partner, and the divine. By approaching these practices with intention, mindfulness, and an open heart, you can transform your sexual relationship into a source of spiritual growth, profound joy, and lasting fulfillment. Let the wisdom of Tantra and astrology guide you on this journey, helping you create a relationship that is not only physically satisfying but also spiritually enriching and deeply connected. Through the conscious integration of Tantric practices and astrological insights, you and your partner can explore new dimensions of intimacy, strengthen your bond, and experience the profound unity of body, mind, and spirit.

By aligning your Tantric practices with the movements of the planets, the phases of the Moon, and the energies of the zodiac, you can harness the power of the cosmos to enhance your sexual experiences. This alignment allows you to tap into the natural rhythms and cycles of the universe, creating a more harmonious and balanced relationship.

As you continue to explore these practices, consider making them a regular part of your relationship, allowing the energy of the cosmos to guide and support your journey together. Whether you're celebrating the fiery passion of Mars, the deep emotional connection of the Moon, or the transformative power of Pluto, these practices can help you and your partner connect on a deeper level, fostering a relationship that is both passionate and spiritually fulfilling.

Ultimately, the combination of Tantra and astrology offers a pathway to a more enlightened, connected, and harmonious sexual relationship. By embracing the teachings of both traditions, you can transform your intimate encounters into sacred rituals that honor the divine within yourself, your partner, and the universe. Let this journey be one of exploration, growth, and love, as you and your partner discover the profound potential of combining these ancient practices for a deeper, more meaningful connection.

Chapter 43: Astrological Sex Magic

Rituals and spells to harness cosmic energy for enhancing sexual pleasure.

Astrological sex magic is a powerful practice that combines the ancient wisdom of astrology with the mystical art of sex magic. By aligning sexual rituals and spells with cosmic energies, individuals and couples can enhance their sexual pleasure, deepen their emotional connections, and manifest their desires. This chapter delves into the art of astrological sex magic, offering a comprehensive guide to harnessing the energy of the planets, stars, and celestial events to elevate sexual experiences and create a deeper sense of connection with the universe.

The Foundations of Sex Magic

Sex magic is a practice that uses sexual energy as a potent force for manifestation, healing, and spiritual growth. It is based on the belief that sexual energy, when focused and directed, can be a powerful tool for creating change in one's life. By combining sex magic with astrology, practitioners can align their rituals with the natural rhythms of the cosmos, enhancing the effectiveness of their magic and creating a more profound connection with the universe.

- **Sexual Energy as a Creative Force:** In sex magic, sexual energy is viewed as a creative force that can be harnessed to manifest desires, heal emotional wounds, and achieve spiritual enlightenment. This energy is believed to be one of the most potent forms of magic, capable of transforming both the individual and the external world.
- **The Role of Intention:** Intention is central to the practice of sex magic. By setting clear, focused intentions, practitioners can direct their sexual energy toward specific goals, whether they are related to love, pleasure, healing, or spiritual growth. Intention acts as the guiding force that shapes the energy generated during sexual rituals.
- **The Power of Ritual:** Rituals are structured practices that help to focus the mind, body, and spirit on a specific goal. In sex magic, rituals often involve a combination of meditation, visualization, chanting, and physical actions, such as sexual intercourse or self-pleasure. Rituals create a sacred space where the practitioner can connect with the divine and channel their energy toward their intentions.

Astrological Alignment in Sex Magic

Astrology offers a framework for understanding how cosmic energies influence our lives, including our sexuality. By aligning sex magic rituals with astrological energies, practitioners can amplify their intentions and tap into the natural rhythms of the universe. Key astrological factors to consider in sex magic include the positions of the planets, the phases of the Moon, and significant celestial events.

- **Planetary Energies:** Each planet in astrology governs specific aspects of life, including love, desire, communication, and transformation. By aligning sex magic rituals with the energy of a specific planet, practitioners can enhance the potency of their intentions.
    - **Venus:** Venus is the planet of love, beauty, and sensuality. Rituals aligned with Venus are ideal for enhancing romantic connections, increasing sexual pleasure, and manifesting love and attraction.
    - **Mars:** Mars governs desire, passion, and assertiveness. Rituals aligned with Mars are powerful for igniting sexual energy, increasing confidence, and manifesting desires related to sexuality and personal empowerment.
    - **Pluto:** Pluto represents transformation, power, and deep emotional connection. Rituals aligned with Pluto are suited for profound sexual healing, exploring taboo desires, and manifesting transformative sexual experiences.
    - **Mercury:** Mercury is the planet of communication and intellect. Rituals aligned with Mercury can enhance communication in sexual relationships, increase mental stimulation, and manifest desires related to learning and exploration in sexuality.
- **Lunar Phases:** The Moon governs emotions, intuition, and cycles of growth and release. The phases of the Moon play a crucial role in sex magic, as they influence the flow of energy and the timing of rituals.
    - **New Moon:** The New Moon is a time for setting intentions, new beginnings, and planting seeds for the future. Rituals performed during the New Moon are ideal for initiating new sexual practices, manifesting new relationships, and setting goals related to sexual exploration.

- ◦ **Waxing Moon:** As the Moon grows from new to full, its energy is expansive and growth-oriented. Rituals during the Waxing Moon are powerful for building sexual energy, increasing pleasure, and nurturing the growth of intimate connections.
- ◦ **Full Moon:** The Full Moon represents the peak of energy, a time of culmination and celebration. Rituals during the Full Moon are ideal for amplifying sexual pleasure, deepening emotional connections, and manifesting desires with full intensity.
- ◦ **Waning Moon:** As the Moon wanes from full to new, its energy turns inward, focusing on release and reflection. Rituals during the Waning Moon are suited for releasing sexual blockages, healing past traumas, and letting go of unfulfilled desires.
- **Celestial Events:** Eclipses, solstices, equinoxes, and planetary alignments are powerful celestial events that offer unique opportunities for sex magic. These events can create portals of energy that amplify the effectiveness of rituals, making them ideal times for deep, transformative work.
  - ◦ **Eclipses:** Eclipses are times of sudden change, revelation, and transformation. Rituals performed during eclipses can be used to uncover hidden desires, release deep-seated blockages, and manifest profound sexual and emotional transformations.
  - ◦ **Solstices and Equinoxes:** The solstices and equinoxes mark the turning points of the year, representing balance, transition, and renewal. Rituals performed during these times are powerful for aligning with the natural cycles of growth and rest, manifesting long-term sexual goals, and deepening the connection between sexuality and spirituality.
  - ◦ **Planetary Alignments:** When planets align, their combined energies create potent influences that can be harnessed for sex magic. For example, a Venus-Mars conjunction is an ideal time for rituals that combine love and passion, while a Saturn-Pluto conjunction can be used for rituals focused on transformation and empowerment.

Rituals and Spells for Astrological Sex Magic

The following rituals and spells are designed to harness astrological energies for enhancing sexual pleasure, deepening connections, and manifesting desires. Each ritual is aligned with specific astrological factors to maximize its effectiveness.

- **Venus Love Spell:** This ritual is designed to enhance love, attraction, and sexual pleasure by harnessing the energy of Venus.
  - **Timing:** Perform this ritual on a Friday (Venus's day) during a Venus transit or on a New Moon.
  - **Materials:** Pink or red candles, rose petals, rose quartz, essential oils (such as rose or jasmine), and a piece of paper with your intentions written on it.
  - **Instructions:** Begin by creating a sacred space where you feel comfortable and relaxed. Light the candles and place the rose petals and rose quartz around them. Anoint yourself with the essential oils, focusing on areas where you want to attract love and pleasure. Hold the piece of paper with your intentions, and as you read them aloud, visualize the energy of Venus infusing your words with love and attraction. Engage in a sexual ritual, either alone or with a partner, focusing on channeling the energy of Venus into your desires. When you're finished, thank Venus for her guidance and let the candles burn out naturally.
- **Mars Passion Ritual:** This ritual is designed to ignite sexual energy, increase confidence, and manifest desires related to sexuality and empowerment.
  - **Timing:** Perform this ritual on a Tuesday (Mars's day) during a Mars transit or on a Waxing Moon.
  - **Materials:** Red candles, a piece of red fabric, a small mirror, a piece of iron (such as a small iron tool or jewelry), and a piece of paper with your intentions written on it.
  - **Instructions:** Create a sacred space that feels dynamic and energizing. Light the red candles and place the iron and mirror nearby. Wrap yourself in the red fabric, symbolizing the fire and energy of Mars. Hold the piece of paper with your intentions, and as you read them aloud, look into the mirror and visualize yourself as confident, empowered, and sexually vibrant. Engage in a sexual ritual, focusing on channeling the energy of Mars into your desires. As you climax, visualize your intentions being sent out into the universe with the power of Mars. When you're finished, thank Mars for his energy and guidance, and let the candles burn out naturally.
- **Pluto Transformation Spell:** This ritual is designed to facilitate deep sexual healing, release blockages, and manifest transformative sexual experiences.

- **Timing:** Perform this ritual during a Pluto transit or on a Waning Moon.
- **Materials:** Black or dark purple candles, obsidian or black tourmaline, a cauldron or fireproof dish, a piece of paper with your intentions or blockages written on it, and sage or palo santo for cleansing.
- **Instructions:** Begin by cleansing your space with sage or palo santo, focusing on releasing any negative or stagnant energy. Light the candles and place the obsidian or black tourmaline nearby. Hold the piece of paper with your intentions or blockages, and as you read them aloud, visualize Pluto's transformative energy enveloping you. Burn the paper in the cauldron or dish, symbolizing the release and transformation of old patterns and blockages. Engage in a sexual ritual, focusing on the theme of transformation and renewal. As you climax, visualize yourself being reborn, free from the past and open to new, powerful experiences. When you're finished, thank Pluto for his guidance, and let the candles burn out naturally.

- **Lunar Manifestation Ritual:** This ritual is designed to harness the energy of the Moon for manifesting sexual desires, deepening emotional connections, and enhancing intuitive insights.
  - **Timing:** Perform this ritual during a Full Moon or New Moon.
  - **Materials:** Silver or white candles, moonstone or selenite, a bowl of water, and a bowl of water, a piece of paper with your intentions written on it, and essential oils such as lavender or sandalwood.
  - **Instructions:** Begin by creating a serene and sacred space, ideally in a place where you can see the Moon. Light the silver or white candles and place the moonstone or selenite next to them. Add a few drops of essential oils to the bowl of water, symbolizing the reflective and intuitive qualities of the Moon. Hold the piece of paper with your intentions, and as you read them aloud, gaze into the water and visualize the Moon's light infusing your desires with its energy.
  - **New Moon Focus:** If performing this ritual during the New Moon, focus on setting intentions for new beginnings, planting seeds for future growth, and manifesting new desires in your sexual relationship. As you engage in a sexual ritual, either alone or with

a partner, concentrate on the energy of potential and the excitement of what is yet to come.

◦ **Full Moon Focus:** If performing this ritual during the Full Moon, concentrate on the culmination of your desires, celebrating the peak of energy and the fullness of your emotional and sexual connection. During the sexual ritual, focus on amplifying pleasure and fully embodying the energy of your desires as they come to fruition.

◦ **Conclusion:** After the sexual ritual, thank the Moon for its guidance and energy. Pour the water outside under the Moonlight as an offering, symbolizing the release of your intentions into the universe. Allow the candles to burn out naturally.

◦ **Solar Equinox or Solstice Ritual:** This ritual is designed to align sexual energy with the transformative power of the Sun during solstices or equinoxes, marking the transitions in the cycle of the seasons and channeling the Sun's life-giving energy into your sexual practices.

◦ **Timing:** Perform this ritual during the Spring or Autumn Equinox, or the Summer or Winter Solstice.

◦ **Materials:** Gold or yellow candles, a small sun-shaped symbol or charm, a piece of paper with your intentions, and sun-related herbs such as cinnamon, sunflower petals, or orange peel.

◦ **Instructions:** Begin by creating a bright, warm space that reflects the energy of the Sun. Light the gold or yellow candles and place the sun-shaped symbol at the center of your altar. Sprinkle the sun-related herbs around the candles. Hold the piece of paper with your intentions, and as you read them aloud, visualize the Sun's light and warmth energizing and infusing your desires with life.

◦ **Equinox Focus:** During the equinoxes, focus on balance and harmony in your sexual relationship. Engage in a sexual ritual that reflects this balance, ensuring that both partners feel equally engaged, satisfied, and connected.

◦ **Solstice Focus:** During the solstices, focus on the extremes—whether it's the peak of the Sun's power during the Summer Solstice or the deep reflection of the Winter Solstice. Engage in a sexual ritual that celebrates the abundance of energy (Summer) or the intimacy of the darkness (Winter).

- **Conclusion:** After the ritual, thank the Sun for its life-giving energy. Keep the sun-shaped symbol as a talisman of your ritual's energy. Allow the candles to burn out naturally.
- **Enhancing Astrological Sex Magic with Personalization**
- While the above rituals provide a framework for practicing astrological sex magic, personalizing these rituals to fit your unique astrological chart, relationship dynamics, and spiritual practices can enhance their effectiveness.
- **Astrological Chart Integration:** Consider the positions of Venus, Mars, and other significant planets in your birth chart and your partner's chart when designing your rituals. For example, if Venus is in Taurus in your chart, you might incorporate earthy, sensual elements into your rituals, focusing on touch, taste, and physical pleasure.
- **Personal Symbols and Talismans:** Integrate personal symbols or talismans into your rituals that resonate with your astrological sign or your specific intentions. These could be gemstones, herbs, or objects that hold personal significance and enhance your connection to the ritual's energy.
- **Guided Meditations and Visualizations:** Create guided meditations or visualizations that align with your astrological influences. For example, if you're working with a Neptune transit, you might meditate on the themes of dreams, illusions, and spiritual connection, using visualization techniques to deepen your experience.
- **Collaborative Rituals:** If practicing with a partner, involve them in the creation of the ritual. Discuss your astrological charts together, decide on the timing and focus of the ritual, and share the responsibilities of setting up the space and guiding the practice. This collaboration can deepen your connection and ensure that both partners' energies are fully integrated into the ritual.

Conclusion

Astrological sex magic offers a powerful, personalized approach to enhancing sexual pleasure, deepening emotional connections, and manifesting desires. By aligning sexual rituals and spells with the cosmic energies of the planets, stars, and celestial events, you can tap into the natural rhythms of the universe and create profound, transformative experiences.

As you explore astrological sex magic, remember that this practice is deeply personal and flexible. Allow yourself to experiment with different rituals, adapt practices to your unique needs and desires, and embrace the creative, spiritual aspects of sex magic. By combining the ancient wisdom of astrology with the powerful energy of sex magic, you can unlock new dimensions of pleasure, connection, and spiritual growth, creating a sexual relationship that is as profound as it is fulfilling.

Let the cosmos be your guide in this journey of exploration and transformation, and may your practice of astrological sex magic bring you closer to the realization of your deepest desires and the embodiment of your highest potential.

Chapter 44: Creating Personalized Sexual Astrology Charts

Step-by-step guide to creating and interpreting personal sexual astrology charts.

Astrology offers a profound understanding of how cosmic energies shape various aspects of our lives, including sexuality. By creating and interpreting personalized sexual astrology charts, individuals and couples can gain valuable insights into their sexual desires, compatibility, and challenges. This chapter provides a comprehensive, step-by-step guide to creating and interpreting sexual astrology charts, allowing you to explore the unique dynamics of your sexual energy and relationships.

Understanding Sexual Astrology Charts

A sexual astrology chart is a specialized version of a natal chart that focuses on the planets, aspects, and houses that most directly influence sexuality, desire, and intimate relationships. While a standard natal chart provides a broad overview of an individual's life, a sexual astrology chart hones in on the factors that shape sexual expression, compatibility, and dynamics.

- **Key Planets:** The primary planets of interest in a sexual astrology chart include Venus, Mars, the Moon, and Pluto, though other planets like Mercury, Jupiter, and Saturn can also provide valuable insights.
    - **Venus:** Governs love, attraction, beauty, and how one gives and receives affection.
    - **Mars:** Governs desire, passion, sexual energy, and how one pursues their desires.
    - **Moon:** Governs emotions, instincts, and how one seeks emotional intimacy and security.
    - **Pluto:** Governs transformation, power, deep emotional connections, and the exploration of taboo or intense experiences.
- **Key Houses:** In a sexual astrology chart, specific houses play a significant role in understanding sexual energy and relationships.
    - **5th House:** Governs romance, creativity, and sexual pleasure.
    - **7th House:** Governs partnerships, marriage, and long-term relationships.
    - **8th House:** Governs sexuality, intimacy, shared resources, and transformation.

- ◦ **12th House:** Governs the subconscious, hidden desires, and karmic patterns.
- **Aspects:** Aspects between planets (such as conjunctions, trines, squares, and oppositions) reveal the dynamics of how different energies interact in a chart. In sexual astrology, aspects involving Venus, Mars, the Moon, and Pluto are particularly important for understanding sexual compatibility and challenges.

Step-by-Step Guide to Creating a Sexual Astrology Chart

Creating a personalized sexual astrology chart involves several key steps, from gathering birth data to interpreting the chart's elements. This guide will walk you through each step, providing you with the tools to create and analyze your own chart or one for a partner.

Step 1: Gather Birth Data

To create an accurate sexual astrology chart, you'll need the following information:

- **Date of Birth:** The day, month, and year of birth.
- **Time of Birth:** The exact time of birth, preferably down to the minute.
- **Place of Birth:** The city, state, and country of birth.

This data is essential for calculating the positions of the planets, houses, and aspects in the chart.

Step 2: Calculate the Natal Chart

Use an astrology software program, website, or mobile app to input the birth data and generate a natal chart. Many online tools allow you to create a detailed chart with all the necessary astrological information. Ensure that the chart includes the positions of the planets, houses, and aspects, as well as the astrological signs associated with each element.

Step 3: Identify Key Planets and Houses

Once the natal chart is generated, identify the positions of the key planets (Venus, Mars, the Moon, and Pluto) and the key houses (5th, 7th, 8th, and 12th). Note the sign and house each planet occupies, as well as any aspects between these planets and others in the chart.

- **Venus:** Identify the sign and house where Venus is located. This will reveal how the individual expresses love, attraction, and sensuality.

- **Mars:** Identify the sign and house where Mars is located. This will reveal how the individual expresses sexual desire, passion, and assertiveness.
- **Moon:** Identify the sign and house where the Moon is located. This will reveal how the individual experiences emotional intimacy and seeks emotional security in relationships.
- **Pluto:** Identify the sign and house where Pluto is located. This will reveal how the individual experiences transformation, power dynamics, and deep emotional connections in sexuality.

Step 4: Analyze Aspects Between Key Planets

Examine the aspects (conjunctions, trines, squares, oppositions, sextiles) between the key planets (Venus, Mars, the Moon, Pluto) and other planets in the chart. Aspects reveal how different energies interact and influence the individual's sexual expression and relationship dynamics.

- **Conjunctions:** When two planets are close together, their energies combine and intensify. A conjunction between Venus and Mars, for example, can indicate a strong connection between love and desire.
- **Trines:** When two planets are 120 degrees apart, their energies flow harmoniously. A trine between Venus and the Moon suggests an easy, natural connection between love and emotional intimacy.
- **Squares:** When two planets are 90 degrees apart, their energies are in tension. A square between Mars and Pluto may indicate challenges related to sexual power dynamics or control issues.
- **Oppositions:** When two planets are 180 degrees apart, their energies are in opposition. An opposition between Venus and Pluto might suggest a conflict between love and the desire for deep, transformative experiences.

Step 5: Interpret the Sexual Astrology Chart

Interpret the chart by synthesizing the information from the planets, houses, and aspects. Focus on how these elements interact to shape the individual's sexual desires, challenges, and compatibility. Consider the following questions:

- **How does Venus influence the individual's approach to love and attraction?**
- **How does Mars influence the individual's expression of sexual desire and assertiveness?**
- **How does the Moon influence the individual's need for emotional intimacy and security?**
- **How does Pluto influence the individual's experience of transformation and deep emotional connections in sexuality?**
- **What do the aspects between these planets reveal about the dynamics of the individual's sexual relationships?**

Step 6: Compare and Contrast Partner Charts (Synastry)

For couples, synastry (the comparison of two charts) can provide insights into sexual compatibility and relationship dynamics. Overlay one partner's chart onto the other, focusing on how the key planets and houses interact between the two charts.

- **Venus and Mars Compatibility:** Examine how each partner's Venus and Mars interact. Harmonious aspects (e.g., trines, sextiles) between these planets suggest strong sexual chemistry, while challenging aspects (e.g., squares, oppositions) may indicate areas of tension or conflict.
- **Moon and Emotional Intimacy:** Consider how each partner's Moon interacts with the other's chart. This reveals how well the partners connect emotionally and how they fulfill each other's need for security and intimacy.
- **Pluto and Transformation:** Look at how Pluto interacts between the charts. This can indicate the potential for deep, transformative experiences within the relationship, as well as areas where power dynamics may need to be navigated carefully.

Step 7: Use Transits and Progressions for Timing

Transits (current planetary positions) and progressions (symbolic movements of planets over time) provide insights into how sexual dynamics evolve. By analyzing transits and progressions in relation to the natal chart, you can identify favorable or challenging periods for sexual relationships.

- **Venus Transits:** Look for Venus transits to natal planets, which can indicate periods of enhanced love, attraction, and pleasure.
- **Mars Transits:** Mars transits can reveal periods of increased sexual energy, passion, and assertiveness.
- **Pluto Transits:** Pluto transits often bring deep transformations in sexual relationships, highlighting times when old patterns may be released or new, intense connections may form.

Conclusion

Creating and interpreting a personalized sexual astrology chart offers a powerful tool for understanding the complex dynamics of sexual energy, desire, and relationships. By exploring the positions of key planets, houses, and aspects, you can gain valuable insights into your own sexuality and the dynamics of your relationships.

As you work with your sexual astrology chart, remember that astrology is a tool for self-awareness and growth. Use it to explore your desires, understand your challenges, and enhance your relationships with others. Whether you're creating a chart for yourself or a partner, the insights gained from sexual astrology can lead to a deeper, more fulfilling connection with your sexual energy and your relationships. Let this exploration of the cosmos guide you on your journey toward a more enlightened and harmonious sexual life.

Appendices:

Glossary: Key Terms and Concepts in Astrology and Sexual Positions

This glossary provides definitions and explanations of key terms and concepts related to astrology and sexual positions. It serves as a comprehensive reference for readers seeking to deepen their understanding of the language and practices discussed throughout this book.

Astrology Terms

- **Ascendant (Rising Sign):** The sign of the zodiac that was rising on the eastern horizon at the exact moment of birth. The Ascendant represents the outer self, how others perceive you, and your initial approach to life.
- **Aspect:** The angular relationship between two planets in a natal chart. Aspects can be harmonious (trine, sextile) or challenging (square, opposition), influencing how the energies of the planets interact.
- **Conjunction:** An aspect where two planets are close together (within 0-10 degrees) in the same sign, intensifying their combined energies.
- **Trine:** A harmonious aspect (120 degrees apart) where two planets are in signs of the same element (fire, earth, air, water), allowing their energies to flow easily together.
- **Square:** A challenging aspect (90 degrees apart) where two planets are in signs of the same modality (cardinal, fixed, mutable) but different elements, creating tension that requires resolution.
- **Opposition:** An aspect where two planets are directly opposite each other (180 degrees apart), representing a dynamic of conflict and balance between their energies.
- **Natal Chart (Birth Chart):** A snapshot of the sky at the exact time, date, and place of birth, showing the positions of the planets and their aspects. The natal chart is the foundation for understanding an individual's astrological influences.
- **Synastry:** The comparison of two natal charts to assess compatibility and relationship dynamics, particularly in romantic and sexual contexts.
- **Transit:** The current movement of planets in relation to the positions they occupied in a natal chart. Transits influence current events and life changes.

- **Progression:** A method of advancing the planets in a natal chart to reflect the inner growth and development of an individual over time, often used to predict future trends.
- **Venus:** The planet of love, beauty, attraction, and relationships. Venus governs how one gives and receives love and pleasure.
- **Mars:** The planet of desire, action, and sexual energy. Mars influences how one asserts themselves, pursues desires, and expresses sexuality.
- **Pluto:** The planet of transformation, power, and deep emotional connections. Pluto is associated with intense experiences, rebirth, and the exploration of taboo subjects.
- **Moon:** The celestial body governing emotions, instincts, and the subconscious. The Moon influences how one experiences emotional intimacy and seeks security.
- **5th House:** The house of romance, creativity, pleasure, and children. It governs love affairs, sexual pleasure, and personal expression.
- **7th House:** The house of partnerships, marriage, and long-term relationships. It represents how one interacts in committed relationships and partnerships.
- **8th House:** The house of sexuality, shared resources, transformation, and death. It governs deep emotional connections, intimacy, and the merging of energies.
- **12th House:** The house of the subconscious, hidden matters, karmic patterns, and spiritual growth. It influences secret desires, fears, and the process of letting go.

Sexual Position Terms

- **Missionary Position:** A sexual position where one partner lies on their back while the other partner lies on top, facing them. This position allows for deep eye contact and emotional connection.
- **Cowgirl Position:** A position where one partner sits or kneels on top of the other, who is lying on their back. This position allows the partner on top to control the rhythm and depth of penetration.
- **Doggy Style:** A position where one partner kneels on all fours while the other partner enters from behind. This position allows for deeper penetration and a focus on physical sensation.
- **Lotus Position:** A Tantric position where one partner sits cross-legged while the other sits on their lap, facing them. This position encourages deep emotional and physical connection through close contact and synchronized breathing.
- **Spooning:** A position where both partners lie on their sides, with one partner behind the other, creating a sense of closeness and comfort. This position is often used for gentle, intimate sex.
- **Yab-Yum:** A traditional Tantric position similar to the Lotus Position, where both partners sit facing each other with their legs intertwined. This position emphasizes spiritual and energetic connection, often involving synchronized breathing and eye contact.
- **Bridge Position:** A position where one partner lies on their back and lifts their hips into a bridge, while the other partner engages from above. This position combines physical strength and flexibility with deep penetration.
- **Standing Lover:** A position where one partner stands while the other wraps their legs around the standing partner's waist. This position requires balance and strength, allowing for spontaneous and adventurous sex.
- **Reverse Cowgirl:** A variation of the Cowgirl Position where the partner on top faces away from the partner lying down. This position allows for a different angle of penetration and can increase physical stimulation.

- **Cobra Position:** Inspired by the yoga pose, this position involves one partner lying face down, lifting their chest off the ground while the other partner enters from behind. This position combines physical flexibility with sexual intensity.

Tantric and Ritual Terms

- **Tantra:** An ancient spiritual practice that views sexuality as a sacred act capable of leading to spiritual enlightenment. Tantra emphasizes the connection between body, mind, and spirit, using sexuality as a path to personal and relational growth.
- **Chakras:** Energy centers in the body that govern different aspects of physical, emotional, and spiritual well-being. In Tantra, sexual energy is often associated with the sacral chakra (Svadhisthana) and the root chakra (Muladhara).
- **Pranayama:** A yogic practice of breath control, used in Tantra to cultivate and direct sexual energy throughout the body. Pranayama enhances mindfulness and connection during sexual rituals.
- **Sex Magic:** A practice that uses sexual energy as a powerful force for manifestation, healing, and spiritual growth. By focusing intention and energy during sexual rituals, practitioners can manifest desires and create change in their lives.
- **Sacred Union:** A concept in Tantra that views sexual union as a sacred act, merging the divine masculine and feminine energies. Sacred union rituals focus on deepening spiritual and emotional connections through sexuality.
- **Astrological Rituals:** Practices that align sexual activities with astrological events, such as lunar phases or planetary transits, to enhance the effectiveness of rituals and deepen the connection between partners.
- **Mantra:** A word or phrase repeated during meditation or ritual to focus the mind and align with a specific energy or intention. Mantras are often used in Tantric practices to enhance the spiritual aspects of sexual rituals.
- **Mudra:** A symbolic hand gesture used in yoga and Tantra to direct energy and focus during meditation or ritual. Mudras can enhance the flow of sexual energy and deepen the spiritual connection between partners.

- **Kundalini:** A form of spiritual energy believed to reside at the base of the spine. In Tantra, Kundalini energy is awakened and directed through the chakras to achieve spiritual enlightenment and heightened sexual experiences.

This glossary provides a foundational understanding of the terms and concepts that are essential for exploring the intersection of astrology, sexuality, and spirituality. Use this resource as a guide to deepen your knowledge and enhance your practice as you continue your journey into the world of sexual astrology.

Charts: Planetary Influence, Moon Phases, and Zodiac Compatibility

This section provides detailed charts that outline the influences of planetary positions, the effects of moon phases, and zodiac sign compatibility in the context of sexual astrology. These charts are designed to serve as quick reference guides for understanding how cosmic energies impact sexual dynamics, timing, and relationships.

Planetary Influence Charts

Planetary Influence on Sexuality and Relationships

Planet	Keywords	Influence on Sexuality	Impact on Relationships
Sun	Vitality, Ego, Self-Expression	Represents one's core identity and sexual vitality. Enhances confidence and attraction when positively aspected.	Governs how one expresses their individuality in relationships and seeks recognition and validation.

Planet	Keywords	Influence on Sexuality	Impact on Relationships
Moon	Emotions, Intuition, Subconscious	Governs emotional needs, nurturing instincts, and the desire for emotional intimacy in sexual relationships.	Influences how one seeks comfort and security in relationships, and how they emotionally connect with others.
Mercury	Communication, Intellect, Expression	Affects verbal and mental stimulation in sexual relationships, influencing how desires are communicated.	Governs how partners communicate and express their thoughts, influencing the clarity and understanding in relationships.

Planet	Keywords	Influence on Sexuality	Impact on Relationships
Venus	Love, Attraction, Sensuality	The planet of love and beauty, Venus influences romantic attraction, sensuality, and the pursuit of pleasure.	Governs how one expresses affection, love, and desires harmony and balance in relationships.
Mars	Passion, Desire, Action	Represents sexual drive, passion, and the pursuit of desires. Mars governs physical attraction and assertiveness in sexual encounters.	Influences how one pursues their goals in relationships, including sexual and romantic pursuits.

Planet	Keywords	Influence on Sexuality	Impact on Relationships
Jupiter	Expansion, Growth, Abundance	Expands and amplifies sexual and romantic experiences, encouraging exploration and growth.	Promotes optimism, generosity, and growth in relationships, encouraging mutual exploration and expansion.
Saturn	Discipline, Structure, Responsibility	Brings structure and discipline to sexual relationships, focusing on long-term commitments and stability.	Governs responsibility, commitment, and the challenges that arise in maintaining long-term relationships.

Planet	Keywords	Influence on Sexuality	Impact on Relationships
Uranus	Innovation, Change, Freedom	Introduces unconventional and spontaneous elements into sexual relationships, encouraging experimentation and novelty.	Influences sudden changes, independence, and the need for freedom in relationships, promoting individuality.
Neptune	Dreams, Illusion, Mysticism	Adds a mystical, dreamy quality to sexual experiences, often blurring the lines between fantasy and reality.	Governs idealism, spirituality, and the potential for illusions or misunderstandings in relationships.

Planet	Keywords	Influence on Sexuality	Impact on Relationships
Pluto	Transformation, Power, Intensity	Represents deep, transformative sexual experiences, power dynamics, and the exploration of taboo subjects.	Influences the dynamics of control, power, and deep emotional connections in relationships, often leading to profound changes.

Moon Phase Charts
Moon Phases and Their Influence on Sexual Energy and Relationships

Moon Phase	Keywords	Influence on Sexual Energy	Impact on Relationships
New Moon	Beginnings, Intention, Potential	A time for setting intentions and initiating new sexual practices or exploring new relationships. Energy is introspective and focused on potential growth.	Ideal for starting new relationships, setting goals, and planting the seeds for future emotional and sexual connection.

Moon Phase	Keywords	Influence on Sexual Energy	Impact on Relationships
Waxing Crescent	Growth, Development, Optimism	Energy is building, making this a time to develop and nurture sexual relationships and desires.	Encourages the growth of new relationships and the deepening of emotional bonds. Focus on building and expanding connections.
First Quarter	Action, Challenges, Decision	A time for taking action on sexual desires and facing any challenges that may arise in relationships.	Ideal for making decisions about the direction of a relationship and overcoming obstacles together.

Moon Phase	Keywords	Influence on Sexual Energy	Impact on Relationships
Waxing Gibbous	Refinement, Progress, Preparation	Sexual energy is high, making this a time for refining and enhancing sexual practices and relationships.	Focus on improving and fine-tuning relationships, preparing for the culmination of desires and intentions.
Full Moon	Culmination, Clarity, Intensity	Sexual energy peaks, offering intense, fulfilling experiences. A time of heightened emotions and clarity in relationships.	Ideal for celebrating love and connection, deepening emotional bonds, and achieving the full potential of relationships.

Moon Phase	Keywords	Influence on Sexual Energy	Impact on Relationships
Waning Gibbous	Gratitude, Sharing, Reflection	A time to reflect on sexual experiences and relationships, expressing gratitude and sharing insights with partners.	Focus on giving back, sharing emotional and sexual wisdom, and nurturing the relationship after the intensity of the Full Moon.
Last Quarter	Release, Letting Go, Adjustments	Energy begins to wane, making this a time for releasing old patterns and making necessary adjustments in sexual relationships.	Ideal for letting go of what no longer serves the relationship, making changes, and preparing for renewal.

Moon Phase	Keywords	Influence on Sexual Energy	Impact on Relationships
Waning Crescent	Rest, Reflection, Renewal	A time for introspection, rest, and renewal of sexual energy. Focus on inner healing and preparing for the next cycle.	Encourages quiet reflection, healing, and the gentle renewal of relationships as the lunar cycle comes to a close.

Zodiac Compatibility Charts
Zodiac Sign Compatibility in Sexual Relationships

Sign	Best Matches	Challenging Matches	Sexual Compatibility
Aries	Leo, Sagittarius, Libra	Cancer, Capricorn	High energy and passion, seeks excitement and adventure in sexual relationships. Needs partners who can match their intensity and desire for spontaneity.

Sign	Best Matches	Challenging Matches	Sexual Compatibility
Taurus	Virgo, Capricorn, Scorpio	Leo, Aquarius	Sensual and indulgent, Taurus values physical pleasure and emotional security. Thrives with partners who appreciate slow, deep, and meaningful sexual experiences.
Gemini	Libra, Aquarius, Sagittarius	Virgo, Pisces	Playful and communicative, Gemini enjoys variety and intellectual stimulation. Needs partners who can keep up with their curiosity and adaptability in the bedroom.

Sign	Best Matches	Challenging Matches	Sexual Compatibility
Cancer	Scorpio, Pisces, Capricorn	Aries, Libra	Deeply emotional and nurturing, Cancer seeks security and intimacy in sexual relationships. Best with partners who value emotional connection and sensitivity.
Leo	Aries, Sagittarius, Aquarius	Taurus, Scorpio	Confident and passionate, Leo enjoys being adored and seeks partners who can match their enthusiasm and creativity in sexual expression.

Sign	Best Matches	Challenging Matches	Sexual Compatibility
Virgo	Taurus, Capricorn, Pisces	Gemini, Sagittarius	Attentive and detail-oriented, Virgo values precision and care in sexual relationships. Thrives with partners who appreciate their dedication to service and improvement.
Libra	Gemini, Aquarius, Aries	Cancer, Capricorn	Romantic and harmonious, Libra seeks balance and beauty in sexual relationships. Best with partners who value equality and mutual pleasure.

Sign	Best Matches	Challenging Matches	Sexual Compatibility
Scorpio	Cancer, Pisces, Taurus	Leo, Aquarius	Intense and transformative, Scorpio craves deep, emotional connections in sexual relationships. Needs partners who can handle their depth and passion.
Sagittarius	Aries, Leo, Gemini	Virgo, Pisces	Adventurous and free-spirited, Sagittarius seeks exploration and excitement in sexual relationships. Thrives with partners who appreciate their need for freedom and variety.

Sign	Best Matches	Challenging Matches	Sexual Compatibility
Capricorn	Taurus, Virgo, Cancer	Aries, Libra	Disciplined and grounded, Capricorn values stability and commitment in sexual relationships. Best with partners who respect their ambition and desire for long-term connections.
Aquarius	Gemini, Libra, Leo	Taurus, Scorpio	Innovative and unconventional, Aquarius enjoys experimentation and intellectual connection in sexual relationships. Needs partners who value independence and originality.

Sign	Best Matches	Challenging Matches	Sexual Compatibility
Pisces	Cancer, Scorpio, Virgo	Gemini, Sagittarius	Dreamy and empathetic, Pisces seeks spiritual and emotional connection in sexual relationships. Thrives with partners who appreciate their sensitivity and creativity.

These charts offer a practical and accessible way to understand the interplay between astrology and sexuality, providing valuable insights into how cosmic influences shape sexual energy, relationship dynamics, and compatibility. Whether you're exploring your own chart, working with a partner, or simply seeking to deepen your understanding, these charts serve as essential tools for navigating the complex and fascinating world of sexual astrology.

Reading Material

Suggested books, articles, and resources for further exploration of astrology and sexual techniques.

Exploring the intersection of astrology and sexuality is a rich and multifaceted journey that draws from various disciplines, including astrology, psychology, spirituality, and sexual health. This section provides a curated list of books, articles, and online resources that delve deeper into these subjects, offering additional insights and practical guidance for those interested in expanding their knowledge and practice.

Books on Astrology and Sexuality

1. **"Sexual Astrology: A Sign-by-Sign Guide to Your Sensual Stars" by Martine**: This classic book provides an in-depth exploration of how each zodiac sign influences sexual preferences, desires, and compatibility. It offers practical advice on how to use astrology to enhance sexual relationships and deepen emotional connections.

2. **"The Astrology of Love & Sex: A Modern Compatibility Guide" by Annabel Gat**: Annabel Gat offers a modern, inclusive approach to understanding sexual compatibility through astrology. The book covers each zodiac sign's approach to love, sex, and relationships, and provides practical tips for creating harmony and passion in your love life.

3. **"Erotic Astrology: The Sex Secrets of Your Horoscope Revealed" by Phyllis Vega**: This book reveals the sexual secrets of each zodiac sign, offering insights into desires, turn-ons, and sexual compatibility. It also includes information on astrological aspects and how they influence sexual dynamics.

4. **"Astrology and the Art of Healing: Utilizing the Birth Chart for Health and Well-Being" by A.T. Mann**: While not exclusively focused on sexuality, this book explores how astrology can be used as a tool for healing, including emotional and sexual healing. It provides insights into how planetary influences can affect overall health and well-being.

5. **"The Only Astrology Book You'll Ever Need" by Joanna Martine Woolfolk**: This comprehensive guide covers all aspects of astrology, including sun signs, moon signs, and plane-

tary influences. It includes sections on love and relationships, making it a valuable resource for those exploring sexual astrology.

6. **"The Secret Language of Birthdays: Your Complete Personology Guide for Each Day of the Year" by Gary Goldschneider and Joost Elffers**: This book combines astrology, numerology, and psychology to offer detailed personality profiles based on birth dates. It includes insights into love, sex, and relationships, making it a useful tool for understanding sexual compatibility.

7. **"Planets in Composite: Analyzing Human Relationships" by Robert Hand**: This book delves into composite charts, which combine the charts of two individuals to explore the dynamics of their relationship. It offers insights into how planetary influences shape sexual and emotional connections.

8. **"Astrology, Karma & Transformation: The Inner Dimensions of the Birth Chart" by Stephen Arroyo**: Stephen Arroyo's work explores the deeper, spiritual aspects of astrology, including how karmic influences and planetary transits affect relationships and personal growth. This book is particularly valuable for those interested in the transformative power of sexual astrology.

Books on Tantra and Sexual Techniques

1. **"Urban Tantra: Sacred Sex for the Twenty-First Century" by Barbara Carrellas**: This modern guide to Tantra offers practical advice on integrating Tantric practices into contemporary life. It includes exercises, meditations, and techniques for enhancing sexual pleasure and deepening intimacy.

2. **"The Art of Sexual Ecstasy: The Path of Sacred Sexuality for Western Lovers" by Margo Anand**: Margo Anand's book is a comprehensive guide to sacred sexuality and Tantra. It provides step-by-step instructions for Tantric rituals, meditations, and sexual techniques designed to elevate sexual experiences to a spiritual level.

3. **"Tantra Illuminated: The Philosophy, History, and Practice of a Timeless Tradition" by Christopher D. Wallis**: This book offers a deep dive into the history, philosophy, and

practices of Tantra. It is an excellent resource for those interested in understanding the spiritual foundations of Tantric sexuality.

4. **"The Multi-Orgasmic Couple: Sexual Secrets Every Couple Should Know" by Mantak Chia and Douglas Abrams**: This book provides practical techniques for couples to enhance sexual pleasure and achieve multiple orgasms. It incorporates Taoist sexual practices and offers insights into energy flow and sexual health.

5. **"The Heart of Tantric Sex: A Unique Guide to Love and Sexual Fulfillment" by Diana Richardson**: Diana Richardson's guide to Tantric sex emphasizes the importance of presence, mindfulness, and slow, conscious lovemaking. The book offers practical advice for couples seeking to deepen their emotional and sexual connection.

6. **"The Tantric Guide to Divine Sexuality" by Devi Ward Erickson**: This book explores the intersection of Tantra and sacred sexuality, offering techniques for healing sexual trauma, enhancing pleasure, and connecting with the divine through sexual practice.

7. **"The Kama Sutra: The Ultimate Guide to the Secrets of Erotic Pleasure" by Vatsyayana (Various Translations)**: The Kama Sutra is a classic text on love and sexuality, offering a wealth of information on sexual positions, techniques, and the art of love. While it is often associated with sexual positions, the text also provides insights into the emotional and spiritual aspects of relationships.

Articles and Online Resources

1. **Astro.com (www.astro.com)**: One of the most comprehensive astrology websites, offering free natal chart calculations, transits, and in-depth articles on various astrological topics. It includes resources for exploring relationship dynamics and sexual astrology.

2. **Cafe Astrology (www.cafeastrology.com)**: A popular astrology resource that provides detailed information on natal charts, love compatibility, and relationship astrology. The site offers articles on Venus, Mars, and other key planets that influence sexuality.

3. **Astrology for the Soul by Jan Spiller (www.janspiller.com)**: Jan Spiller's website offers insights into astrology from a soul-centered perspective, with a focus on personal growth and transformation. The site includes articles on relationships, sexuality, and karmic astrology.

4. **AstroStyle (www.astrostyle.com)**: Run by The AstroTwins, this website provides accessible astrology content, including horoscopes, love compatibility reports, and articles on how astrology influences love, sex, and relationships.

5. **The Astrology Podcast (www.theastrologypodcast.com)**: Hosted by astrologer Chris Brennan, this podcast covers a wide range of astrological topics, including relationship astrology, Venus and Mars dynamics, and sexual astrology.

6. **The Dark Pixie Astrology (www.thedarkpixieastrology.com)**: A resource for learning about various aspects of astrology, including relationship astrology and the influence of transits on love and sex. The site offers articles, guides, and free astrological tools.

7. **MindBodyGreen (www.mindbodygreen.com)**: A wellness site that occasionally features articles on astrology, including how planetary influences affect love, sex, and relationships. It also covers topics related to Tantra and sexual health.

8. **Tantra.com (www.tantra.com)**: A resource dedicated to Tantric practices and sacred sexuality, offering articles, guided meditations, and online courses. The site provides insights into how Tantra can enhance sexual experiences and deepen spiritual connections.

9. **Good Vibes Astrology (www.goodvibesastrology.com)**: This site offers astrology courses, articles, and resources focused on relationship and sexual astrology. It provides practical advice for using astrology to enhance love and sexual compatibility.

10. **Elephant Journal (www.elephantjournal.com)**: An online magazine that covers spirituality, relationships, and wellness, including articles on astrology and Tantra. The site offers insights into how these practices can be integrated into daily life for greater fulfillment.

Workshops and Courses

1. **The Astrology University (www.astrologyuniversity.com)**: Offers online courses and workshops on various astrological topics, including relationship astrology and Venus/Mars dynamics. Courses are taught by leading astrologers and provide in-depth knowledge and practical applications.

2. **The Tantric Institute of Integrated Sexuality (www.tantrinstitute.com)**: Offers online courses, workshops, and coaching on Tantra, sacred sexuality, and sexual healing. The insti-

tute's courses are designed to help individuals and couples deepen their sexual experiences and connect with their spiritual selves.

3. **The Shift Network (www.theshiftnetwork.com)**: Provides online courses and summits on topics related to spirituality, wellness, and personal growth, including astrology and Tantra. The platform offers resources for those interested in exploring the intersection of astrology and sexual practices.

4. **Sacred Wild Woman (www.sacredwildwoman.com)**: Offers workshops and retreats focused on feminine spirituality, including Tantric practices and sexual empowerment. The site provides resources for women interested in exploring sacred sexuality and astrological insights.

5. **The School of Evolutionary Astrology (www.schoolofevolutionaryastrology.com)**: Founded by Jeffrey Wolf Green, this school offers courses and resources on Evolutionary Astrology, which explores the soul's journey and karmic influences. It includes content on relationships and sexual dynamics from a spiritual perspective.

This reading material provides a wealth of resources for those interested in deepening their understanding of astrology, sexuality, and the interplay between the two. Whether you're a beginner or an advanced practitioner, these books, articles, and courses offer valuable insights and practical guidance for enhancing your sexual relationships and exploring the cosmic dimensions of love and desire.

Bibliography

This bibliography provides a comprehensive list of references and sources used in the creation of this book on sexual astrology. It includes books, articles, academic papers, and online resources that have informed the content and provided a foundation for the exploration of astrology, sexuality, and their intersections.

Books

1. **Arroyo, Stephen.** *Astrology, Karma & Transformation: The Inner Dimensions of the Birth Chart.* CRCS Publications, 1978.
    ◦ A foundational text exploring the spiritual and karmic aspects of astrology, including the influence of planetary transits on personal growth and transformation.
2. **Anand, Margo.** *The Art of Sexual Ecstasy: The Path of Sacred Sexuality for Western Lovers.* TarcherPerigee, 1989.
    ◦ This book provides a comprehensive guide to sacred sexuality and Tantra, offering practical techniques and insights for deepening sexual experiences.
3. **Carrellas, Barbara.** *Urban Tantra: Sacred Sex for the Twenty-First Century.* Celestial Arts, 2007.
    ◦ A modern guide to integrating Tantra into contemporary life, with a focus on enhancing sexual pleasure and intimacy through spiritual practices.
4. **Gat, Annabel.** *The Astrology of Love & Sex: A Modern Compatibility Guide.* Chronicle Books, 2019.
    ◦ A contemporary exploration of astrological compatibility, offering insights into how planetary influences shape love, sex, and relationships.
5. **Green, Jeffrey Wolf.** *Pluto: The Evolutionary Journey of the Soul.* Llewellyn Publications, 1985.
    ◦ A deep dive into the transformative power of Pluto in astrology, exploring its influence on the soul's journey, including themes of sexuality and power dynamics.
6. **Hand, Robert.** *Planets in Composite: Analyzing Human Relationships.* Whitford Press, 1975.

    ◦ This book explores composite charts, which combine the natal charts of two individuals to analyze the dynamics of their relationship, including sexual compatibility.

7. **Richardson, Diana.** *The Heart of Tantric Sex: A Unique Guide to Love and Sexual Fulfillment.* John Hunt Publishing, 2003.
    ◦ A guide to Tantric sex that emphasizes mindfulness, presence, and the deepening of emotional and sexual connections between partners.

8. **Spiller, Jan.** *Astrology for the Soul.* Bantam Books, 1997.
    ◦ A book focused on Evolutionary Astrology, exploring how planetary influences shape the soul's journey, with insights into relationship dynamics and sexual energy.

9. **Vega, Phyllis.** *Erotic Astrology: The Sex Secrets of Your Horoscope Revealed.* Adams Media, 2009.
    ◦ This book provides a detailed exploration of sexual preferences, desires, and compatibility based on zodiac signs and astrological influences.

10. **Woolfolk, Joanna Martine.** *The Only Astrology Book You'll Ever Need.* Quarto Publishing Group USA, 2001.
    ◦ A comprehensive guide to astrology, covering all aspects of natal charts, including sections on love, relationships, and sexual compatibility.

Articles and Journals

1. **Arroyo, Stephen.** "Astrology, Psychology, and the Four Elements." *The Mountain Astrologer*, 1992.
    ◦ An article exploring the psychological dimensions of astrology, including how the elements (fire, earth, air, water) influence sexual dynamics and relationships.

2. **Gat, Annabel.** "Astrology for Sexual Compatibility: How the Signs Align in Love." *Cosmopolitan*, 2018.
    ◦ A popular article that provides an overview of sexual compatibility based on astrological signs, with practical tips for understanding relationship dynamics.

3. **Greene, Liz.** "The Astrological Neptune and the Quest for Redemption." *Journal of Analytical Psychology*, 1996.

- This academic paper examines the influence of Neptune in astrology, particularly in the context of romantic and sexual relationships, exploring themes of idealism and illusion.

4. **Tarnas, Richard.** "Cosmos and Psyche: Intimations of a New World View." *Journal of Humanistic Psychology*, 2006.
   - An exploration of the relationship between astrology and psychology, focusing on the impact of planetary transits on human behavior and sexuality.

Online Resources

1. **Astro.com.** "Understanding Venus and Mars in Astrology." Accessed March 15, 2024. https://www.astro.com.
   - A comprehensive online resource offering detailed explanations of Venus and Mars' roles in astrology, including their influence on love and sexual dynamics.
2. **Cafe Astrology.** "Compatibility in Astrology: How to Read Your Love Chart." Accessed February 20, 2024. https://www.cafeastrology.com.
   - An accessible guide to understanding astrological compatibility, with a focus on reading synastry charts and interpreting planetary aspects in relationships.
3. **The Astrology Podcast.** "Sexual Astrology: Exploring Venus and Mars." Hosted by Chris Brennan. February 2023. https://www.theastrologypodcast.com.
   - A podcast episode dedicated to exploring the influence of Venus and Mars on sexuality, featuring discussions with leading astrologers on how these planets shape sexual behavior and relationships.
4. **The Dark Pixie Astrology.** "The Role of Pluto in Sexual Astrology." Accessed April 5, 2024. https://www.thedarkpixieastrology.com.
   - An article that delves into Pluto's transformative power in sexual astrology, exploring how this planet influences deep emotional connections and sexual experiences.
5. **AstroStyle.** "Love, Sex, and Astrology: How the Planets Influence Your Love Life." Accessed January 10, 2024. https://www.astrostyle.com.
   - A comprehensive resource on the intersection of astrology and sexuality, offering insights into how planetary transits affect romantic relationships and sexual dynamics.

Courses and Workshops

1. **The Astrology University.** "Understanding Relationship Astrology: A Course on Synastry and Composite Charts." Taught by Frank Clifford, March 2024. https://www.astrologyuniversity.com.
   - An online course focused on relationship astrology, covering synastry, composite charts, and the astrological factors that influence love and sexuality.
2. **The Tantric Institute of Integrated Sexuality.** "Sexual Healing and Tantra: A Comprehensive Guide to Sacred Sexuality." Taught by Devi Ward Erickson, April 2024. https://www.tantrinstitute.com.
   - A workshop that integrates Tantra with sexual healing practices, offering tools for deepening intimacy, enhancing sexual pleasure, and exploring the spiritual aspects of sexuality.
3. **The Shift Network.** "Astrological Wisdom for Love and Relationships: Exploring Venus and Mars." Taught by Rick Levine, February 2024. https://www.theshiftnetwork.com.
   - A course that explores the astrological influences of Venus and Mars on love, sex, and relationships, with practical guidance for using these insights to enhance personal and romantic connections.

This bibliography reflects the diverse range of sources that have informed the content of this book, providing readers with a wealth of additional resources for further exploration. Whether you're interested in deepening your understanding of astrology, exploring sacred sexuality, or learning practical techniques for enhancing relationships, these references offer valuable insights and guidance.

<u>Message from the Author:</u>

I hope you enjoyed this book, I love astrology and knew there was not a book such as this out on the shelf. I love metaphysical items as well. Please check out my other books:

-Life of Government Benefits

-My life of Hell

-My life with Hydrocephalus

-Red Sky

-World Domination:Woman's rule

-World Domination:Woman's Rule 2: The War

-Life and Banishment of Apophis: book 1

-The Kidney Friendly Diet

-The Ultimate Hemp Cookbook

-Creating a Dispensary(legally)

-Cleanliness throughout life: the importance of showering from childhood to adulthood.

-Strong Roots: The Risks of Overcoddling children

-Hemp Horoscopes: Cosmic Insights and Earthly Healing

- Celestial Hemp Navigating the Zodiac: Through the Green Cosmos

-Astrological Hemp: Aligning The Stars with Earth's Ancient Herb

-The Astrological Guide to Hemp: Stars, Signs, and Sacred Leaves

-Green Growth: Innovative Marketing Strategies for your Hemp Products and Dispensary

-Cosmic Cannabis

-Astrological Munchies

-Henry The Hemp

-Zodiacal Roots: The Astrological Soul Of Hemp

- **Green Constellations: Intersection of Hemp and Zodiac**

-Hemp in The Houses: An astrological Adventure Through The Cannabis Galaxy

-Galactic Ganja Guide

Heavenly Hemp

Zodiac Leaves

Doctor Who Astrology

Cannastrology

Stellar Satvias and Cosmic Indicas

Celestial Cannabis: A Zodiac Journey

AstroHerbology: The Sky and The Soil: Volume 1

AstroHerbology:Celestial Cannabis:Volume 2

Cosmic Cannabis Cultivation

The Starry Guide to Herbal Harmony: Volume 1

The Starry Guide to Herbal Harmony: Cannabis Universe: Volume 2

Yugioh Astrology: Astrological Guide to Deck, Duels and more

Nightmare Mansion: Echoes of The Abyss

Nightmare Mansion 2: Legacy of Shadows

Nightmare Mansion 3: Shadows of the Forgotten

Nightmare Mansion 4: Echoes of the Damned

The Life and Banishment of Apophis: Book 2

Nightmare Mansion: Halls of Despair

Healing with Herb: Cannabis and Hydrocephalus

Planetary Pot: Aligning with Astrological Herbs: Volume 1

Fast Track to Freedom: 30 Days to Financial Independence Using AI, Assets, and Agile Hustles

Cosmic Hemp Pathways

How to Become Financially Free in 30 Days: 10,000 Paths to Prosperity

Zodiacal Herbage: Astrological Insights: Volume 1

Nightmare Mansion: Whispers in the Walls

The Daleks Invade Atlantis

Henry the hemp and Hydrocephalus

10X The Kidney Friendly Diet

Cannabis Universe: Adult coloring book

Hemp Astrology: The Healing Power of the Stars

Zodiacal Herbage: Astrological Insights: Cannabis Universe: Volume 2

<u>Planetary Pot: Aligning with Astrological Herbs: Cannabis Universes: Volume 2</u>

Doctor Who Meets the Replicators and SG-1: The Ultimate Battle for Survival

Nightmare Mansion: Curse of the Blood Moon

<u>The Celestial Stoner: A Guide to the Zodiac</u>

Cosmic Pleasures: Sex Toy Astrology for Every Sign

Hydrocephalus Astrology: Navigating the Stars and Healing Waters

Lapis and the Mischievous Chocolate Bar

Celestial Positions: Sexual Astrology for Every Sign

Apophis's Shadow Work Journal: **:** A Journey of Self-Discovery and Healing

Kinky Cosmos: Sexual Kink Astrology for Every Sign

Digital Cosmos: The Astrological Digimon Compendium

Stellar Seeds: The Cosmic Guide to Growing with Astrology

Apophis's Daily Gratitude Journal

Cat Astrology: Feline Mysteries of the Cosmos

If you want solar for your home go here: https://www.harborsolar.live/apophisenterprises/

Get Some Tarot cards: https://www.makeplayingcards.com/sell/apophis-occult-shop

Get some shirts: https://www.bonfire.com/store/apophis-shirt-emporium/

Instagrams:
@apophis_enterprises,
@apophisbookemporium,
@apophisscardshop

Twitter: @apophisenterpr1

Tiktok:@apophisenterprise

Youtube: @sg1fan23477, @FiresideRetreatKingdom

Podcast: Apophis   Chat   Zone: https://open.spotify.com/show/5zXbr-CLEV2xzCp8ybrfHsk?si=fb4d4fdbdce44dec

Newsletter: https://apophiss-newsletter-27c897.beehiiv.com/

www.ingramcontent.com/pod-product-compliance
Lightning Source LLC
Chambersburg PA
CBHW081357130726
47998CB00011B/2995